Grass-Clearing Man

A Factional Ethnography of Life in the New Guinea Highlands

D0222726

Paul Sillitoe
Durham University

Jackie Sillitoe

WAVELAND

PRESS, INC.

Long Grove, Illinois

For past and present friends in the Was valley
who appreciate that
"it is in giving that we receive" (St. Francis of Assisi)

For information about this book, contact:
Waveland Press, Inc.
4180 IL Route 83, Suite 101
Long Grove, IL 60047-9580
(847) 634-0081
info@waveland.com
www.waveland.com

Cover: An *ol howma* speaking prior to a large pig kill.

10-digit ISBN 1-57766-601-1
13-digit ISBN 978-1-57766-601-1

Printed in the United States of America

7 6 5 4 3 2 1

Contents

Preface

"What's life like in the New Guinea Highlands?" Students frequently ask this question and this book tries to answer it from the viewpoint of a life spent in the Was valley of the Southern Highlands. It is a *factional* account and so something of an experiment. It is a fictional story that features ethnographic facts—a genre that we think makes ethnography more accessible, even fun to read. That, at least, is the book's aim.

It is our experience that students seem reluctant to read ethnographies, which is alarming as these are central to the discipline of anthropology. It is perhaps even more alarming that some anthropologists maintain that ethnography is boring compared to sociological speculation and theorizing on the nature of humanity. And it is puzzling because one of the few points on which this fractious academic tribe seems to agree in defining their discipline is that it involves ethnography. In its attempt to make ethnography readable, this book deals with a range of issues that teaching indicates students find interesting.

While the book is in the tradition of Elenore Smith Bowen's (Laura Bohannan's) *Return to Laughter*, it does not feature us, the authors, until the last chapter. It is consequently not in the reflexive style that became popular subsequently, which self-consciously includes the authors, such as David Hayano's *Road through the Rain Forest* or William Mitchell's *The Bamboo Fire*, to cite two New Guinea examples. It adopts a standard ethnographic approach in reporting various activities, recounting these generally, as one might describe the game of soccer as opposed to a particular match. When it sets factual activities in a particular context, it is fictional with respect to the actors who participated in the events.

The book has the structure of a standard biography. It follows a life from birth to death—that of a man called Ongol, living in the Was valley. It contrasts with other New Guinea biographies such as Andrew Strathern's *Ongka* or Roger Keesing's *Elota's Story* in that Ongol is a fictional person. Furthermore, it deliberately marshals and orders the ethnography topically in chapters rather than presenting it as a pastiche dependent on the subject's life history. It explores a series of related events in Ongol's life and connects them to tell a story. It is akin to the extended case method of anthropology, which traces a chain of events, which are often disputes, through a detailed personal history. So the book is a history, too, of events in the Was valley during the twentieth century.

On a more academic note, and to show that we are not entirely theoretically unaware, the factional genre is a response to postmodern criticism that argues anthropological accounts grossly distort ethnographic reality—or in extreme versions, they are fictions. This book is fictional in that the story it tells never happened and the characters it describes have never lived to our knowledge in the Was valley. Ongol, Wasnonk, Mindiy, Kot, and the others who are featured in the tale never existed. Nonetheless, Wola friends, to whom we dedicate the book, may recognize episodes in the lives of individuals they have known. While the characters that populate these pages are made-up, they are not entirely the products of our imagination but borrow, as in many novels, traits and experiences from various persons we have known. The events described are based on real events that we heard about or saw during our stay in the Was valley but are arranged in a fictional narrative. We have included a genealogy that shows the *dramatis personae*, for readers who lose track of the characters and their relations to one another. It gives both fictional personal names and Wola terms for the kin relationships (with the central character Ongol as ego).

The ethnography, on the other hand, is factual. The practices described occur, or occurred, in the Was valley. We saw many of them. The exchange transactions and rituals happened, the spells are genuine and recorded as recited, the customs surrounding marriage and kinship and the subsistence regime all exist. A map shows the places mentioned, which are real locations in the Was and neighboring valleys. The principle of ethnographic-determinism informs the documentation of these data; that is, we seek to let the ethnography speak for itself and set the agenda for any anthropological explanation/interpretation—a principal source of distortion identified by postmodernism. It would be erroneous to claim that the documentation of the ethnographic facts features no distortion, and even more so our explanation/interpretation of them. But we seek to keep explanation/interpretation to a minimum, sufficient for the reader to make sense of what is going on, as we understand it.

The book contains a great deal of information on various rituals and associated supernatural beliefs. While we witnessed some of these, much of it comes from the accounts of those who took part in various ceremonies, sometimes years previously. Missionaries had followed a surprisingly effective scorched earth policy with respect to local rites, which they thought pagan, even the work of Satan, which had to be suppressed in converting people to Christian beliefs and saving their souls. Nonetheless, participants had lively memories of their past customs that they willingly shared with us, recounting and discussing various rituals. While some of these featured secret acts and spells known to only a few, people spoke openly about them knowing that we intended to make them public in a book. They agreed, as they are now Christians, commenting that it would ensure that "our ancestors' ways are not lost forever," which would otherwise be their fate as participants in the events pass away. Ironically, we probably obtained more information than if observing the extant rites, with people guarding their secrets, which would have also put publication out of the question.

In addition to our friends in the Was valley, who generously allowed us, uninvited, to share their lives, we thank Doris Sillitoe, Laura Sillitoe, and Sheila Harding for acting as lay readers of the manuscript and making valuable suggestions as to how we might improve its readability.

A note on the pronunciation of words in the Wola language:

As far as possible the transcription of Wola words has been kept simple; we have used ordinary English letters in preference to less familiar linguistic signs. Broadly speaking, the consonants sound much the same as in English with a few strange sounds—ng, mb, nd, nj—used at the beginning of some words. The vowels sound as follows:

The **a** as in father, **ae** as in bat, **au** as in how, **ay** as in say and **ai** as in nice.

The **e** as in bet and raised **e** (**ᵉ**) as in nut.

The **i** as in bit and **iy** as in bean.

The **o** as in hot, **or** as in shore, **ow** as in low, and **oi** as in groin.

The **u** as in put, **uw** as in true.

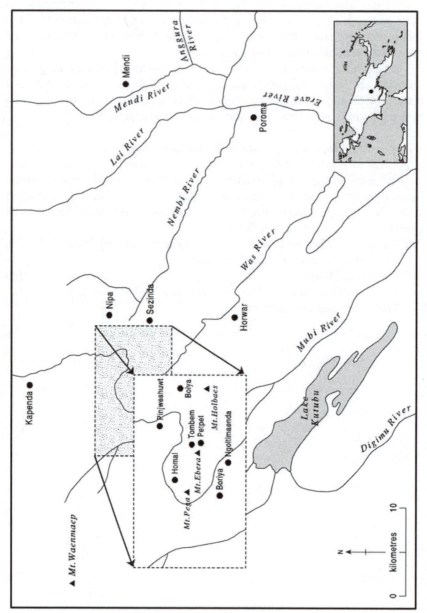

Map of Wola speaking region (Was River area where Ongol lived enlarged).

Chapter 1

A Birth and a Death

*I*t is just as well, perhaps, that we cannot recall our birth. Ongol came into the world just before dawn on a chilly night, on a ridge above the Was valley in the mountains of New Guinea. It was sometime early in the twentieth century, on one of those nights when the clouds sink down into the valleys, filling them with a wispy mist that makes everything damp with fine dew. His mother Wasnonk sought to keep him warm by hugging him between her swollen breasts. His thin cries filled the forest, where she squatted with him exhausted after several hours of labor. She had delivered the baby alone, crouching on hand and knees. After what seemed interminable contractions she had caught him between her legs as he finally emerged and cuddled his clammy body into her chest. She thought that he was dead as he was so still and silent but when she poked a finger into his mouth to clear away the mucus he took a lungful of air and bawled. "Good pair of lungs," she thought, not knowing how right she was, as Ongol was later to prove one of the loudest yodelers in the Was valley.

They were all alone. Wasnonk could see a thin line of light silhouetting the mountains on the other side of the valley, which gradually became wider as the dawn edged away the night darkness. She had been on her way back from a garden, her net bag weighed down with harvested sweet potato tubers, when her water broke, taking her by surprise, and she went into labor. She struggled on between contractions, becoming increasingly worried that she would not make it back to her homestead at Tombem. She arrived at the fringe of the forest where gardens and settlement begin and found a sheltered spot off the path between the buttresses of a large beech tree. She sank to her knees. A while later, another woman coming along the path heard her groans and called out asking if she was all right. She came over and Wasnonk told her what was happening, and she confirmed that her labor was advanced. She went off and returned some time later with two other women, one of whom was Wasnonk's mother-in-law, Saemten, bringing some hot embers and firewood and some baked sweet potato tubers, still warm, although they said they doubted Wasnonk would feel like eating. They left again soon afterward as darkness fell.

1

A view eastward across the Was valley.

Ongol was Wasnonk's first child, and she did not really know what to expect, like any first time mother perhaps; she had no benefit of prenatal classes nor had she received much information about giving birth. Her culture discouraged discussion of sexual matters, treating them with something of a Puritanical attitude. Her mother was deceased, and whenever she tried to ask her older sister about what to expect she told her not to worry as her body would do it all for her and expel the infant when ready. "It's unlike anything you've experienced before," she said grinning. "You have no control really," intimating that entry into the motherhood club was a racking affair. It had been a frightening prospect, and the previous night had confirmed Wasnonk's worries.

While her sister had told her to position herself on hand and knees and catch the infant, she seemed more concerned about the "carry bag" (afterbirth) than the birth itself. "Do not pull it, whatever you do," her sister had warned. "The 'carry bag' will come out when it is ready." Wasnonk waited for the placenta to be expelled as instructed, the umbilical cord snaking up inside her body. Damp with dew mixed with the sweat of her exertions, she started to feel cold for the first time. She huddled over the small fire that smouldered before her, blowing on it to bring up flames that she fed with some dry wood. She shivered. She felt strangely disembodied. Although shattered and in some pain, she felt elated looking down at the tiny human being cradled in her arms. The terrifying prospect of labor was behind her. She was a mother. She checked his fingers and toes—all there. Suddenly she felt ravenous and reached for the cold sweet potato tubers, which she ate greedily.

After a while, she felt some further mild contractions and the afterbirth came away, looking, she thought, more like a strange internal organ than any bag. She let it plop onto the forest floor. The smell of damp decaying leaves would always remind her of this night, she thought, having spent much of it with her forehead pressed into them. She pulled her net bag toward her and took out a bamboo knife. She peeled a thin sliver off the edge with her teeth to give a razor sharp blade. She also unravelled a short length of string from the strap end of her bag. She measured the length of one finger along the umbilical cord from her son's belly-button-to-be, as her sister had told her, and she firmly tied the string around it, "but not so tight as to cut through it," she recalled her sister saying. Her hand trembling slightly, she sliced through the cord. All seemed well with Ongol, who had found the breast by this time. The cord left attached to his little body would shrivel and drop off of its own accord in the following days.

Wasnonk's sister had been particular about disposal of the placental "carry bag." It was polluting and she had to get rid of it. She parcelled it up in some leaves and secured it with thin vine pulled off a nearby tree. There was a deep limestone pothole adjacent to the path that she would pass returning home, and she would throw the parcel down there. She also carefully turned over the leaves between the tree buttresses to remove all traces of birthing blood, also fatally polluting to men. She spent considerable time carefully wiping blood-streaked, pale, caking amniotic fluid off the baby with soft leaves. She collected them from a Piper tree that was conveniently nearby. Later she unwrapped a leaf parcel containing a new string bag that she had recently netted for her baby and arranged her pandan leaf rain cape in a scoop shape at the bottom and lined it with a generous layer of the soft leaves to make a bed for Ongol, before placing him carefully on it. She arranged the bag of sweet potato tubers first from her head and then gingerly lifted Ongol's bag on top of it. The

A mother carries her infant in a net bag—soles of feet and buttocks visible.

sun was up and had burned the low clouds from the valley by the time Wasnonk set off with Ongol cradled in his string bag on her back. It took her a
long time to reach her house. She walked slowly and painfully, using a stick
for support.

No one took any notice of her return, although word must have spread
about her confinement. It is customary among Wola speakers of the Was valley for women and men to occupy separate houses. She had to pass close by
the men's house, where her husband Haebay lived, but neither he nor his
brother took any interest. Indeed, he ignored the arrival of his son for some
weeks, as did other male relatives, until the pollution of the birth had worn
off mother and child. When she arrived at her women's house, some 50
meters further up the path, she kindled a fire and put some tubers to bake in
the ashes. Wasnonk curled up on her side with Ongol snuggled into her
breast and fell into a deep sleep. She half woke to feed the baby, dropping off
again as he suckled. This would be their routine at night for months to come.
Wasnonk spent four days confined to her house recovering from the exertions
of birth and waiting for its immediate contagion to pass. Her mother-in-law
Saemten brought her food, water, and firewood and sat with her, sometimes
cradling her new grandson. Over the following weeks Wasnonk's life gradually returned to its everyday routine, except now, she had Ongol with her
wherever she went.

* * * * * * * * * * * * * * *

Ongol's early years were relatively uneventful, at least from his infant
perspective. He accompanied his mother daily to her gardens, where he spent
hours sleeping on a bed of soft leaves in her string bag hanging from a nearby
tree stump or fence stake. She fed him on demand, spending long periods sitting with him at her breast, sometimes talking with others. Wasnonk did not
resent these intrusions into her activities; rather she welcomed them as breaks
from whatever she was doing. Her tasks included pulling up thick mats of
grassy vegetation to prepare the soil for tilling, spreading the vegetation to
dry and subsequently heaping it onto fires, breaking up the soil with her digging stick and heaping it up into mounded beds, planting these beds with
sweet potato vines, among other cultivation tasks.

Ongol and his mother shared her house with the pigs that were in her
charge, housed at night in stalls along one wall, their soft grunts contributing
to the sound of home life. The throaty call of Wasnonk, *"urrrrrr jiya urrrrrr
aumuw,"* summoning pigs home for their evening feeding was among the first
words he learned, along with *am* [mother]. His *ab* [father] Haebay did not
pay him much attention until Ongol had cut several teeth at about 18 months,
when Haebay decided that it was time to give him a name. Until then Ongol
had no agreed-upon name; he was Nais-G^{c}nkden-Imbiy-Na-Wiy, the customary epithet meaning "Tiny-Nameless-Boy." A child is not recognized as a
social being in the Was valley until named; with infant mortality high, families refrain from openly acknowledging children until they have a fair chance

of survival. Socially unrecognized by the wider family, the mortuary payments are minimal should they die. Up to this time, children are largely the mother's preoccupation.

This is not to say that Wasnonk had no name for her baby. She called him Na-Iyziy, "My-Son," for some months and subsequently Olnay, "Man-Biter," because he sometimes nipped her nipple painfully when feeding, particularly when hungry. Her husband Haebay did not much care for the name and started to call the boy Ongol, and it was this name that subsequently caught on. If asked why he called his son Ongol, Haebay would have shrugged his shoulders and said, "I don't know." It had nothing to do with the *ongol* [Indian bead ash] tree[1] that men culti-

Mother and infant.

vate around house yards, the leaves of which they sometimes use for hair decoration. It was a name that appealed to him; it sounded right for his son. Personal names do not necessarily have any meaning, even when they refer to something else such as, to give three other popular names, Sab "marsupial," Naway "cockatoo," or Nolai "cicada." They are homonyms it appears. Other names have no meaning at all, such as Unguwdiyp, Neleb, or Mayja. They are "just men's names."

Nonetheless, people can explain the derivation of some names, such as Olnay or Wasnonk. It is not possible to generalize. Wasnonk means literally "Was-river-girl"; she was named after the valley in which she was born. Likewise, Ongol's *ab* [uncle] Kot and his *hay* [cousin] Pes had names that derived from events in their early lives. Ongol's grandfather, Shong, had named Ongol's uncle Kot because of his joy when he had to *kot bay* [yodel] news of his son's survival as a robustly healthy infant, after the several miscarriages and stillbirths that preceded his arrival. If he had known what the future held, Kot's father may have tempered his celebration and its subsequently bitter recollection in the boy's name. It was Pes' mother who had named him, after the *pes* [soft nappy leaves] with which she lined her net bag, because he was always messing these and she had constantly to collect handfuls of fresh leaves. Other names may not relate directly to the child at all but derive from events that occur while a person is still an infant or from relations between other persons. Ongol's uncle, Korobol, was called "Wrong-man" by his mother because of her grievances about her husband's wrongful behavior. Unfortunately, for Korobol the name stuck, but it was not an enduring slight because even names that have a literal meaning become "just names" in everyday life, rather like Sillitoe or Shufflebottom in England.

* * * * * * * * * * * * * *

Some of Ongol's first memories, while fragmentary, concerned dramatic events. Similar to many small boys the world over, one such memory was the first spanking he received from his *ab*. The occasion, physically emblazoned on his memory, concerned a prized pearl shell that Haebay had received from the bridewealth exchanged at the marriage of Wasnonk's sister. Ongol was present in the men's house one day, left in the care of his father, when Haebay got the shell out, unwrapped it, and sat discussing it and his exchange plans with some relatives. He intended to give it in an *ol bay* [man maker] mortuary transaction, which is part of an exchange sequence that customarily follows sometime after a person's death, possibly years later, when kin invest wealth with one another in a payment called the *ol tobway* and expect a threefold return in the *ol bay* repayment. Haebay had received a pig in *ol tobway* from his father's mother's relatives in the name of his deceased father's brother. It is an exchange that measures men's transactional ability and social standing par excellence, and Haebay was planning carefully for it.

Ongol was fascinated by the shell. He had seen men handling such pearl shells before in transactions but had not been so close to one. They were rare and highly valued objects. Later, his father carefully wrapped the shell in a sheet of silken moth cocoon with moss and white cockatoo down and slid it into its pandan spathe and fern leaf envelope before binding it up again with meters of string in an elaborate crisscross pattern.

When Ongol subsequently told his *hay* Pes, who was on an extended visit to Tombem with his family, that he had seen his father's prize pearl shell, Pes said that he did not believe him because only *ol howma* [renowned men] handled such treasures. Stung by the disparagement of his father's status, Ongol said that he would prove it. It was midday and nobody was around the homestead. They went down to the men's house and opened the low door into the sleeping quarters at the rear where Haebay had cached the shell. Ongol brought it through the door to the sitting area. After looking at it, Pes said that he could not tell if it was a shell of any real size or not, because it was wrapped up. Ongol foolishly allowed this jibe to prompt him to unwrap the shell. They both peeked at it and, suddenly realizing the seriousness of their actions, tried to wrap it up again. They could not reproduce Haebay's neat binding and bundled the misshapen package back where they had found it.

Haebay returned home late that afternoon, having walked a considerable distance from a settlement in the neighboring Nembi valley to witness a mortuary exchange. After baking and eating some sweet potato tubers, he went to turn in for the night. Noticing that the wooden slats that served as a door to the sleeping room were oddly lodged in position, he feared that someone had entered to steal the shell. He pulled the slats out and crawled in hurriedly to the dark room. He found the shell cached where he had left it and felt a surge of relief, which soon turned to flaming rage when he took out the package and saw the state of it. He challenged his brother Kot who had a ne'er-do-well reputation, but Kot denied any knowledge of what had happened to it. Haebay stormed up the path to Wasnonk's house to ask if she had seen anything. She had been working in a distant garden all day, but "I left Ongol here with Pes

Binding up a pearl shell in a pandan spathe envelope.

and they may have seen something," she said. When Haebay turned to the two boys, he could see from their frightened faces that they were guilty. He had no time for Ongol's mumbled excuses about defending his father's maligned reputation and grabbed the nearest thing that came to hand, which was a pig tether hanging on the wall, and proceeded to beat the pair.

In his blind fury, he caught Wasnonk with some lashes too, as she sought to protect the boys after they had received several blows each. The result was that ugly wheals formed on the boys, and Wasnonk departed the next day to live with her brother's family at his place, and Haebay had to indemnify her with a cowry shell necklace before she would return some weeks later. It was a vivid lesson in the value of pearl shells and other wealth to adults, and by extension the transactions in which they hand them on to one another. Ongol witnessed a number of these exchanges as he grew up and slowly learned about the complex series of transactions that mark social and political life. One such exchange was to make up another of his earliest memories, the large *ol sond* compensation payment for Kot, his uncle.

* * * * * * * * * * * * * *

The problem with Kot was that he was socially out of control. His behavior was unpredictable; it did not always conform to what people expected and was sometimes outright unacceptable. "He's like a big child, has never grown up," Haebay his *haemay* [brother] would say. "He doesn't know right from wrong." He caused his relatives endless problems, embroiling them in one dispute after another. He would, for example, regularly help himself to produce from others' gardens as the fancy took him. The time he killed a pig that he came across rooting in the forest, surreptitiously butchering and cooking it, was memorable. Haebay felt certain guilt because, when Kot arrived one evening with cooked pork and shared it, he accepted Kot's explanation that the father of Huwniy, a girl he was courting from a community on the other side of the valley, had given it to him, he should have known better. Subsequently implicated in the theft, Kot's relatives tried to cover up the deed when the pig owner, who lived further down the Was valley, started to sound off about the mysterious disappearance of the animal. They would have gotten away with it, if Kot had not stupidly bragged about his actions. Consequently, they found themselves involved in a heated dispute, which cost them two pigs in compensation.

The dispute was a drawn out affair, as is common. The two parties met on several days at one another's homesteads to argue the case, sometimes spilling over onto the adjacent grassy *howma* [communal clearing] found at the center of most settlements with homesteads dotted around it. The meetings were informal, there is no court system to supervise hearings nor is there a judge to officiate and adjudicate. While the principal parties to the dispute do most of the talking, others express an opinion, too, often in support of their kin, and sometimes act to restrain them if they become overexcited and likely to come to blows. There is widespread agreement as to what comprises wrongful behavior. Those present seek to establish culpability and may argue over the evidence of wrongdoing. The opinions passed indicate to the two parties what the majority thinks and the appropriate way to settle their differences, such as the level of compensation; in this event, two pigs would indemnify the owner. The aim is settlement and closure, not justice and punishment. However, with no authority to enforce a settlement, it is necessary to convince those in the wrong to make amends as necessary.

Those concerned about their social reputations, such as Haebay and his cousins, tend to heed the majority opinion, particularly what their kin have to say, because to ignore it can damage their standing as responsible persons. It was absence of such a social conscience that made Kot such a difficult character, apparently impervious to community opinion. Furthermore, those who ignore the views of their kin may forfeit their support, especially if blatantly in the wrong. To have kin at your back defending you is a necessary feature of any tribal regime lacking central authority. If you lose their support, you become more vulnerable to physical attack from others. The threat of violence is another consideration that inclines those in the wrong to settle a dispute, primarily by offering appropriate compensation. When disputes become deadlocked with neither party giving way, violence is likely to erupt in frustration as one tries to force acceptance of his or her views on the other. This can lead to armed hostilities with serious consequences for both sides. No one in his right mind wants to trigger such fighting if embroiled in a dispute. All of these forces incline those involved in a dispute to reach a settlement, albeit the arguments leading up to it, extending over several days, may be heated, alarmingly so sometimes.

Kot's behavior became increasingly difficult with time, and as a young adult, he got himself into progressively more serious scrapes. One day he ran off with Huwniy, the young woman he was courting from a nearby community. The pair moved from place to place, spending much time at remote forest locales, where they used unoccupied houses and helped themselves to food from adjacent gardens, avoiding their kin who were after them. When they were finally caught, a fierce dispute erupted. Kot's relatives offered to pay compensation but would not agree to go the whole way and arrange a *hort bay* [attenuated bridewealth] transaction to marry the couple. When Kot ran off to the Nembi valley in the midst of all this, even Huwniy and her kin realized that he would make a hopeless husband. The problem for Huwniy was that she had gotten pregnant during the weeks they were on the run. When she informed her father, he arranged for her to marry an older polygynously married man whom he knew was seeking a fourth wife. Few people knew that the daughter she subsequently bore was not her husband's but was Kot's child. The concealment would embarrass young Ongol in the future.

When he returned to the Was valley, Kot continued with his wayward behavior. As if failing to pull his weight with daily tasks, such as cultivating gardens, constructing houses, and so on, was not enough to exasperate his kin, he stole ripe pandan nuts, pilfered from gardens, and helped himself to others' property. There was even another episode involving a pig. Many of these wrongdoings cost Haebay and his relatives further compensation payments. What were Haebay and his relatives to do about such an uncontrollable personality? Kot's extreme behavior raises the intriguing question of how stateless societies maintain social order with no police, law courts, or other formal means of social control. Instead, order depends on persons acknowledging that they have mutual rights and responsibilities with respect to one another and realizing that the support of kinsfolk is vital. Behavior such as Kot's that threatens these assumptions is irrational. It pushed the status quo to a breaking point.

* * * * * * * * * * * * * *

It was inevitable that Kot would one day overstep the mark. He was smitten by Huwniy's sister but she would have nothing to do with him. One day, rebuffed while visiting her settlement, he attacked another woman in frustration and violently raped her, injuring her seriously. She was entering her house, halfway in on all fours, when he jumped on her from behind. Kot disappeared again into the forest, after helping himself to the largest of the woman's harvested sweet potato tubers. Her furious kin set out to take revenge, saying that no compensation could make up for what he had done this time. When Kot's equally angry relatives heard the news yodeled across the valley, they were inclined to agree but they felt obliged to find Kot first and see what they could salvage from the debacle. They searched for two days over into the Ak valley before returning home, saying that he would turn up again soon enough. Sadly, prophetic words it turned out.

Some five days later a yodeled message from the Ak valley said Kot was dead. Haebay and some relatives rushed over. They heard how someone had seen his corpse in the Ak River, tangled in the roots of a large tree that had been swept downstream and jammed between boulders in the turbulent water-course, adjacent to some gardens, from where someone had spotted him. The river had evidently carried his body some distance to judge from its horrendous injuries, limbs broken akimbo. His kin retrieved his mangled body by balancing along the tree trunk and carried him back to Tombem lashed under a pole. They arranged the pole on two forked uprights driven into the ground in the center of the *howma*, as is customary at funerals, and three days of mourning followed. A group of female relatives sat around the corpse wailing gently and chatting, their lament increasing in volume whenever someone arrived at the *hombera* [funeral]. They could hear new arrivals approaching from a distance, as it is customary to start wailing loudly as one nears, walking up to a corpse to keen and sometimes stroke it in grief. When women and children arrive, they join those sitting around the suspended corpse, while men go to the nearest men's house where they congregate to smoke and talk. The wailing

Handing over a pearl shell as a contribution to an *ol gwat* mortuary exchange; women sitting and mourning around the deceased's corpse.

expresses both anguish and fear. The *wezow* [life force] of individuals becomes a *towmow* [spirit] at death, which is malicious, assailing relatives, causing sickness and even death. A newly emerged *towmow* is believed particularly vindictive, and during a funeral people avoid going out at night for fear of attack.

Much talk at funerals concerns the associated series of mortuary exchanges. Many of those arriving bring valuables to contribute to the first payment called the *ol gwat* that occurs following interment. They present these to people more closely related to the deceased than they are. These donations indicate something about the state of their relations, as people say that they help to ease the recipient's sorrow. They also signal something about the giver's feelings of loss. A paltry gift suggests jaded associations. The wealth flowing through the hands of the deceased's kin shows the health of the social network. The recipients in turn pass on what they receive to the deceased's closest relatives, who also receive contributions via their social networks and orchestrate the *gwat* distribution. At Kot's funeral, it was Haebay and his *haemay* [brother-cousins] who coordinated the exchange. The wealth accumulates in the men's house, and people say that the sight helps assuage the grief of close kin.

After some days of public mourning, it is time to dispose of the corpse. Two men, not close relatives, accept responsibility for preparing the grave. The Wola disposed of corpses in a number of ways: buried in a grave, exposed on a rock ledge or wooden platform erected on a rock face, laid in an enclosed coffin raised some two meters off the ground, or placed in an open-fronted lean-to-style coffin erected at waist height. It was decided to inter Kot in a raised coffin under the graceful casuarina trees on the edge of the *howma*, which served to remind young Ongol for years to come of these tumultuous events.

The coffin comprised four straight poles driven into the ground in pairs a shoulder width apart, a body length between them. The makers lashed two stout pieces of wood in place between the more distant poles on either long side of what would comprise the coffin. They cut a series of matching grooves in the top edge of these at close intervals and placed some whittled spindlelike pieces between them to make the floor of the coffin. They hewed and then lashed in place the planklike sides and ends. The one at the head end had a hole carved in it through which the deceased's head was visible. If the deceased wore a wig or had long hair suitable for wig making, someone might take it, the hair coming away easily with the scalp skin after a period of decomposition. No one availed themselves of Kot's hair with its ill-fated associations. The plank at the foot end was larger, extending from the coffin to the ground, and sometimes people painted a design on it in charcoal, ocher, and white clay, similar to the anthropomorphic designs on shields. They decorated the other boards with designs, too, sometimes red crescents depicting pearl shells. The coffin-makers cut another series of matching grooves at close intervals in the top edges of the long planklike sides and put more whittled spindlelike pieces in place to make the coffin roof. They lined the inside with large tough pandan leaves,[2] and they erected a fence around the entire structure to stop pigs rooting around it; the thought of them dislodging and eating pieces of decomposing corpse was horrific. When the coffin was ready, they transferred the corpse on its funeral pole amid loud wailing and laid it to rest. They covered it with further pandan leaves, put the wooden spindles in place along the top edge, and finally enclosed the coffin with grassy sods. (This coffin, accorded to men only, was subject to much variation depending on the feelings of kin; sometimes, for instance, they erected a small thatched roof over the coffin—a popular or socially renowned man dying in his prime might have a particularly elaborate structure.)

An event involving his father and uncles during the funeral particularly impressed young Ongol's memory. On the first day of mourning, distraught with grief, acting as if somehow responsible for Kot's untimely death, they each hacked off a finger joint. The cuts were not clean, as they used polished stone axes. Ongol's abiding recollection was of their mixed cries of grief and pain as they wandered around the corpse with blood streaming down their forearms and dripping to the ground. It was a customary way of showing grief. Another involved the mourning attire of women closely related to the deceased, such as Kot's *am*, Saemten, and his *boliy* [sister-in-law], Wasnonk.

Ongol hardly recognized them at first, their strange appearance initially frightening him. They had donned long, ankle-length grass skirts, daubed their bodies and faces entirely with white clay, and made and wore voluminous necklaces of Job's tears seeds, which signify grieving and withdrawal from everyday life, indeed making it awkward to undertake routine tasks.

* * * * * * * *

Following the interment came the distribution of the accumulated *gwat* wealth on display at the men's house. It comprised cowry shell necklaces, pearl shells, pigs, bundles of salt, possum teeth pins, and *wombok* [cosmetic oil]. A proportion of the wealth went to Saemten's kin. It is customary for the kin

A woman in mourning apparel.

with whom the deceased resided (usually his father's relatives if a man, as here with Kot, and a husband's if a woman) to amass the *gwat* and distribute it to those living elsewhere (usually the deceased's maternal kin if a man and both paternal and maternal if a woman), although this was not always so. The coffin builders also received something, as is usual, for interring the corpse. In addition, Haebay and his relatives presented some of the wealth to Huwniy's kin to meet their demands for compensation for Kot's final misdemeanor. However, this was not the end of the compensation payments or the mortuary transactions. Over the next few days, Saemten's kin arrived with valuables for the next stage in the sequence, reciprocating the *gwat* in an *ol tobway* exchange. It included the customary *gwat kaend* of pigs and sides of pork. Haebay and his relatives added some animals from their herds and a week after the interment staged the funeral pig slaughter and pork distribution, cooking the meat with hot stones in a long earth oven running along one side of the *howma*. Many people turned up and received some pork, in particular those who had contributed to the *gwat* payment.

During the funeral, there was predictably much discussion about Kot's death and softly spoken conjecture as to what might have happened. Many suspected Huwniy's relatives of waylaying him, but they vehemently denied it, pointing out that they had many witnesses to being elsewhere in the Was valley. Furthermore, no one could recall seeing them in the neighboring Ak valley for a month or so previously. Kot's close relatives, including his two *haemay*, did not press the charge, possibly for fear of sparking off a violent confrontation—the wayward Kot had cost them enough already. His death consequently entered the local memory as an unsolved mystery. Nonetheless, while protesting that they were not directly involved, Huwniy's relatives acknowledged a certain culpability, for if Kot surmised they were searching for him with malicious intent, he may have been careless when crossing the river, trying to escape when the river was too high, or, it was whispered, he might have committed suicide (although those who knew him thought this improbable; his infamy never seemed to worry him).

Huwniy's kin subsequently entered into, as party to the tragedy, an *ol sond* compensation exchange with Kot's *ab*, Shong, and his relatives. In doing so, they reflected Wola ideas about responsibility for violent death, where anyone present or involved is accountable (e.g., if someone on a journey has a fatal accident, those with him are responsible, for they should have been looking out for his welfare). It signaled that they did not wish it to damage relations between them; the transaction again communicating something about their intentions regarding their social affairs. The first stage of the transaction, the *ol komb*, took place a month or so after the funeral. Anticipation started to build among Haebay's kin when they heard the *hor kobay* "*Ooooooo*" yodel echoing periodically from across the valley. This marks the slaughter and butchery of pigs for the forthcoming exchange by those preparing the presentation, who display the sides of pork destined for the payment on a chest-high horizontal pole at their homesteads.

All those contributing to the exchange kill pigs in the days preceding the event. On the agreed day they put on their second-best finery—various feathers in the hair (such as cassowary pompoms) and faces painted with black and white designs—and converge on the recipients' place, each man carrying a side of pork draped across his shoulders. They yodel the characteristic "*Ooooooo*" cry as they approach. When they arrive at the recipients' *howma*, they trot around in a large circle hooting loudly, and others who are present may join in, though not those closely related to the deceased. After dancing for a while, they display the pork together with any other wealth, such as seashells, and formally hand it over. One of Huwniy's relatives gave a standard oration along the lines of "these things are to help Shong, Haebay, and their *sem* [family] to assuage their sorrow at their loss," although truth be told they felt a sense of relief at no longer having Kot on the loose, mixed with guilt for feeling so. They would never have dreamed of openly admitting to their feelings, even to themselves, as these feelings infringed on the cardinal value placed on kin supporting one another. Once the donors handed over the pork, the recipients shared it with those in their sociopolitical network, usually according to the wishes of the deceased's close relatives.

Witnessed by Ongol as a small boy, these events served to further his education in the centrality of exchange in Was valley social and political life. But recalled dimly by him in later life—the *gwat* mortuary and *komb* compensation transactions conflated in his memory—they also planted the seeds of future misunderstandings. The implications of the large *ol komb* compensation exchange were that Huwniy's relatives had tacitly accepted responsibility for Kot's death. It was as if he was executed with the unspoken acceptance of his kin, as someone beyond social control, impervious to the sanctions that ensure normal behavior. He had strained the stateless tribal order to a breaking point and, leaving his relatives little option, had paid the ultimate penalty of his life, for which they sought to take no customary *luwzimb* [revenge.]

Genealogy showing relations between persons (words in brackets are Wola kinship terms).

Note: The Wola language classifies kin differently to English, and some of the kin terms in this book may consequently strike the reader as strange. For example, Wola does not distinguish between father and uncle on the father's side (including 2nd uncles or father's father's brother's sons), all are *ab*, whereas it does distinguish maternal uncles, called *mai*, from paternal ones (the *mai* term is used reciprocally for maternal nephews too). Nor does it distinguish between father's and paternal uncles' daughters, both are *mboliy* (male speaking).

Genealogy diagram (Wola kinship terms in brackets):

- △ = ○ [moma] [mom]
- ○ = Shong = Saemten [mom] [moma] [mom]
- △ [ab]
- Lem [ab]
- Sab [ab]
- Huwniy
- Kot [ab]
- Kombaem [mboliy]
- △ [boliy]
- △ = ○ [mboliy]
- ○ [kaykay] [kaykay]
- △ = ○ [ab] [bap]
- △ [yaegin]
- △ = ○ [bap] [raem]
- △ [hay]
- Haebay = Wasnonk [ab] [am]
- Twaen [mboliy]   Hond [haemay]
- Naway [mai]
- Mindiy = Ongol = Wat [weray] [ego] [weray]
- △ [iyziy]   ○ [waenay]   △ [iyziy]
- ○ = Korobol [bap] [mai]
- Pes [hay]
- ○ = Nap [bap] [nyaegin]
- △ [haemay]

Chapter 2

Growing Up and Ensuring Health

Life has its shocks, although none can perhaps compare with entering the world or leaving it, both of which events we all experience but cannot recount to others. One of Ongol's earliest upsets was the arrival of Twaen, his *mboliy* [sister]. It made him so angry, interrupting his agreeable existence monopolizing his mother's attention. He was always an avid feeder and was reluctant to give up the breast, even after years on solid food. There was nothing untoward in his behavior; it is common in the Was valley for children to breast-feed for years, not months. Mothers try gradually to wean their offspring, in keeping with their measured and easy approach to child rearing generally. While Wasnonk encouraged Ongol not to suckle from toddlerhood onward, he was reluctant to stop altogether, even when his father and other male relatives started to ridicule him. When she was several months pregnant with his sister, Wasnonk realized that she would have to take some action.

One evening when Ongol demanded a comfort feed, he received the most appalling surprise. Instead of his mother's sweet warm milk, he took a mouthful of foul tasting stuff that caused his mouth to burn. His mother laughed at his shocked expression until tears came to her eyes, which only exacerbated Ongol's bewilderment and anger. She handed him a gourd of water to wash the bitter taste out his mouth. He threw an enormous tantrum, which only made matters worse because, when he smote his mother across the head with her digging stick, she retaliated with a hefty slap to his legs. He was reduced to frustrated tears. His comfortable life with his mother was falling apart. As if to underline this, she called to her husband, who carried him off kicking to the men's house for the night, where he was increasingly to spend his time. Over the next few days, whenever he gingerly approached his mother for a feed, cautiously testing her nipple with the tip of his tongue, he sensed the same

A woman eats pork while breast-feeding her daughter after a pig kill.

awful caustic taste. Before the week was out, he was thoroughly weaned. Later he learned that his mother had smeared her nipples with tar, scraped from the inside of his father's tobacco pipe.

All in all, Ongol had no reason to complain, having dominated his mother's life for some time. He could have been a taken off the breast as an infant to make way for a new sibling. The extended period of nursing, suppressing ovulation, had contributed to Wasnonk not conceiving again for some time. On top of this, men customarily observe a lengthy postpartum taboo to protect themselves from the polluting effects of childbirth. The taboo on intercourse also ensures that a mother does not have another child until the previous one has developed some independence. If she falls pregnant too soon, this may make a "mother's milk bad" such that an infant will refuse the breast and wean prematurely, or make her milk dry up, resulting in a weak, sickly child. If she tried to feed both a baby and a toddler, both might be under nourished. The parents of children who are taken off the breast too soon with the arrival of a new baby may resort to a small rite to ward off stunted growth. Someone who knows the appropriate spell mutters it as the child drinks some water, representing the mother's breast milk, and sucks on a length of peeled sugarcane of the *maesep* variety that grows vigorously—just as they wish the infant to develop.

Ideally, weaning is a gradual process, as with stubborn Ongol, and reflects the steady pace of growing up in the Was valley. While Ongol felt shoved to one side by his baby sister and spent more time, at his parents' encouragement, with his father in the men's house after her arrival, he nonetheless continued to spend much time with his mother, taking sly pokes at his sister when he thought he could get away with it, as he experienced a strange pleasure from hearing her cry. Childhood should be a carefree time of life. Ongol's was by and large, aside from a few bothersome occasions, expectable, as any boy's enthusiasm is likely to run away with him occasionally, such as in the pearl shell episode. He enjoyed an ordinary upbringing by New Guinea Highland standards. Reflecting the stateless sociopolitical order where no one has authority over another, children are neither frequently forced to do things against their will nor chastised for their actions, unless seriously out of line, notably damaging others' interests. They have much freedom, although they have to learn, and keep within the limits of, what others accept as tolerable or normal behavior. This comprises the process of socialization, as in all societies, and occasionally juveniles demand guidance, and, if willful, rebuke. However, as long as they are not wayward and provoke the ire of adults, Was children enjoy a free and easy life. They face relatively few restrictions, and to those familiar with the straightjacket of school education, learning is informal.

Ongol spent his childhood years living alternately at two places, Homal and Tombem, on Meng territory. Meng was the name of his father's *semgᵉnk* [small family]. These kin groups comprise some 30–40 close relatives. The Was valley comprises a patchwork of such "family" territories. The "small family" groups occupying the same part of the valley make up a *semonda* [large family]. These comprise 100–200 distantly related persons. Ongol's "large family" was called Aenda. In referring to someone, people may preface their personal name with that of a *sem* to which they are related, in reverse order to English usage, putting the *sem* [surname] first; so that Ongol, for example, was Meng Ongol. More often he was Pol Ongol, using the name of the *sem* through which his mother's father had claimed land. This naming convention, while extending on individuals' personal names and serving as a part of their self, applies to only one aspect of their kin-defined identity. The aspect is not culturally specified, in the sense of necessarily relating to the *sem* with which they are currently living, nor following any rule such as being their father's *sem* affiliation or what anthropologists call a patrilineal connection.

You should not marry anyone from a "family" group to which you are related through a close relative such as your mother or father; marriages are exogamous. You can live and cultivate on the territory of any "small family" where residents recognize that you have rights to do so, that is, have the necessary exchange-validated extant kin relationships. Many men, such as Ongol's father Haebay, opt to live where there fathers did before them, which is likely the place where they grew up and feel most at home. However, they are free to move elsewhere if they wish to do so, anywhere they can claim access to land.

Tombem is situated high up the wall of the valley above the Was River in a fairly densely settled area where there are several gardens. The vegetation in such places is largely secondary, predominantly consisting of dense stands of two- to three-meter-high cane grass interspersed with patches of shorter coarse grass and areas of secondary woodland. Homal is some three hours' walk downstream, situated in a small side valley adjacent to Mount Puga. The roaring white waters of the turbulent Was River are nearby and plainly audible. Fewer households have gardens here. The vegetation is largely primary rainforest interspersed with patches of cultivation and regrowth. When he was young, Ongol found it a slightly scary place with the dark forest nearby, home to dangerous demons, creatures that he was told are part human and part animal or plant that attack and kill humans in horrible ways. In adolescence, when he sometimes sought solitude, it became his favorite home, particularly with its opportunities to hunt.

* * * * * * * * * * * * * *

After his sister's arrival, Ongol accompanied Wasnonk less often to the gardens and soon was hardly going at all. He had long since stopped going daily. He gradually spent more time in the company of other children. On occasion, his mother had initially left him in the care of one of his older cousins, at first against his wishes, provoking temper tantrums to their amusement. Subsequently he wandered off on his own and increasingly became independent of his mother. It was a gradual process, epitomized in the slow swap from Wasnonk's house to the men's house, with his parents encouraging him to stand on his own two feet and not to rely so much on his mother. He came to subscribe to the view of boys his age that "only sissies hang around with their mothers," an attitude that he would expand on as an adult regarding female company generally. After his induction to his peer group, he came to prefer its company, roaming around settled areas and hanging about house yards and *howma* with other children. They did not venture far afield, no further than nearby gardens. Sometimes they could be heard charging noisily along paths, giving voice to the irrepressible energy and excitement of youngsters.

They played a variety of games, which passed in and out of vogue, one craze giving away to another. The games they played included "tops" where they spun wooden tops at sticks driven into the ground, scoring a point if they hit a stick. Another was a version of fives where they rapidly tossed some polished river pebbles repeatedly between the palm and back of the hand to see how many times they could do it before dropping them. Sometimes on rainy days they played "string figures," deriving much fun from tying such smutty designs as "wiping your bottom" and "man and woman bonking" in addition to more staid representations such as "vine bridge," "grasshopper" and "cassowaries." But Ongol always thought this a girls' game, preferring more boisterous activities. Favorites included the "swing," comprised of a length of vine suspended from a tree branch over a steep slope, arranged to swing out high above the ground and back again, and the "toboggan," comprised of a large tough leaf, used sledgelike to slide down slopes—the steeper and scarier the better. Sometimes they attached a whirligig of entwined pandan leaf strips to a stick that spun around when held aloft as they ran along paths—what later generations would call "airplanes." Other times they played in streams, splashing around and building "dams" of stones and mud.

Some days they would play at being adults. They would build small leanto houses thatched with cane grass. They cut pearl shells and sides of pork from large leaves and played at exchanges and pig kills, and sometimes they decorated themselves with featherlike leaves or bird feathers, if available, and painted designs on their faces with colored clay and held dances. A favorite with the boys was to pretend that hostilities had broken out, and armed with small bows made by their fathers or other kin, they would run around shooting soft green cane grass stems at one another, albeit this game regularly ended in tears with someone hurt. On occasion, the boys used their bows and blunt-ended arrows to stun birds, or they stalked and threw stones at them. They plucked and roasted the ones they caught over a fire, frequently squabbling over their share of the game. They became increasingly accurate bowmen as time passed, until in their teens they were proficient hunters. The shift from play to serious hunting was again gradual. The boys spent

A little girl plays with a whirligig of pandan leaf strips on a stick.

increasing amounts of time hunting until in their teens it became a regular activity, when Ongol spent extended periods at Homal.

Adolescent boys venture into the forest with its richer game; the grasslands around settlements are home to small birds and rodents only, but taking potshots at these small targets is good training and helps them improve their accuracy. They stalk game as previously, only now armed with an array of sharp pointed arrows, including the three-pronged bird arrow. They learn to set both spring and deadfall traps for marsupials and, equally important, to read spoor so that they locate them correctly on the "paths" of animals. A popular ruse in dry spells is to erect a hide, comprising a rough frame covered with foliage, overlooking a pool of water to which birds come to drink as other sources dry up. They arrange a pole as a perch over the pool to entice birds; the pole extends into the hide where it has a length of hollow bamboo lashed to its top edge. The hunter sits quietly in the hide with a pronged arrow ready in his bow and lined up in the bamboo tube along the perch, ready for any hapless bird that alights there. Another common hunting technique involves using dogs to flush out game, although only some men own dogs. As a young man approaches adulthood, his relatives may include him on hunting trips further afield with dogs, and also take him stalking nocturnal animals by

A boy holds a bow and arrow; his companion has a "car," a wheel mounted on a cane stem, making a vroooming noise when he pushes it.

moonlight, another successful strategy. Some become particularly good hunters, skilled at reading the forest and regularly bag possums, cuscus, and wallabies in addition to large birds such as colorful parrots, doves, honeyeaters, and, if lucky, birds of paradise with their highly valued headdress plumes.

* * * * * * * * * * * * * * *

The shift from play to other adult pursuits is similarly a gradual transition. A boy may decide to accompany his father or other close relative when he is pioneering an area for a new garden and help in a desultory way to clear undergrowth, erect fences, burn cut vegetation and so on, although he is not able to give serous assistance with heavy tasks until well into his teens when he is strong enough. At this age, he may establish a small garden of his own, and by the time he marries, he is likely to have more than one. Similarly, a boy may give some spasmodic help to relatives constructing a house such as fetching materials, holding things, and undertaking small tasks, but only older boys can contribute significantly to heavy work. Boys may also help their households by collecting firewood, often with their parents' encouragement, although some are reluctant to take on such responsibilities.

When it comes to wealth transactions, which occupy much of men's time, boys do not really become involved until their late teens, although youngsters may receive valuables in an exchange and invest them following their father's advice. Again, taking on exchange responsibilities is a gradual process; a boy starts slowly, maybe receiving a pearl shell to invest or a small pig for his mother to keep. Thus, he begins in a small way to make contributions to exchanges and receive wealth. The sons of more successful men do not start sooner or necessarily receive more wealth as youngsters. A boy may start to take an active interest in exchanges in his mid-teens and attend events, helping relatives display wealth, for example, by collecting the fern fronds on which to arrange it. Ongol could remember the first time he had eagerly run off to gather ferns, returning with an armful and proudly helping his father and uncles arrange them along the eaves of their men's house for a display of valuables.

Twaen's childhood was somewhat different. While girls and boys are treated the same when they are babies and toddlers, girls never stop accompanying their mothers to the gardens when older, although they may stay behind some days and play with boys around homesteads. Even then, they may find themselves with some responsibility that inhibits their play, as girls are more likely to be called on to undertake child care; for example, mothers expect them to look after smaller siblings while they are away in gardens. A girl takes on adult tasks sooner than a boy does, being in her mother's company much of the time and helping her. Again, she assumes tasks gradually. When small she may carry a couple of sweet potatoes or a small piece of firewood home in her little net bag, and as she grows up her load increases. We see here the instigation of the sexual division of labor arrangements that characterize Wola daily life, where men and women undertake different activities.

Initially a girl, like a boy, accompanies her mother for security and plays in the garden, but she is soon encouraged to help her mother with the cultivation work. This is largely playful at first, and includes help with small tasks such as fetching embers to light fires, but slowly her help becomes more substantial and she lends a hand with tilling the soil and heaping up and planting mounds. In her early teens, her father and possibly other relatives will allocate her areas in gardens for which she is solely responsible. When she marries, she may continue to cultivate these areas if her husband's place is nearby. Similarly with pig keeping, a girl graduates from assisting her mother to being responsible for the care of her own pig. She may do this for a man other than her father and receive a *showmay hentiya* [pig rope] payment for her services, wealth that she will pass on to a close male relative such as her father.

Boys enjoy more freedom than girls do to play as they grow up and appear to mature more slowly. The difference in dress between infant girls and boys reflects the differing rates at which they mature into their roles. Almost as soon as they can toddle, small girls wear a grass skirt and carry a small net bag like the ones their mothers carry; whereas boys run around naked until five or six years of age. People expect little girls to help their mothers and act like small women, whereas boys do not shadow adults, are not made responsible for tasks, and behave like children. No one thinks they should participate in adult activities, many of which are physically beyond them or cannot be undertaken until they approach adulthood.

Both girls and boys learn their roles by observing adults, playing at grown-up activities, and gradually taking on adult tasks. The line between

Children learn through play: a boy experiments with an axe during clearance of a new garden.

play and work is not clear; children slowly spend increasingly more time on serious pursuits. There is no formal education; life is an education. They learn naturally by observing and doing in their own time. Indeed, children are unaware that they are learning much of the time, acquiring tacit knowledge and skills by watching and experimenting until able to undertake tasks. If you asked someone when he or she learned to do something and who taught him or her, you would likely receive a blank look, as the person just picked up the knowledge in the course of everyday life. If we asked Twaen, for example, when she was an adult, who taught her to cultivate sweet potato mounds, she would probably say that she has always known, which in a sense, so far as her memory goes, she has, having observed her mother Wasnonk since infancy and subsequently experimenting as a girl working alongside her and mastering the skill.

* * * * * * * * * * * * * *

"How would you like to be a *kem*?" asked Ongol's father and uncles one evening as they sat in the foyer of their men's house scraping sweet potato tubers and putting them to bake in the ashes of the fire. The question did not come entirely as a surprise, as Ongol had recently heard people discussing the staging of a *sor kem* ritual, which was performed to ensure the well-being of the community. He was ambivalent about taking on a central role in the ritual as one of the two *kem* boys. While he was flattered to know that people thought him responsible enough and were talking about him in the role, he

Under her mother's watchful eye, a small girl helps heap up soil for a sweet potato mound.

was reluctant to volunteer because he knew that it involved a tiresome period of seclusion and the observation of some taboos. After thinking about it for a few days, he agreed; what had swung his decision was the prospect of feeding on the generous cuts of pork given to the *kem* boys, which would compensate for the irksome aspects of the ritual.

Ongol and his partner, another young man from one of the other Aenda *semgᵉnk*, had little idea of what to expect and quizzed the two men who had performed the *kem* role when the community last staged the ritual about three decades previously. Their memories were hazy on some points and they disagreed over others. But there was nothing untoward about that because rites invariably differed from one performance to another; there is no immutable liturgy, although the same rite will follow similar procedures on different occasions. Furthermore, there was a man from across the river living at Kapenda who would officiate at the ritual. He was the only person in that part of the valley who knew the necessary spells and manipulations, which he had learned from his father. Before the ritual, some men built a cane-grass-thatched house on a knoll below the *howma*, large enough to accommodate several people and an earth oven pit.

On the first day of the ritual men congregated at the *kem* house where the Kapenda man killed a small pig and cut off a wide strip of fatty pork belly, which he cut up into chunks. He distributed them to those present on pieces of maroon cordyline leaf,[1] while muttering the following spell (or incantation):[2]

Hulu	wuwno	iba	wido,	baiyaba	iba wido.
Girl	boy	keep	well,	all possessions	plenty.

Hulu	igidi	iba	wido,	baiyaba	iba wido.
Girl	boy	keep	well,	all possessions	plenty.

It expresses the ritual's objectives, which are to ensure the well-being of the hosts and their prosperity, notably that they handle much wealth in coming transactions. The recipients of the chunks of meat, including Ongol and his partner, cut them into smaller pieces. Then, running in a circle around the house, they threw these in all directions over it and into the surrounding cane grass chanting repeatedly, "*buragaib, buragaib, buragaib,*" a phrase that has no apparent meaning beyond calling on the community's *towmow* [ancestor spirits] to come and receive the offering, called the *buragaib kalay*. It was necessary to throw the scraps of meat over the house, which represented a barrier between the living and the dangerous *towmow*. The Kapenda man again whispered his spell as he threw his meat. This noisy offering placated the *towmow*, reducing the likelihood that they would attack living relatives, inflict illness, and kill them.

Later that day the Kapenda man prepared a plaque of *kem* palm cockatoo[3] feathers and a *tomtay* arrow for the next day's proceedings. The plaque comprised a half-meter length of robust pandan leaf smeared in red ocher, with seven large black palm cockatoo feathers arranged around its edges, three down either long side and one at the top. He painted the arrow's black palm[4] point with red ocher, too, and tied on two *ngai* lily leaves.[5] He whispered the following spell as he tied the leaves and arranged the feathers around the plaque:

Ku taegali	winini.	Ku taegali	winini,	urukemba	haezida.
A large river	is.	A large river	is,	palm cockatoo	is.

Yaeka yaeka	laeru	yaeka- la	babu	bidu.	Ku taegali	winini.
Chirping	palm cockatoo	chirping	does	well.	A large river	is.

Urukemba	haezida.	Yaeka yaeka	laeru	yaeka- la	babu	bidu.
Palm cockatoo	is.	Chirping	palm cockatoo	chirping	does	well.

When a young anthropologist asked about the meaning of the spell some years later, he was told that those staging the ritual would enjoy long life just as a large river flows for a long way, even endlessly. It reiterates the ritual's aim to ensure good health, longevity, and material prosperity. The *kem* bird is an apt symbol for this as it is a particularly strong bird; it has a powerful hooked beak capable of cracking hard nuts and is believed to be long lived. Black palm is likewise a particularly hard wood that does not rot quickly. Although both bird feathers and palm wood are black, no one could think of any meaning related to the color black. Nor could they for the red ocher, except saying that the palm cockatoo has a striking red face.

Before dawn of the second day, Ongol and his *kem* partner stood on a knoll above the *howma*, one holding the feathered plaque upright on top of his head and the other doing the same with the decorated arrow. Below them was a crowd of people from Aenda, their *semonda*. Many stood in a common Highlands pose, with their arms wrapped across their chests, a hand on either shoulder hugging themselves to keep warm in the chilly air. All looked to the east, toward the double peaks of Mount Holbacs, waiting for the sun to come up over the horizon. When it appeared and shone on the two boys' bodies the pair retired to the nearest men's house and on the clearing below men proceeded to kill 40 or more large pigs, hitting them across the bridge of the snout with heavy wooden clubs.

* * * * * * * * * * * * * * *

It was the start of a pig kill. These are a common feature of communal events, such as the *kem* ritual. For some weeks before, people prepare for them. They have to ensure that there are sufficient stones for the oven in which they will cook the pork, men and women ferrying these back from the river's edge when on trips that take them that way. Men erect long horizontal poles, supported on forked stakes driven in at chest height along the edge of the clearing. In front, they build a long table of split wood slats that will hold the banana leaves and tree fern fronds collected for the oven a few days before the pig kill. They deposit the oven stones under the table and in front dig a long ditch for the earth oven; in all probability it will be where there was a previous oven and they will unearth many more stones to add to the pile. Men have to collect and chop up much firewood, too, to heat the oven stones. There is also frenetic exchange activity before a pig kill, as men seek to settle their outstanding transactional commitments to demonstrate that they can afford to kill pigs, without exchange partners worrying that they may, as a consequence, default on their obligations to them. They also have to present valuables to the women who have looked after their pigs, largely their wives, before they can kill the pigs.

There is a great deal of excitement on the day of the kill. Men scorch and scrape the bristles off the clubbed pigs over fires. They arrange the carcasses on their backs, legs sticking stiffly skyward, on banana leaves to butcher them. The conventional way is to make two parallel cuts down either side, between the chest and belly, and remove the strip of fatty pork. Next, butchers peel the flesh away from the ribs until the legs are splayed on the ground, breaking the pelvis with a hammer stone or axe. They abrade the exposed ribs on either side of the chest with a chert knife and break them by pushing down on the sternum bone, removing this with the broken ribs attached. They remove the internal organs, tying off the gullet before pulling the innards through to prevent chyme spurting out. Female relatives take the offal and wash it out in a nearby stream. Finally, they sever the animal's head and cut through the flesh along the spine, ending up with two sides of pork, each with a front and rear leg attached. They display these on the horizontal pole, and the heads are frequently put on pronged sticks driven into the ground. The show of pork is a highlight of the event, displaying what, when cooked, they will distribute among their kin and friends.

While the butchering proceeds, others lay a fire over the oven pit, arranging the stones on top of the wood before lighting it. Clouds of thick smoke bellow upward and waft across the clearing. When the fire has burned through, men remove many of the stones that have fallen into the pit, together with charred and smouldering wood, using split wood tongs. They line the pit with banana leaves on which they place the pork together with hot stones and tree fern fronds to soak up blood and fat during cooking. They cover the contents with more banana leaves and a layer of hot stones, and finally scrape earth up over the pit to create a long, steaming bed. During the two hours or so that the pork takes to cook, people mingle around talking, smoking, and eating; they cook small cuts of pork, either by roasting them over flames or stewing them in lengths of bamboo tube cut especially for the occasion. There is an air of anticipation about the opening of the oven and coming distribution of pork.

Finally, the time comes to open the oven. Men lift the pork onto banana leaves and cut it up into joints for distribution to kin and friends. When they have worked out to whom they are going to give which cuts, men stand up and shout the names of the recipients while holding the piece of meat above their heads for the selected individual or a representative to collect. This share-out is the high point of the event, at which participants reaffirm their relations with one another. It is an insult to omit someone who expects to receive some pork and signals a breakdown in relations. There is no collective feast; instead, people eat the meat with their families in the privacy of their homesteads. The gathering disperses slowly during the afternoon, or quickly if rain comes, as is common, leaving the debris of the kill scattered about the clearing.

* * * * * * * * * * * * * * *

While men were slaughtering and scorching the pigs at the *sor kem* ritual, the Kapenda man joined Ongol and his friend in the men's house where he rubbed red ocher onto two bark cloth hats that the two boys were to wear. He told them that it was important that the sun "does not see your hair." They wore the hats for the next month throughout their period of seclusion. The bodies of the two boys were also painted with alternate red and yellow clay stripes. The ritual officiant again whispered an incantation, similar to the previous one, of which the boys only heard snatches:

Kwi mana	*baeraeno*	*urukemba*	*haezida.*	*Yaeka yaeka*	
Type of tree	branch	palm cockatoo	is.	Chirping	

	laeru	*yaeka- la*	*babu*	*bidu.*	*Ku taegali*	*winini.*	*Urukemba*
	palm cockatoo	chirp	does	well.	A large river	is.	Palm cockatoo

haezida.	*Yaeka yaeka*	*laeru*	*yaeka- la*	*babu*	*bidu.*
is.	Chirping	palm cockatoo	chirp	does	well.

This spell makes specific reference to a hardwood tree, symbolizing the strength of those sponsoring the ritual and their long lives. The large river named again alludes to the "river of life," may it be long for all participants.

While all of these activities were taking place, some men arranged a small oven inside the *kem* house, lighting a fire to heat stones. The newly hatted and decorated pair went there with the Kapenda man. Ongol was feeling rather important and enjoying himself greatly. Men arrived from the clearing above with neck cuts of pork.[6] They cut these into small pieces and threw them into the fire that was heating the stones inside the house, as a further offering to their *towmow*. They called out to them to come and eat the meat; they did so with such phrases as, *"Ab njay ngo nabay"* ["Father you eat it"] or, *"Naway njay ngo nabay"* ["Naway (or whichever dead relative they named) you eat it"], naming several deceased relatives. Someone from each *semg^{e}nk* took along a side of pork, too. They draped these over a short pole inside the house. The Kapenda man cut the front haunch off each, while again muttering a variation of his spell. He also butchered the small pig from the previous day's rite and cooked it together with the other pork in the *kem* house oven.

While the majority of men had returned to the clearing to continue pig butchering and communal oven preparation, the Kapenda man and the boys, together with a few others, prepared the small oven. Ongol and his partner learned that they would receive three of the pork haunches, while the officiant would take two, together with the small pig, as his fee. In addition to this pork, the man also received for his ritual services a *towmow habuw bay* [spirit stand make] reimbursement, contributed to by those related to the host *semonda*, comprising a cowry shell necklace, a pig, a salt parcel, some *wombok*, a new woman's net bag, and a grass skirt. Ongol remembered looking at the haunches of pork and then around the house, which would be his

The *kem* dancers.

home for the coming weeks, and wondering if they would be sufficient compensation for being a *kem* boy. He hoped that he was not going to regret agreeing to it, for it was only a temporary construction and a large one at that, which would be difficult to keep warm at night.

He did not have time to brood on that busy day. When they had closed the oven, the spellholder led them both back up to the clearing where they were closing the long communal oven. He told them to fetch the *kem* feather plaque and ochered *tomtay* arrow to perform the *kwimb liy* [moss hit] dance. Two men met them who had also painted their bodies with alternate red and yellow clay stripes and blacked their faces with charcoal. When an anthropologist subsequently suggested that the decoration might represent the rays of the sun driving away the darkness of night, it was dismissed as fanciful; the participants did not know the meaning of the body painting, if anything, it was simply "how our ancestors did things." The two men also wore lesser-bird-of-paradise[7] headdresses, their beautiful wispy yellow and white tail plumage waving to and fro as they moved, and each carried an hourglass-shaped drum. The boys were told to follow the men in a square formation. Drumming rhythmically, they led the pair around the clearing, one holding the plaque and the other the arrow on his head, as they had when welcoming the sunrise. The spectators sang the refrain of "*Ar... ar... uw, ... ar... ar... uw, ... ar... ar... uw...*" They repeated the performance intermittently while the pork cooked, sometimes resting to talk, smoke, and share tidbits of cooked meat. It was said that the performance further pleased the *towmow*; it "made them happy." Among these was Kot, his overgrown grave (now supporting a dense raised bed of foliage) overlooking proceedings from the edge of the clearing, his legacy soon to return to cause Ongol's family further trouble.

* * * * * * * * * * * * * * *

During the pork distribution to kin and friends that marked the ritual's finale on the clearing, some men gave Ongol and his partner special rear leg cuts to add to the haunches received earlier. They called him Kem and his partner Sor when they held up their cuts for the boys to collect, as they had throughout the ritual. These new names were to stick with them for the rest of their lives. The acquisition of such additional names is common. It proved a bane for the anthropologist, making it difficult to follow conversations sometimes, without having intimate knowledge of personal histories and various names, and the compilation of genealogies became a headache as he sought to add individuals two or more times under different names. Another occasion on which persons may acquire a new name is following the death of someone in their community with the same name as theirs. It would remind close relatives of their grief to hear the deceased's name, which they are prohibited from uttering for fear of attracting the unwelcome attention of the *towmow* [ghost]. The living person's new name is an alternative name, not a nickname.

The pair deposited the meat they received in the *kem* house, where the small oven was also opened and the pork distributed. They were told that they were to stay secluded in the house for the next four days, that it was critical the "sun does not see you," nor do other people. They could emerge at night to relieve themselves in the nearby thicket of cane grass. During the day, they had a pandan leaf arranged gutterlike through the wall of the house, which they used when they urinated. It was the source of some amusement; although the first time Kem, as Ongol was called throughout, used it, he had a painful accident catching his testicles in the gloom on the sharp spines that ran along the pandan leaf. The boys fed on the pork mostly. Another young bachelor fetched them some vegetables, water, and firewood. They needed a good supply of wood because it was a cold house, as Ongol had foreseen. The Kapenda man told them if they came out during the day they would anger the *towmow*, fall ill, and in all probability die.

The seclusion became less rigid after four days and the boys could leave the house in the daytime, so long as they did not remain around settled areas but went into the forest. They were not to meet or even see a woman during the next "moon" (month), and when outside the house they carried a whistle to blow and warn women if they were somewhere they might meet them, such as on a path. They could meet and speak with men. During this month their young bachelor helper continued to supply them with food, as under no circumstances could they accept food from women. The only meat they could eat was pork, and they consumed what they had received during the ritual within a few days. They could not eat the flesh of marsupials, birds, or even insects. They could not eat sugarcane or Highland pitpit stems either. Ongol did not find these prohibitions onerous. They lived on the normal, mainly vegetable diet comprising sweet potato tubers mostly. The entire community had to observe these food taboos, too. During the seclusion period, couples also had to refrain from sexual relations. If anyone broke these taboos, they would suffer leprosy, the displeased *towmow* gnawing off their fingers and toes in anger. They would also jeopardize the beneficial effects of the ritual for the whole community.

A month later, the bachelor helper turned up at the *kem* house with a small pig, which the boys slaughtered and cooked. Before sharing the pork among themselves, Kem and Sor took a leg each and pushed the now grubby bark-cloth hats from their heads with the trotter. This marked the end of their ritual seclusion; "the sun could see their hair again," and after eating the pork, the boys returned to normal life. The food and other taboos were lifted for everyone. Nevertheless, it was not the last time that Ongol hid his hair from the sun's gaze, or more strictly, from that of women.

* * * * * * * * * * * * * * *

Young men, concerned to ensure their well-being and appearance, may perform rites to promote their health. They focus on the growth of a fine head of hair, a sign of vitality. When a man is sick, his hair becomes lifeless, dry, and wispy and may even start to fall out, particularly if "eaten by a woman," that is, sick because of female pollution. Ongol took part in the "magical plant hair" rite with a few bachelor friends. They approached someone who knew the relevant spell and gave him some cowries for his help. They spent their days in the forest hunting for marsupials and birds, which they shared with him, too. They depended on him to cook their food because the rite forbade them to approach a fire. It was necessary to remain cool because this makes hair grow and promotes good health. One of the symptoms of pollution sickness is a hot, burning body, and the ritual aimed to keep their temperatures down. Hence, they spent their time in the dank and cool rain forest.

Another reason for staying in the forest was that it reduced potentially polluting contacts with other people, notably women but also men who had recently had sexual congress. While the bachelors might meet women, they could not linger in their company or accept food from them. They and their helper friend collected their food from garden areas pointed out to them by their mothers. They wore bark cloth hats, similar to those Ongol and Sor had worn during the *kem* ritual, so that if they met women or tainted men they could not see their hair and "stop it from growing well." When the boys were alone, they inserted small twirls of *leb* [sweet flag[8]] leaf in their hair. They did this because the blades of the *leb* plant grow long in the way that they wished their hair to grow. They also use *leb* in some contexts to attract women when courting; it symbolized the contradiction between the danger of women and their desirability, something that was subsequently to fascinate the anthropologist, who was alerted by structuralist thinking to investigate the mediation of such oppositions.

In addition, every few days their helper took a ball of "moss"[9] and crumbled it onto their hair. This variety of moss grows in long strands and forms dense mops of foliage, just as they wished their hair to grow. It "showed their hair how to grow." The helper recited the following spell as he crumbled the moss, all the boys coming to learn it (Ongol could recall it decades later as an old man, rather as we can recall a poem learned by heart in school):

Hiyt	*gahow gep.*	*Hiyt*	*gahow gep.*	*Waegiyael*	*gahow gep.*
Mount Hiyt	chorus.	Mt. Hiyt	chorus.	Mt. Waegiyael	chorus.

Oliy	*gahow gep.*	*Hiyt*	*gahow gep.*	*Oliy*	*gahow gep.*
Mt. Oliy	chorus.	Mt. Hiyt	chorus.	Mt. Oliy	chorus.

Moi	*gahow gep.*	*Kiybael*	*gahow gep.*	*Boron*	*tay*	*pebay.*
Mt. Moi	chorus.	Mt. Kiybael	chorus.	Silkwood[10] tree's	trunk	go.

Bort	*tay*	*tonguwluw.*	*Bort*	*tay*	*pebay.*
Silkwood tree	trunk	ants.	Silkwood tree	trunk	go.

Waen	*ten*	*tonguwluw.*	*Waen*	*ten*	*pebay.*
Woolly cedar[11]	trunk	ants.	Woolly cedar	trunk	go.

The spell compares the boys' heads with the well-forested tops of mountains and infers that the heads will be similarly densely "forested" with hair. The tree ants represent hair lice, the speaker telling them not to climb up and swarm in the foliage, for when lice infest a man's hair the irritation forces him to cut it off.

The hair growth rite is as near as those living in the Was valley come to the initiation of young men, unlike other places in New Guinea where they are secluded and subject to painful physical ordeals while ritual knowledge is revealed to them. But adolescence is not necessarily pain free, as most youngsters wish to sport nose decoration, which entails piercing the nasal septum. There is no associated rite, and some opt to put vanity second to comfort and not to submit to the operation. Ongol was not such a character. One day he plucked up the nerve to ask Pes, his older *hay*, to perform the operation. Pes prepared a sharp pin of tree fern wood. He cut the end off a sweet potato and held it firmly against one side of Ongol's nose. The next thing Ongol knew was a sharp stab of pain as his cousin pushed the pin through his nasal septum. His eyes watered but otherwise he took it stoically. It was only the start of his discomfort because to ensure that the wound did not heal he had to twirl the pin every day to break the scab.

He enlarged the hole over a period of time by inserting objects larger and larger in diameter into it, starting with the stem of a raspberry[12] and then of a leguminous plant.[13] It was a painful business. His favorite nose pin would be a cassowary wing quill with a white cockatoo feather pushed into its hollow end. Other nasal decoration includes the dry stem of a cane grass inflorescence or small pieces of bark-stripped polished-wood. Ongol was lucky in that while he had to endure a swollen and painful nose, and the inevitable jibes of "your fig[14] fruit ripens nicely," the wound did not become a puss-filled sore, which would have obliged him to stop and allow it to heal. Ongol's experience was unlike an anthropologist's, who, in his zeal to identify with people and demonstrate that one foreigner at least did not think that they should change their customs, had his nasal septum pierced and ended up on antibiotics with a swollen purple plum of a nose. Ongol avoided tabooed soft foods to prevent his nose from turning soft and squashy with puss, only eating firm things, mainly tubers.

Similar to most young men, Ongol was keen to cultivate a fine head of hair and sport nasal decoration, not only as a mark of his health but also to enhance his appearance and make himself attractive to the other sex. Later in life, he would supplement his natural hair with a wig, of a sort that the first European explorers called "pharaonic" in shape. The interest that Ongol showed in the hair growth ritual and his concern, like other bachelors, to ensure his well-being and defend himself from the potentially enfeebling effects of female contact, were sure indications, paradoxically enough, that some young woman had attracted his attention.

Chapter 3

Courting, Incest, and Sickness

*W*hen children start to show an interest in the opposite sex, parents often become a little anxious. Youngsters can do things they may later regret under the drive of their hormones. If Wasnonk and Haebay had received an inkling of where their son's courting was going to lead, they would have turned white-haired overnight. As it was, they were mildly amused by the interest that he showed in some of the valley's young girls, whose merits or otherwise were a regular topic of conversation among his peers. After a while, a girl called Kombaem, who lived downriver, attracted his attention. She was some years younger than he, which is usual in the Was valley where women commonly marry in their mid to late teens and men in their early twenties or later. One day Ongol's courting antics made his father laugh out loud. They were working on a garden fence when he caught a cockchafer[1] that flew past. He tugged a hair from his head and carefully tied it under the creature's shiny green-blue elytra, and then released it, tossing it downriver in the direction of Kombaem's territory. The insect buzzed off noisily to the accompaniment of Haebay's laughter, "Fat lot of chance that will reach her and help your wooing," he chuckled.

Although they did not see one another regularly, Ongol and Kombaem felt a strong mutual attraction. Not that it showed. By contemporary Western standards, their courting was constrained, even inhibited. Young men and women feel embarrassed in one another's company and behave awkwardly. Yet, they have customary ways to communicate their feelings to one another, without having to put them in words, which would be an uncomfortable prospect. One is to use *leb* magic, which they believe makes them attractive to the other party. Kombaem used it on Ongol one day, when she guessed that they would both be attending a pig-kill festival at a settlement midway

35

between their homes. She took some leaves from the fragrant *leb* plant (distilled oil from the rhizome of which is often in haute couture perfumes) and pushed them in the hollow end of cane grass stem. She also poked some leaves under her armband, as a further message. At the festival, she shyly approached Ongol and tapped him gently with the end of the wand. Before tapping him, Kombaem whispered the following spell over the wand to ensure its efficacy. She had purchased the spell for a cowry shell from a young woman who had recently married into her community:

Iyb	*Bluwshobaenda*	*aena*	*wiya*	*gaimndael.*
Water	a large pond (toward Poroma)	over there	is	hearsay has it.

Hend	*amuwn*	*deraen*	*deraen*	*sa*	*burubtuw.*
Look	over there	outside	outside	men's house	sit.

Na	*nais*	*oliy.*	*Njen*	*Konay*	*kab.*	*Na*	*buwa.*
My	boy	husband.	Your	Thoughts	two.	My	hit.

Na	*kaendowlahendet*	*buwa.*
My	*leb* wand	hit.

The spell instructs her sweetheart to sit gazing out of the foyer of his men's house when she approaches, so that he sees her before any other girl and their two *konay* [minds] may become attracted to one another. It tells how she will ensure his affections by "hitting" him with her *leb* wand, such that he becomes smitten by her. Kombaem subsequently hid a small piece of flag leaf in some pork that she received during the festival before passing it on to Ongol to eat. The smile that he gave her and the few awkward words he spoke showed that he had gotten the message. Young men may resort to similar tactics. The anthropologist faced many demands from friends for "white man's *leb*," or aftershave, and suitable alluring phrases.

Ongol and Kombaem saw one another at intervals in the following months, sometimes talking briefly. While it would be wrong to suggest that the idea of romantic love informed their feelings—male and female relations in Wola society have an anxious, fearful edge—nonetheless when he knew Kombaem better, Ongol told his parents that he felt comfortable, even somehow familiar with her. They had an uncanny understanding, of the sort he imagined made a strong marriage. "We are *turiy* 'happy' with each other." But Kombaem's mother, when she became aware of the budding relationship, showed herself implacably opposed to it. The pair put this down to her being an overprotective mother, widowed with only one daughter, who would be unhappy to see her marry a man from some distance away and move to live with him, such that she would lose regular contact with her. Ongol became anxious that Kombaem might show interest in another boy, because of her mother's pressure and hostility to him. He decided to do something about it.

He had heard his *hay* Pes talk about a practice among the neighboring Huli speakers called *jiya luw waen bay* [frog kill and dry] that prevented someone you liked from being attractive to anyone else, and he approached Pes to learn more. Young men sometimes resort to it to stop a girl from marrying another suitor before they have acquired sufficient *injiykab* [bridewealth]. They catch a *kinja* [green tree frog[2]] and kill it by pushing a sharpened cassowary wing quill up its anus until it emerges from the mouth. Next, they tie a length of string tightly around the dead frog's stomach, reciting a spell such as the following:

Molow	*nonkon*	*yabiy*	*kongonkongon.*		*Ogor*
Over there	girl's		hidden interleaved with.		Large intestine

kongonkongon.	*Ogor*	*kongonkongon.*
hidden interleaved with.	Large intestine	hidden interleaved with.

Tombor	*kongonkongon.*	*Mayow*	*kongonkongon.*
Stomach	hidden interleaved with.	Small intestine	hidden interleaved with.

Molow	*nonkon*	*yabiy*	*kongonkongon.*
Over there	girl's		hidden interleaved with.

Finally, the reciter puts the frog above the fireplace in his house, on the bark-sheet fireguard above the fireplace protecting the roof. The shiny and plump creature—the appearance that people associate with health and attractiveness—dries out, becoming dull and shriveled up—the look they associate with ill-health and ugliness. The spell tells how this will happen to the girl "over there" as the frog dries out, the magic infusing her internal organs so that she falls ill, with pains in her guts. Tying the string around the frog mimics the girl's actions with a painful stomach, as people commonly fasten a length of vine tightly around the abdomen to ease such pain. Unable to eat properly with the stomach complaint, she consequently wastes away, becoming thin and unattractive to others. The small *kinja* frog soon dries out, the magic rapidly taking effect.

When he learned about the magic, Ongol was of two minds because, after all, it was a mean thing to do to someone you found attractive. The thought of reducing buxom Kombaem with her broad hips and full breasts, the epitome of physical beauty in his eyes, to a skinny and bony girl gave him qualms. But, with her mother exerting such pressure on her, he needed to do something. If he let others know what he had done, the news would find its way back to Kombaem's mother and persuade her of his earnestness and need to back off. After all, the effects of the magic could soon be reversed, he told himself. When a young man has amassed sufficient wealth to marry the girl he favors, he puts the shrunken frog and quill in a damp place, such as a pool of water, where the frog swells up and turns soft again; the girl also recovers, "swelling up" in health, her body becoming firm and well.

* * * * * * * * * * * * * *

The next time Ongol saw Kombaem she certainly did not look well. She had come with some other girls on the day of a reparation exchange attended by many people. Her stressed appearance had something to do with the worry of how she was going to respond to seeing Ongol again. She avoided him, until an impromptu dance started in which several young men in face paint and plumes, Ongol among them, formed a bobbing and chanting circle. After

Young girls dance beside men they find attractive as they beat drums.

a while, she pushed into the circle next to Ongol, a customary way for a young woman to show that a man attracts her. Something that stuck in her mind from that exciting day was looking across the clearing and wondering about the fate of the person in the dilapidated raised coffin she saw in the shade of the surrounding casuarina trees. She decided not to return home that night but stay with some friends nearby. When Ongol heard, he went over in the evening with some others to visit. They were feeling bold and, after talking awkwardly for a while, started singing songs, as they sat around the fire. The girls reciprocated with songs of their own. They all knew where they were hopefully headed, namely to singing *turmaen* [courting songs] to one another.

    The *turmaen* is a stylized way of courting that helps young couples overcome their shyness. After some warm-up singing, couples attracted to one another sit side by side and take turns singing *turmaen* chants to each other. At the end of each song, they ostentatiously click their fingers together. It is usual for several to attend such courting sessions, not all necessarily singing courting songs. It is an open declaration of a couple's attraction to one another, although it is not binding until they start to exchange gifts, and at a subsequent courting session, they may sing with another partner. They are public events and there is no further physical contact between couples, involving any caressing or kissing; there are usually some older relatives present, too. Any such intimate behavior would be entirely inappropriate. If a woman wishes to indicate that she is available for sexual intercourse, she may blink her eyes at the man who attracts her in a sly seductive way or scratch the palm of his hand; she may make such secret signals at any place and time.

Young women singing songs of an evening.

Ongol had his courting song ready for such an occasion, and in the falsetto voice that characterizes such performances, he softly chanted the following to Kombaem:

Buwol buwa	*bort*	*tongort buwa*	*na*	*Agem,*	*waenor*
I cut up pollard branches	at	I split logs	my	place name,	elm tree[3]
buwael buwa	*bort*	*tongort buwa,*	*esbaymwaen*
I cut up pollard branches	at	I split logs,	secondary regrowth
buwael buwa	*buwol tongol buwa*	*na*	*Shuwol,*	*waenor*
I cut up pollard branches	I cut fence stakes	my	place name,	elm tree
buwael buwa	*buwol tongol buwa*	*na*	*Kuwbul,*	*waenor*
I cut up pollard branches	I cut fence stakes	my	Place name,	elm tree
buwael buwa	*buwol tongol buwa,*	*wolapot*	*kabuw*
I cut up pollard branches	I cut fence stakes,	winged bean[4]	dry wood
piybuw	*lengowmaen,*	*hond*	*kabuw*	*tobmonol.*
wind sways	like so,	banana cultivar	dry wood	pick up.
Ebay	*bay*	*paendiyp monol*	*bay*	*na*	*oliy*	*ken kaba.*
Come	?	fumble and drop	?	my	husband	you choose.

It is difficult to convey the poetry of the song and what Ongol had in mind and sought to share with Kombaem, because, as with many of the chants in this book, much is lost in translation. The reference to chopping up tree branches and cutting fence stakes involves the pioneering of new gardens in which his wife-to-be will cultivate crops. It alludes to his marriage preparations and their subsequent cooperation as a family. It also refers to him amassing the valuables necessary for the *injiykab* exchange. He cannot mention the seashells and pigs directly without feeling shame at appearing to boast about the wealth that he will collect but alludes to its quantity, likening it to pollard branches and wood chips. The allusion to driving in a line of fence stakes is a metaphor for the wealth lined up at the marriage exchange, particularly the pigs. The beans, bananas, and leaves swaying in the wind suggest the many children in their future family. The last part of the song teasingly asks whether the girl will pick him up or fumble and drop him to another man. It is her choice.

Later that evening, Ongol retrieved the dried frog and placed it in a puddle of water behind his house. He considered that they had entered into a *turmaen* [engaged] relationship and would marry soon.

* * * * * * * * * * * * * *

The pair subsequently reaffirmed their intentions not only at further *turmaen* [courting sessions] but also in making small gifts to one another at intervals. Kombaem gave Ongol bananas and pandan nuts, in addition to netting him a new string bag, and he reciprocated with some cowry shells, salt, and a cuscus that he caught. When the courting gifts reached the pitch of signaling Ongol's relatives' intentions of initiating *injiykab* negotiations—namely they made the conventional opening payment of pigs and shells to Kombaem's kin that formally confirms the would-be groom's plans to the bride-to-be's relatives—her mother, who was the hapless Huwniy, turned to a sister in desperation. She went to visit her in the Nembi valley, where her sister had married, and told her the identity of her daughter's true father, that he was the infamous Kot. She was the only person living who knew it. Her father and a few uncles who knew the truth had told no one and had all passed away. It was unclear if Huwniy's deceased first husband knew the truth, as she never dared mention Kombaem's paternity to him in case he was ignorant of it. If he had known, he had told no one. His behavior suggested that he was unaware of it, as he had always acted as if Kombaem was his daughter, and everyone assumed that this was so. "How can I stay silent and allow my daughter to enter into an incestuous marriage?" Huwniy wailed. It was shameful enough that she had entered into a *turmaen* relationship with Ongol, which is prohibited between related persons. Seeing how tormented Huwniy was, her sister decided that she had to tell their brothers what she had learned. They in turn tackled Huwniy and her husbands' kin and all hell broke loose.

Two of Huwniy's brothers crossed the Was River to inform Haebay and his kin, and alert them that Ongol could not possibly marry Kombaem. When they arrived at the Tombem men's house, they found Ongol with his father and some uncles filling an earth oven with vegetables. They invited them to stay and join the meal. There was no easy way to break the news and they came straight out with it, turning to Ongol and telling him that a marriage with Kombaem was out of the question because any relationship between them would be *boliy tumay* [sister climbing] incest. When he learned that Kombaem was Kot's daughter and so his cousin, he was dumbfounded, and he could see from the astonished look on his father's and other relatives' faces that they were equally shocked. He slumped as if "pig-clubbed" and remained silent for a long time trying to take in the information, as Kombaem had the previous day. She had been amazed to think that the overgrown grave on the edge of the clearing contained the bones of her father, a man she never knew. "How could everyone let me make such a fool of myself?" Ongol asked. He heard how no one had known until Huwniy told one of her sisters (his relatives, although aware of who Huwniy was, had not connected Kombaem with the long ago Kot episode). Life became difficult for Huwniy and Kombaem when the truth about Kombaem's paternity became known.

When Huwniy's husband, who was considerably older than she, had died, Huwniy married one of his brothers. He had also recently passed away, and Huwniy had remained living as a widow at their place with her daughter. Now that the cat was out of the bag or, more appropriately, "the pig was now loose of its tether," her husbands' relatives shunned her. They were furious that Huwniy had apparently duped her first husband and made fools of all of them. She decided that it would be better to return to live with her brothers. Life returned to normal, until a few months later when a young man from the Ak valley started to court Kombaem, subsequently signaling his wish to marry her. At the ensuing marriage negotiations, Kombaem's mother's brothers and relatives, who took a leading role as she was now living among them, became embroiled in a dispute with her deceased stepfather's rela-

An overgrown raised coffin grave on edge of a *howma* clearing.

tives over the distribution of the *injiykab*. (Haebay and his kin kept their distance and made no claims as close relatives of the biological father. It was up to those distributing the *injiykab*, Haebay said, to decide if they would give them any valuables, as a sign of their ongoing, if tortured, relations and wish to put the unwelcome resurgence of the Kot saga behind them.) A vociferous argument erupted over the following days, developing into a brawl on one occasion, at which the bride's parentage became the subject of widespread public debate and comment.

Events now took a tragic turn. The young woman was wretched. She felt intense shame, even thinking that she was somehow responsible for the violent argument. The sense of rejection that she felt by those she had grown up to consider as her paternal relatives intensified her dark depression, as did the hurt she had suffered over the debacle of her courtship with Ongol for whom she had genuine feelings. One morning, as the *injiykab* negotiations warmed yet again, she was seen for the last time walking down to the Was River where she threw herself into the raging torrent from a place known for suicides; the turbulent foaming water dashed her body against the rocks, causing nearly instant death. She was not missed until midday, when some women set off to gardens adjacent to the river where they thought she was harvesting tubers. They called out her name. It was a while before someone spotted her bag and digging stick, which she had left on the large boulder she had jumped off. The news was yodeled to those arguing on the clearing above, and a frantic search started, which went on all afternoon. They never found her sad body. When he heard the news, Ongol was distraught and rushed across the valley to the funeral with a cowry necklace to contribute to the *gwat* mortuary payment. He arrived to find a group of women sitting around Kombaem's net bag hanging from her digging stick driven into the ground, all that was left of her life. They started to keen gently as Ongol approached wailing loudly. He spent the day there in a daze.

The *injiykab* dispute came to an abrupt end, and another one started over responsibility for the girl's death. The two parties to the *injiykab* negotiations

Women sit in mourning around the net bag and possessions left by a young woman who has committed suicide.

joined forces in suggesting that Ongol was at the root of the tragedy, because if he had not persisted in his courtship of the girl the facts about her parentage would not have become public knowledge with the resulting dispute over the distribution of her *injiykab*. He should have been more responsive, they said, when Huwniy tried to warn him off. During the ensuing dispute, which dragged on intermittently over weeks, Ongol, supported by his father and relatives, argued that this was ridiculous and refused to acknowledge any responsibility for paying compensation. Some harsh things were said about him and his relatives; even Kot's deeds were dragged into the remarks, as if to say that one could not expect much else of such a man's nephew. But it was not only Ongol who suffered; poor Huwniy went out of her mind with grief and subsequently made little sense to anyone who spoke to her, until she died a broken soul.

* * * * * * * * * * * * * * *

Soon after these tragic events, Ongol fell seriously ill and his *mai* Korobol died in his prime. Korobol's illness was sudden and acute; he had a painful chest, was feverish and was short of wind. His relatives performed the "pandan seedling planting" rite in an attempt to save him. It is resorted to when there is an omen of impending death, such as a person dreaming of his own demise or, as in Korobol's case, of seeing a relative's corpse. It is a message from the *towmow* world. Someone who knew the "pandan seedling" spell tied some string around a tuft of hair on Korobol's head. The Wola believe that the *wezow* enters and exits a person through the top of the head and that tying a clump of hair here seals the "door" so that it cannot leave. The threatened person wears the knot until it falls out. The spellholder smeared the knot of hair with pig's blood and red ocher while muttering the following spell:[5]

Haela	*waembow*	*kiniy*	*wiyalow.*	*Kaembo*	*haelo*
Pandan[6]	*waemb* variety	aerial root	planted well.	Cane grass[7]	shoot

piniy	*wiyalow.*	*Oromaeno*	*wiyalow.*	*Winiy-dinopiniy*
root	planted well.	Aerial root	planted well.	Variety of grass[8] root

wiyalow.	*Oromaeno*	*wiyalow.*	*Delbaswiy*	*piniy.*
planted well.	Aerial root	planted well.	Single crown pandan	root

wiyalow	*Oromaeno*	*wiyalow.*	*Baera*	*tombuga*	*muwkabow*
planted well.	Aerial root	planted well.	Black	pig	take

ladiydagow.	*Obadiy*	*ladiydagow.*	*Waro*	*amuwmuw,*	*talo*
eat.	Take	eat.	Back off	that way (NW),	back away

amuwmuw	*waro*	*amuwmuw,*	*Talo*	*amuwmuw.*
that way (NW),	back off	that way (NW),	back away	that way (NW).

Akaliy	*diniy*	*waro*	*amuw*	*haeruw.*
Man's	life force	back off	that way (NW)	together.

Nokodino	*waro*	*naena*	*waro*	*naena*	*haeruw.*
Pig's life force	Back off	that way (SE)	back off	that way (SE)	together.

Talo	*amuwmuw,*	*waro*	*amuwmuw.*
Back away	that way (NW),	back off	that way (NW).

Next, Korobol stood clenching the liver, tongue, some meat, and a rib from a slaughtered pig between his teeth. The spellholder took a pandan seedling and red-leaved balsam plant[9] in one hand and a cane grass[10] shoot and the club used to kill the pig in the other, and holding these on either side of Korobol's body, he passed them down Korobol's trunk and legs. Finally, he pushed them firmly into holes scooped out at his feet. The victim will be like the things planted—all vigorous growers—strong and healthy, not fatally sick as the dream foretold. The rite also substitutes the slaughtered pig's *wezow* for that of the dreamed person. Death occurs when the *wezow* wanders off too far from the body. By holding the pig's organs in his mouth, Korobol symbolized holding tightly onto his *wezow* in place of the pig's. The spell's symbolism repeats these themes. The "life force" of the person in the dream is not "well planted"; it is in danger of wandering off. It mentions the plants rooting well; it refers to pandans that have only single crowns, which grow up vigorously straight and high. The victim will thus be "well planted" in this life. It refers to the victim's wandering "life force," and that of the pig substituting for it, going off in the opposite direction. It invites the spirit force causing the person's unease to come and eat the pig.

Finally, those present shared the earth-oven-cooked pork, giving the invalid choice cuts. Sadly, these ritual efforts did not keep Korobol rooted in

The *aenk way boi* rite, preparing to run plants and a pig club down an ailing boy's body.

this life, and not long afterward, he passed away. His relatives, anxious to establish the cause of his premature death, resolved to arrange an *ol sond beray* divination. It is staged on a moonless night. The afternoon before, they made a circle, some three meters in diameter, by pushing short stakes (about half a meter long) into the ground, in a clearing some distance from any homesteads—for the divination is a hazardous undertaking involving dangerous spirits. Each stick represented a possible cause of death, such as a *towmow* "ghost" from the deceased's mother's or father's side, a sorcery attack, *mogtomb* [poison/poisoning], or pollution. They balanced a leaf on the top of each stake. That evening Haebay and another relative carried Korobol's corpse, lashed on its mourning pole, to the spot and, after checking that all the leaves were in place, sat in the middle with the pole resting across their thighs. They carried bows and arrows tipped with points of human bone, the most lethal in the Wola arsenal.

They sat waiting for some movement in the vicinity. It was a chilly overcast night and they shivered occasionally, partly from the cold and partly in fear. It was pitch dark, dead quiet, and eerie. The stake nearest the first movement or sound shows the cause of the person's death. It is unequivocal if a leaf falls off a stick. The malignant force responsible for the death may make its presence known as a mouse, an insect, the wind, or some other being or phenomenon. The first sound came from the sorcery stake. Haebay and his partner should have jumped up and fired their arrows in that direction, for if they were quick, they may have "shot" the sorcerer's *wezow*, preventing it from returning to his sleeping body and so causing his death, too. Instead they lost their nerve, running off in fear, coming back a while later to collect Korobol's corpse and return it to its place of mourning on the *howma*. The sorcery verdict of the leaves-on-sticks divination unnerved the community for it showed that they were under a supernatural attack.

* * * * * * * * * * * * * * *

The combination of fear and grief in the community found expression in a *woktoiz ungbiy* episode. This occurs when the *wezow* of a recently deceased *woktoiz* [sorcery] victim enters an individual's anus, instead of going off immediately to the *towmow*, and makes the person behave madly. It happens at night only. One of Korobol's sister's sons, a *haemay* of Ongol, was so possessed, rushing around wildly tearing up crops, pulling down bananas, wrenching up fence stakes, and shouting dementedly at the top of his voice. This behavior occurred on several nights. It reached a peak on the night that he carried Korobol's decomposing, maggot-infested, and stinking corpse from its resting place at a nearby rock face necropolis and deposited it, sitting up in a grim, putrid pose, outside the foyer of his men's house. The eyeless collapsed face was no longer recognizable. This crazy, grief-stricken act distressed his relatives greatly, but there was little they could do to moderate his berserk behavior. He had been close to his mother's brother and felt his loss keenly. They had to wait for the possession to finish of its own accord; meanwhile, they took care at night to keep weapons such as bows and arrows out of his reach because such crazed men can cause serious harm. The spirit attack ended within two weeks or so.

It was perhaps inevitable that when Ongol fell seriously ill within weeks, complaining of chest pains and fatigue, he should conclude that he was a victim of the sorcery attack too. His relatives arranged a *woktoiz kobay* [sorcery takeaway] ritual to establish if he was "hit" and, if so, to ward the sorcery off. A man who knew the necessary spells came over from the neighboring Ak valley. He built a small platform outside Ongol's men's house from *wok* wood,[11] driving in four stakes to form a rectangle, lashing cross members between these with *maip ya* vine,[12] and arranging slats across these. He decorated the structure by tying sprays of *shwimb*[13] and *bat*[14] leaves on it together with moss. Next, he decorated himself to frighten and intimidate the attacking sorcery force, blackening his face with charcoal, painting on a design in white clay, and pinning a cassowary feather pompom on his head. When he was ready, Ongol sat on the structure, and the healer rushed around the house yard and environs, whistling loudly. He was calling to Ongol's *wezow* and after a while heard it whistle in reply. The time that it took to respond indicated that Ongol was the probable victim of a sorcery attack. Various relatives sat on the structure, too, after Ongol (for their own protection, women and children were not present during the communication with dangerous spirit forces). The strength and speed with which their *wezow* whistled back indicated their state of health (no response indicates imminent death).

Next, the officiant scraped a shallow hole and lined it with banana leaves. He took one of Ongol's pigs, which Wasnonk had tethered in the house yard earlier, and bound a length of *maip ya* vine around its snout, while muttering the following spell:

| *Winiy* | *Yomavay,* | *Wagay* | *wiya* | *bay* |
| Wind | Name of mountain near Margarima, | Was River | is | ? |

Sorcery is believed to "bite" victims, and tying the animal's mouth shut symbolizes keeping it from biting. The spell refers to the powerful forest spirits living on Mount Yomavay near Margarima that travel like the wind, spirits such as those summoned by the sorcerer to attack and bite the victim. It asks, "Have the forest spirits from Yomavay traveled here like the wind to attack us?" It also asks, "Is the victim's *wezow* going down the Was River?"—an allusion to the belief that the spirits of the dead travel along rivers.

The healer rammed a long needle-like cassowary wing quill repeatedly up each of the pig's nostrils and, holding the squealing animal over the banana leaf lined bowl, caught the blood streaming from its snout. Then he clubbed the animal with a round stone, which he subsequently threw into the nearby cane grass. While someone butchered the pig, he dipped *taziy* [parsley] leaves[15] into the carcass to soak up more blood that he squeezed into the bowl, finally topping it up with water. He would come back to the bowl of blood later. Meanwhile, while repeating his spell, he took a hot stone from the fire and wrapped the pig's liver around it, packaging it up in a banana leaf bundle to cook while he continued with the rite. Next, he took a cassowary quill and cut it in two, taking the larger piece from which he made a hollow tube. He put one end in a bamboo container that he produced and sucked on it. He followed this with the whistling routine again, before placing the quill end on Ongol's chest and sucking hard on it again. He turned and spat into the pool of blood. He repeated this four or five times, closely inspecting his saliva on each occasion. He was looking for bloodstains in it, as these indicate the person will recover following the ritual. If there is no blood in the spittle, the victim is probably close to death because "blood does not flow from a corpse as it does a living person." He repeated the sucking and spitting routine somewhat perfunctorily on the chests of the others present, as none showed symptoms of sorcery attack.

Peering into a bloody pool of water to see one's reflection.

Next, Ongol came and sat by the leaf-lined bowl, called the "pig's blood mirror." The Ak valley man studied the surface of the liquid intently, searching for Ongol's *wezow* [reflection]. It took him a while to see it, but when he did, he said that its clarity indicated that he should recover following the ritual. Other relatives present, who might also be targeted by the sorcery, checked to see their reflections, too, in the "mirror," the clarity indicating their health status. If they see no reflection, this indicates that their *wezow* [life force] is dangerously enfeebled by the attack, and death is likely. *Woktoiz* entices the victim's *wezow* away from his body, thereby killing him. Both the whistling and the searching for the reflection in the pool of blood are ways of checking for the presence of the *wezow* (the slower the *wezow* is in coming, the weaker the victim, indicating that it may be about to depart forever, resulting in death). When the pig's liver was well cooked, all those taking part in the ritual ate a small piece. This marked the end of the ritual and everyone relaxed except Ongol, who was still feeling lousy. They sat around chatting and smoking while the pork cooked in a nearby earth oven, which some of those present had organized. Later, they shared the meat, after giving the Ak valley man the head and a side of pork, together with a string bag, cowry necklace, and gourd of *wombok* to reimburse him. Normally, there was nothing Ongol liked more than a fatty cut of pork, but he only picked at his share; nonetheless, the ritual's diagnosis gave him some hope of recovery soon.

* * * * * * * * * * * * * *

Further confirmation of Ongol's recovery came a few days later when Wasnonk insisted that he allow an elderly visiting relative of hers to perform the "hair take" procedure. It focuses again on hair as a sign of health status. She twirled some of his hair into a thick strand that she put into her mouth and bit sharply. She declared that the result was sound. Her teeth had not cut into the strand and banged together noisily as they would if his hair had been brittle and tired, an indication of serious sickness. Inevitably, Ongol and his kin asked themselves who could be responsible for the sorcery attack. It was a recurring topic of conversation in their men's house, as they puzzled over who could want to attack them with malevolent magic. They had their suspicions, and topping the list were Huwniy's relatives.

When a cousin of Ongol returned after a couple of days in the forest with two mountain cuscus that he had caught, they decided to perform the "earth oven pit" divination to establish who was responsible for the sorcery. They harvested some taro tubers from a nearby garden and heated stones for an oven in their house yard. They arranged the tubers around the eviscerated marsupials, nominating one for each *sem* whose members might conceivably wish them harm. When they opened the oven later in the afternoon, they inspected each taro closely to see if a hot stone had burned any. If one is scorched, it indicates that the *sem* represented by that particular taro is responsible for sorcery. They all expected to find a scorched tuber, as the previous rituals had established that they were under sorcery attack; not finding a burnt taro would signify that sorcery was not responsible for Korobol's death and Ongol's illness. After some deliberation and comparison of tubers, they decided that the one nominated to represent Huwniy's kin was indeed scorched. No one was surprised. They ate the contents of the oven, except for the one burnt taro, which they kept as evidence of the guilt of her relatives.

Of course, Ongol reasoned, it had to be Huwniy's relatives. Everything pointed in that direction. They blamed him for Kombaem's tragic death. However, when he thought about it, their resentment went back further than that, to his *ab* [uncle] Kot's crimes. While he pondered his position, he recalled Kot's fate. The more he thought about it, the more likely it seemed that Huwniy's relatives had killed him too, in revenge for his mistreatment of her and for the violent rape of the other woman. The large *ol komb* compensation exchange that he had witnessed as a child further confirmed it in his mind; Huwniy's relatives made the payment to prevent full-scale armed hostilities from breaking out to avenge Kot's killing.

Ongol and his kin confronted Huwniy's relatives about the sorcery, and they vehemently denied it. There was an angry dispute about it. They almost came to blows, albeit only delaying what was looking increasingly likely. During the argument, Ongol recalled that Huwniy's relatives only made the first *ol komb* payment of the three-stage *ol sond* sequence following Kot's death, and he raised the "temperature" by demanding that they should meet their full exchange commitments by completing the other two stages. His father Haebay and uncles thought it unwise to push these demands after all this time and were reluctant to support him. "The sorcery accusations are causing more than enough trouble," they reasoned.

Chapter 4

Revenge and Armed Conflict

*R*evenge is sweet. Those living in the Was valley would agree with this sentiment, and Ongol was no exception. While all humans can probably relate to the emotion, they do not regularly act on it, unlike people throughout the New Guinea Highlands. Here it is a duty, a deadly serious business. When Ongol had sufficiently recovered his strength to take action, he was predictably bent on taking revenge, not only for his own illness but also for the deaths of his *mai* Korobol and *ab* Kot. The inflexibility of Huwniy's relatives, he concluded, left him no other option. If they would not admit to their nefarious activities and compensate him and his kin as appropriate, so signaling their wish to continue amicable social relations, it was his right to take action to square their accounts. He resolved to attack them in turn by engaging in sorcery. First, he had to acquire the knowledge.

Rumor had it that someone in Wasnonk's natal community knew how to perform *woktoiz*, and Ongol visited the Nembi valley to find out, staying with some of his mother's relatives there. The man was understandably cagey when Ongol approached him because to admit to knowing the procedure and spells for sorcery is tantamount to admitting to using them, which could open him up to charges of killing others, risking revenge and demands for compensation. At first, he denied any such knowledge. But some days later, when Ongol turned up at his house with a maternal relative who knew the man well and had his trust, he indicated that he might know something or someone else with the knowledge. After hearing Ongol's story, he told him to come back in two days' time, in the evening, and to bring two pigs and cowry shell necklaces as a fee. The man subsequently agreed to return to the Was valley and show Ongol how to make the sorcery attack.

49

There is probably no standard way to conduct a sorcery attack. When the anthropologist inquired into the issue years later, he found that although the sorcery accounts of various men featured the same broad themes, they varied considerably over details. This is understandable for a ritual conducted clandestinely and shrouded in secrecy. It is probable that men modify what they learn, perhaps forgetting some of what they are told or innovating on gossip about the ritual, concocting their own schedule from what they pick up. Whatever, Ongol believed that he was able to lure an enemy's *wezow* to its death, which was what interested him.

* * * * * * * * * * * * * *

One night, some days later, Ongol led a pig to a place called Ebera, a forested ridge that rises behind Tombem. The elevation was to ensure that the sorcery force could "see" over the valley to its target. The Wola perform such rites at night, not only for secrecy but also because this is the time when the *wezow* wanders from the body; they say that they recall this from their dreams, which they believe result from their *wezo*w wandering abroad. When Ongol arrived at Ebera he could sense the tension building up within him. The Nembi valley man had been busy building a small wooden slatted table and making several small *pel* [beech[1] wood] stakes. He had lit a fire from wood collected earlier. After completing his preparations, he told Ongol to hold the pig firmly and tied a length of *maip ya* vine tightly around the animal's neck to choke its cries. He then inserted a cassowary bone dagger into the pig's ear and drove it into its head. He muttered the following spell as the animal writhed in pain and Ongol struggled to stop it from breaking free:

Atma kab,	*atma kab,*	*atma kab,*	*olma kab,*
Go on seize him,	go on seize him,	go on seize him,	man seize him,

olma kab,	*olma kab,*	*atka pip,*	*atka pip,*
man seize him,	man seize him,	smell him out,	smell him out,

olma kab,	*atka pip,*	*olma kab.*
man seize him,	smell him out,	man seize him.

It urges the sorcerer's *wezow* to travel quickly and hunt down and kill the sorcery target. It features the cry that men shout to command a dog to flush out game when hunting: "Go on; smell it out, seize it." In this case, the command refers to the sorcery target. The sorcery secures revenge by sending the operator's *wezow* to kill that of an enemy, by "eating" some vital organs.

The man told Ongol to finish the animal off with a stone. He then took this and put it on the fire to heat up, with other stones heaped there for the earth oven, while Ongol lifted the pig onto the slat table. The Nembi man lit a bundle of dry cane grass stems, which burn with a bright flame, and waved this torch under the table to singe off the animal's bristles, again while repeating his spell. He said that the smell of the burning bristles would attract the victim's roaming *wezow* to the forthcoming pork meal so that they could kill it. He left Ongol to finish singeing off the remaining bristles over the fire, after which they started to butcher the animal. The Nembi sorcerer removed the liver, and grabbing the hot club-stone off the fire with his naked hand, wrapped the liver around it, parceling it up with leaves and securing those with vine. Next, he fenced off a small area with the *pel* stakes and whistled over the enclosure to attract the *wezow* of someone from the target community, luring it to its destruction. The operator has no control over whose life force enters but he only attracts those of enemies. When he judged that a *wezow* had entered the enclosure, he beat the ground inside with the liver and stone parcel to kill it.

While Ongol finished butchering the pig and putting the pork in the earth oven to cook, the Nembi man fashioned a rough spear from a length of *wok gamboge* wood. This is the *woktoiz*, from which the name for the ritual derives. Again whistling and reciting his spell, he drove the spear into the ground to be sure of killing the hapless *wezow* that had wandered into the vicinity. Later, they unwrapped and shared the liver, the man tossing the stone away at random. It bounced off a nearby tree, which he said was an excellent omen that the sorcery had likewise "hit" an enemy. They opened the oven and ate some of the pork before returning to the men's house with the remaining meat to share with the others. Only men can eat such pork. Ongol could now relax. He was well pleased with his night's work and slept contentedly. He believed that a relative of Huwniy would fall sick and die within one or two moons, giving him sweet revenge.

* * * * * * * * * * * * * *

Ongol and his few kin who knew what he had been up to should have kept quiet about it. To admit to performing sorcery is tantamount to admitting to attempted murder in Wola eyes. But Ongol was too fired up with taking revenge for his father's and mother's brothers to remain silent, and he described to others what he had done on Mount Ebera. It was inevitable that the news should find its way back to the ears of Huwniy's relatives, who were dismayed to hear about this black magic attack. It was a tense time. It only needed one of Huwniy's relatives to die unexpectedly for them to conclude that the person was the victim "killed" in the sorcery. Sadly, one of her kin fell seriously ill two or three months later, and he and his relatives attributed his illness to the sorcery. They performed some curing rites and waited anxiously but he died a few weeks later. There was no doubt in their minds as to the cause, nor was there doubt in the minds of Ongol and his kin, who took pleasure in seeing the death as just revenge.

After the funeral, which Ongol and his kin decided they should not attend, the dead man's relatives crossed the river to confront his "killers." An angry dispute soon followed, each side accusing the other of sorcery and demanding compensation for the deaths of their kinsmen. Ongol and his relatives denied the sorcery, as is usual, while intimating that if the other side had admitted to killing Korobol, and Kot too, and done the proper thing in paying adequate compensation, they would not think they had lost someone in revenge. Huwniy's relatives were incensed. "We have killed no one," they cried. The result was deadlock, as both sides believed they were in the right. The temperature was rising and rising, and men started to wave and rattle their bows and arrows at one another in threatening gestures, accompanied by throaty growls. This signals that violence is probable, and sure enough, it culminated in one of the recently deceased's brothers losing his temper and pulling his bow and firing an arrow in rage. The howl of pain that went up and the accompanying cry of dismay showed that he had hit someone. A man fell to his knees with the arrow in his chest. Some men turned to help him, grabbing him by his arms and carrying him from the fray, while others surged forward.

An armed skirmish ensued with Huwniy's relatives as they withdrew down hill toward the river. One of them sustained an arrow wound to the shoulder; otherwise they managed to retreat and cross the river with no further casualties. When they had all crossed the river, some men cut through the vine walkways and railings of the suspension bridge, rendering it unusable by their pursuers. During the next few days, men similarly cut down other bridges that were on paths that led directly between their territories, reducing the chances of surprise attacks. Two days later, the man who took the arrow in the chest died in great pain coughing up blood. Ongol and his relatives were now out for open revenge. Full-scale armed *saend* [hostilities] existed between the two communities, as they sought to take revenge. It was as if Kot, the source of the troubles, was reaching out from his stilted grave under the casuarina trees and stoking the mayhem that characterized his life.

It is intriguing to consider how armed hostilities arise, as they are instructive about the stateless political order. They relate to problems of law and order. They occur when one or several persons try to force their views on another party, which resists, trying in turn to compel the other side to accept its views. In other words, each side seeks to exert power over the other. Each party predictably resists, as it is anathema in a stateless context for anyone to exercise power over another—that is, force a person to do something against his will, depriving someone of his freedom. If the resulting struggle becomes physically violent and results in someone's death, the revenge obligation kicks in. This is the driving force behind armed conflicts when they break out, as kin recognize a duty to seek *ol luwzimb* "revenge" for any relative killed. Here revenge should be taken as soon as possible, in hot and full anger.

We can interpret the revenge principle as an institutionalized way of preventing any party from taking power to itself and depriving others of their freedom of political action. As soon as someone kills another person, in trying to force that person to obey his wishes, the killer becomes the target of the deceased's kin, bent on evening the account. After all, taking away someone's life is the ultimate expression of power and denial of freedom. So, paradoxically, while armed *saend* "hostilities" start with power struggles, they act to prevent any party from exercising power over another. We can see that it is the reverse of state warfare that aims to exert power over enemies, to defeat and control, and to take over resources. In the Was valley the aim is to achieve a balance of losses and damage and to assert equality of relations by evening the account, not to defeat and conquer the enemy. It was in such a struggle that Ongol and his relatives now found themselves.

* * * * * * * * * * * * * *

While there was much talk of exacting revenge, there was no concerted attempt until the shot man's kin had concluded the funeral and mortuary exchange. The conversation during this time was about little else. Several men took the opportunity to prepare their weapons, sitting around the adjacent men's house producing many palm-wood-tipped arrows. Two of them went off to fashion new shields from the flying buttresses of forest trees, which would comprise more or less oval slabs of wood that they would sling from the shoulder on a vine loop, leaving the hands free to pull a bow. They returned one afternoon and proceeded to draw designs on them in charcoal, filling in with white clay and red ocher. Others brought out smoke-stained and battle-scarred shields from their houses, some of which they also decorated to intimidate the enemy, while others made shields from sheets of bark.

Ongol decided to go one better and, as evening fell, went quietly to the nearby necropolis at Petpet to find a human forearm bone. One of the exposed graves there contained the remains of an unrelated man who had married the widow of a kinsman and died locally. It was an unnerving business going there, particularly in the half-light, a known haunt of *towmow* that maliciously attack and kill living kin. But grave robbery was a tricky business that had to be done secretly because if relatives heard about it they would be angry and demand compensation. Furthermore, he had to be careful not to disturb the remains of

Human remains in exposed graves on a rock face.

Smearing ocher onto the shaft of a newly made bone-tipped arrow.

his kin resting there and provoke their ghosts. He came away with two forearm bones that would make excellent arrow points. The Wola say that human bone-tipped arrows are the most lethal because they are prone to break off in a wound, and such splinters are likely to cause blood poisoning and death. While Ongol prepared the shafts of the arrows in the company of the others at the funeral, he pared the bones into needle sharp points and mounted them on palm foreshafts in private, so that no one would ask any awkward questions. He was well pleased with the two finished arrows, smearing the points with red ocher, and was confident that he might exact revenge with one of them.

While an imminent attack did not concern Ongol's kin, as the side that had lost someone, men whose homesteads were nearest enemy territory (and so most vulnerable to assault) decided to refurbish their defenses in anticipation of possible attack later in the conflict. They ensured that the heavy fences that protected approaches to houses were in sound repair and that they had sufficient heavy timber on hand to barricade their narrow entrances at night, when they most feared attack. Thick brakes of cane grass otherwise surround homesteads, usually situated on readily defended ridges and knolls, giving protection from stealthy approach. A few men also built small hidden shelters elsewhere to store their valuables such as shell wealth and bird plumes, and their *hungnaip haen* [ancestor stones], so that in the event of being routed from their houses, these items would not be plundered. They also moved their pigs to the homesteads of relatives elsewhere for the duration of the hostilities. Two men took the precaution of sending their wives and children to other areas too. Families whose houses were located deeper within the *sem* territory were less worried, as an enemy attack was unlikely to penetrate that far for fear of being cut off and suffering losses.

The *towmow* give an added line of defense. Always lurking near the homesteads of their kin, they warn of any raiding party making a stealthy approach by *web kay* "whistling" to them. If men think they hear a whistle, they are immediately on guard against an attack. Sometimes the spirits communicate a warning at night through someone talking in his sleep; such *kombaysol kutubay* "sleep talking" may cause a scramble for the door and weapons for fear of an imminent attack. When asked later by the curious anthropologist why their *towmow* should bother to protect them, when at other times the spirits attack their descendants, "eating their vital organs" to cause illness and death, people rationalized that the *towmow* act like persons looking after their pigs. A family looks after its pigs, feeding them tubers and so on, until one day it decides to kill and eat them. Only a pig's owner can legitimately kill an animal, and so it is with *towmow*, only they should kill and "eat" their kin.

The behavior of two men from Huwniy's community who were related through their mother to the man shot in the chest is also instructive about attitudes toward armed hostilities in the Was valley. Grief stricken, they came to the funeral, bringing wealth to contribute to the *gwat* mortuary exchange. No one thought to exact revenge on them, although the chances were that in the forthcoming skirmishes they would be fighting with the enemy, as it is usual in any armed conflict for men to fight alongside those with whom they reside. The implication of taking sides is not that men ignore their connections to relatives elsewhere. The ramifying kin network that characterizes relations in the region makes it inevitable that some relatives will find themselves on opposite sides in hostilities. Indeed, the classificatory kin system, where people recognize a wide range of relatives and so can trace connections with several of those they meet, results in many finding themselves pitched against relatives in any violent encounter.

While distant classificatory kin may engage in combat with one another, close relatives will avoid fighting if they find themselves on opposite sides, and may even warn one another of danger. The two men from the other side of the valley who attended the funeral would not engage in fighting directly with their mother's kin, but they would fight the relatives of those kin—distant relatives—who were fighting on the other side. The result is that the two sides pitted against one another in hostilities do not comprise two monolithic blocs or armies but are fluid groupings of variously related persons with shared interests. The identification of two sides is not easy. One needs intimate knowledge of relations to predict people's possible behavior and allegiances. In arranging an ambush, for example, a few men will proceed in secret, such that not everyone on their "side" knows about it because some of them are likely to be related to possible targets and may warn them, thereby putting the ambushing party in danger of a counterattack. It is possible that men will support both sides at different times, fighting on one day for one side and on another for the opposing side. The interlinking of relatives across territories makes the idea of one side defeating the other foreign.

* * * * * * * * * * * * * *

Following the funeral, Ongol and his relatives set out to take revenge. Early the next morning, a group of warriors left to *saend buk pobtuw* [take the fight] to the enemy. They did not anticipate meeting any opposition on their side of the river and made for the nearest bridge on a neighboring territory. They approached it carefully, fearing an ambush. When they crossed the river, they split up into small parties to advance quietly, taking different paths toward the enemy territory. While the enemy had been unsure whether to expect armed retaliation or demands for compensation, some men had been preparing to defend their settlement. They had mounted guards on approach paths; three or four men were in temporary lean-to shelters hidden in the cane grass, with a good view across the surrounding country. They might ambush an approaching party of warriors if it was small, or alternatively they might raise the alarm. Such tactics make any advance into enemy territory hazardous, particularly as the defenders know its geography better than the attackers do.

It was during the approach toward the enemy territory that Ongol learned about the *saend iysh shor* [fight tree leaf] that helps men spot ambushes. He watched with interest as his *ab* Lem prepared it. He took a long leaf of *wolahaeriy* bamboo[2] and placed a *ngai ya* vine[3] leaf on it together with some moss before rolling it into a funnel shape. He muttered the following spell[4] into the hole at the top:

Piyaliy	*deno*	*widor.*	*Piyaliy*	*deno*
Mountain toward Kutubu	eye	is.	Mountain toward Kutubu	eye

widor.	*Imiliy*	*deno*	*widor.*	*Huruwguw*	*kaendow,*
is.	Mountain toward Tari	eye	is.	Grass skirt	cut,

kondor	*kaendow.*
edible grass[5]	is.

The reference to mountains and eyes was an allusion to the sharp lookout that men keep over the country to locate any enemy advance, hoping to spot warriors before the warriors see them. Furthermore, when the enemy fired arrows at them they would prove ineffective, as soft as women's skirts and edible grass.

As they advanced, Lem waved the leaf funnel in the enemy's direction to detect lookouts and ambushes.[6] The rest of the party followed him quietly. Ongol could feel his heart pounding with anticipation and grasped his bow and arrows tightly so that they did not rattle. Lem stopped every now and then and whispered again into the leaves before holding them up. The foliage in the funnel helps the bearer "see" any enemy hiding in the shadows who will stand out as light—and not dark-skinned—like the pale colored vine leaf and moss. If the enemy is a long way off, the funnel bearer feels a tingle at his shoulder. If a little way off, he feels the spasm in his elbow, and if nearby and an ambush is imminent, he will feel the twinge in his wrist and hear a "click" sound. This magic allows a party of warriors to advance toward enemies safely, and hopefully spot and surprise them first.

* * * * * * * * * * * * * * *

Neither side, as it happened, was able to surprise the other that day. Both were on high alert for action. When the lookouts spotted Ongol's party, they raised the alarm and a group of warriors quickly assembled to meet it. Initially they engaged in *ab saend bay* [fighting with insults], shouting abusive barbs at one another as they maneuvered gingerly into arrow range. Then someone loosed off an arrow and the skirmish started in earnest. Ongol felt the pent up excitement and anxiety of the stealthy advance explode as he charged forward with others in his party, shouting at the top of his voice. He released two arrows in quick succession before the enemy group rallied and pushed them back. The front moved rapidly from one place to another as men rushed forward in attack and then backward in response to counterattack. They fought everywhere, across gardens, around houses, along paths, in cane grassland, and through pockets of forest. When Ongol's side overran two homesteads, some men set fire to the houses, damaged garden fences, hacked at bananas, and debarked ornamental casuarina trees.

The fighting waxed and waned for several hours, the front extending over half a kilometer, with groups of men pushing forward and falling back again. The action was confusing and fast moving with arrows flying back and forth. By midday, over 100 men had arrived to take part in the skirmish. Such a fast-moving encounter is tiring; men ceaselessly on the move, running back and forth over several hundred meters. When they are within enemy arrow range, men have to dart about quickly so as not to be a static target. Even those carrying heavy wooden shields keep moving to avoid taking a crippling—and if close to the enemy, potentially fatal—arrow wound in their legs. They did not all fight all the time. While others were fighting, some men rested behind the lines, sitting around fires smoking; some even prepared an earth oven to cook food. Others posted themselves on nearby ridges and shouted warnings to kin about enemy movements. Some small boys hung around these groups, learning and soaking up the excitement; some even had small bows, although adults ensured that they did not put themselves in danger by approaching the fighting too closely.

A few men sustained arrow wounds, some in the back or buttocks, common

A house burning down.

wounds suffered when retreating after loosing off an arrow or two into the enemy lines during a sally forward. In mid-afternoon, a man advanced along the edge of the fighting under the protection of a shield until within arrow range of some enemy warriors. During the confusion of a simultaneous rush forward by his side, he shot an arrow into their midst and hit one of them in the chest, the man falling to his knees with a cry. The charge from the other side pushed the wounded man's colleagues back, sealing his fate. He took four or five more arrows in his body before some men reached him and hacked him about his head and shoulders with axes, and grabbed his cowry necklace and bow and arrows. By the time his relatives had regrouped and pushed the attackers back down the hill, it was too late to save him. He was dead when they reached him. The mourning cries that went up confirmed the death to Ongol's side, which was elated to have evened the revenge score.

Later in the afternoon, Huwniy's relatives, sensing that the Ongol's side would soon be withdrawing, pushed the fighters back toward the river. While they were keen to take revenge, they were careful not to allow their anger get the better of them. The retreat would be tricky for Ongol's side, having to cross the river would create a vulnerable bottleneck. The enemy was cautious, not pressing immediately toward the bridge because it feared a claw-like trap. This is a well-known tactic. While some men try to draw a foe forward, for example by setting fire to a house, others set an ambush on the approaching path. There was such a danger of a trap in advancing too quickly to the river, of being attacked from several directions, the enemy turning to confront them while another party blocked their retreat. Dusk was also approaching and darkness falls quickly adjacent to the equator, furthering the

Men fighting a skirmish across a garden.

danger of walking into an ambush. Everyone was tired, too, after several hours of combat. Only one man was wounded among those withdrawing.

While Ongol's side had suffered some casualties, and one man was subsequently to suffer an agonizing death from a septic wound, it was buoyed up by the afternoon's brutal killing. It felt victorious and performed the *ol sowaebay* dance and chant along the path back home. Some men continued the dance and singing the next day, with white clay designs painted on their charcoal blackened faces and feathers in their hair, the dead man's necklace and weapons displayed on the *howma*. They taunted the enemy; their whoops of joy, heard across the valley, intruded offensively into the funeral wailing. Others kept watch expecting a retaliatory attack; several had not slept that night, being too excited and fearing a raid.

* * * * * * * * * * * * * * *

The conduct of skirmishes illustrates the character of group activities generally in the Was valley. They are the product of loosely coordinated actions, decisions reached mob-like. There is no command or leadership; each man fights as he thinks fit in the mêlée. The action is the result of many individual decisions based on numerous simultaneous encounters, each responding as he judges best to the threat he faces. A concerted group endeavor results because all these individual acts have a common goal. A few men may agree at the spur of the moment to coordinate their actions more closely, for example in an attempt to outwit their enemies. They may try outflanking them in a move called *saend mariy pay* [carry the fight to them], establishing an ambush to pick off skirmishers.

During the next three months there were several encounters, some large and others small, when opposing parties met. Their scale depended on warrior movements. There was no element of surprise if large numbers of men advanced; the enemy would soon spot them, raise the alarm, and mobilize to meet the attack. More often small groups sought to approach the enemy stealthily, or set an ambush to trap the unwary. The other side would respond when it saw or heard such activity, and depending on their size, a skirmish would start if the sides were more or less balanced, or the outnumbered party would withdraw. To understand the conduct of armed hostilities, it is necessary to remember that the overall numbers on both sides are about equal. One cannot overwhelm the other by force of arms. When two equally matched parties of warriors meet and engage one another, others are likely to rally in support on hearing the sounds of battle. They often meet somewhere midway between their two territories, and this locale becomes the *saend howma* [fight clearing], a razed area of trampled gardens, destroyed houses, and felled trees, across which the two sides sally back and forth in the fray. In the current conflict, it was the area adjacent to the bridge, the river acting as a barrier because an attacking party was vulnerable when withdrawing across it.

On some days, no fighting occurred because enemy groups either did not advance toward one other or make contact. Men spent some time not fighting, making arrows to replace those fired, although during skirmishes they picked up and re-used some of those shot at them. They also relied on noncombatant relatives, such as the young, wounded, and elderly, to manufacture weapons, mainly arrows. While there were a number of further skirmishes, Ongol only fought in two. An arrow wound to the thigh put him out of action. He had inadvertently exposed himself during a sally toward the enemy, carrying only a small underarm shield that reached to his waist. He was angry with himself for his recklessness. The operation he endured did nothing to improve his temper. Two relatives helped him off the battlefield as he grasped the arrow, and one of them subsequently pulled it out of his thigh, causing him to shout in pain. He limped back with the aid of a stick; at least, he consoled himself, it was not necessary to carry him back on a stretcher lashed under a pole.

The trouble with some palm-wood arrow points is that they splinter readily, leaving slivers in the wound when pulled out. When a relative inspected Ongol's wound the next day, he detected such a large splinter. While one man held Ongol from behind, around the waist, and others held his arms and legs, someone skilled at removing such objects cut into his

thigh with a flint flake. Using a long bamboo needle, he poked and eased the splinter out, until he was able to grasp it between his teeth and pull it. The pain was intense and Ongol groaned in agony through clenched teeth. In addition, as if this were not enough, when the surgeon had removed the arrow tip, he used the flint blade to make two deep cuts on either side of Ongol's chest, along the bottom edge of his ribs, causing him to bleed profusely. He did this to stop the build up of blood from the wound inside the body, particularly in the chest, where, it is believed, internal bleeding can cause death by festering and "stinking." Men do not bandage arrow wounds for the same reason but leave them to hemorrhage until the blood coagulates.

A man with an underarm shield.

The operator was not sure that he had removed all the arrow point, which was not necessarily as serious as it sounds; several men have lived for years with pieces of arrow lodged in their bodies, although many believe that these ultimately killed them. Ongol, understandably, was unwell for some days after the grueling operation. He developed a fever and decided to kill a pig to aid his recovery, sharing the pork with his relatives in the men's house. He took the piece of arrow tip removed from his thigh and sunk it into a piece of fat that he pushed into a bamboo internode tube. When the fat rotted, it would turn puss-like and the arrow fragment slide out. Any splinter left in his body would likewise be expelled by the build up of puss around it. Ongol was unsure if any more fragments emerged from the wound but he slowly regained his strength, if not his mobility. He became increasingly frustrated, unable to take part in further fighting—until, that is, a stunning idea for an ambush occurred to him.

* * * * * * * * * * * * * * *

Stealth and surprise characterize armed conflict, and ambushes are a common tactic. Men maintain a lookout almost constantly during hostilities, so as not to be caught unaware, and only the wiliest ruses are likely to achieve success. Sometimes, under cover of darkness, a party of warriors creeps up to an isolated enemy homestead and surrounds and attacks it. They set fire to the house, shooting the inhabitants as they emerge in panic. Such attacks, penetrating enemy territory, are fraught with danger for the raiders, and retreating without loss is tricky. The commotion and shouts for help bring others to the aid of those attacked and a skirmish is likely to ensue, if the attackers have not fled. Those attacked cautiously pursue their attackers, fearful of further ambushes. Another wile is to arrange an assassination. This is where being related to both sides in a conflict may be turned to advantage—a relative of a person on one side agreeing to lure a person from the other side into an ambush. Alternatively, being related to both sides can prove a disadvantage, if those on one side have a grudge against you and your kin. They may arrange to meet you on some pretext, after organizing a group of warriors to lay an *enj karuw lay* [betray and hit] ambush on the route.

The trick with successful ambushes is to lay in wait somewhere the enemy will not suspect. Men expect ambushes on the route between their settlement and the enemy's, and consequently when they leave their territory, they proceed with caution and may depart from the path and advance in small parties through the surrounding bush. It was in this respect that Ongol had a bright idea. There was a suspension bridge deep in the forest on the other side of his territory, to the rear with respect to the enemy, where the river traversed a large bend. He surmised that a raiding party would likely use the bridge, taking a long route round through the forest, to attack some isolated forest homestead. If Ongol's party set up an ambush at the bridge, the enemy would be unlikely to suspect it, having walked for several hours. It was a perfect location for an ambush with thick vegetation in which to hide, and the enemy would present an easy target swaying above the river. He persuaded three relatives to accompany him, including his cousin Pes and Nap, his mother's sister's husband. It took him much longer than usual to walk there, and toward the end of the journey, his companions had to support him physically because the strain of the journey had caused his wound to bleed.

They spent the night in a relative's vacant house. In the morning, they proceeded to the bridge and concealed themselves behind a large tree overlooking it. They could speak because the roar of the river drowned out the sound of their voices, but they could not light a fire and have a smoke for fear of giving themselves away. After three days of fruitless waiting, the others wanted to call the ambush off, but Ongol managed to persuade them to give it another day. His perseverance paid off the next afternoon. The first they knew that people were on the other side of the river was when someone called out. They silently arranged themselves behind trees above the bridge as agreed previously and waited. The tension built up, such that Ongol could feel himself quivering with nervous excitement. He sought to release his anticipation by muttering the following spell[7] over the arrow that he held in his bow:

Uwduw	*Waegiya*	*hininiy.*	*Kashiy*	*haen*
Over there	mountain near Kutubu	rock.	Outcrop near Aengariya	rock

niniy.	*Buka*	*duwa*	*duwa.*	*Taebor*	*duwa*	*duwa.*
over there.	Blood	flow	flow.	Bamboo blade of arrow	flow	flow.

It imbued the arrow with accuracy and deadly power similar to that of malicious "bush spirits" that live at the two named mountains and kill their victims with a bamboo bladed arrow and suck out their life force. It urged the wounded to bleed profusely until death occurs.

Crossing a vine suspension bridge over the Was River.

After what seemed an age but was only a few minutes, a man's head and shoulders appeared at the bridge entrance. It was one of Huwniy's relatives at the front of a raiding party, which was just as well, for there had been a chance that it was some men not involved in the conflict returning from a trading trip to Lake Kutubu. The sense of expectation was terrific. Ongol signaled to the others with his hands to wait before firing until the man was on the bridge. They allowed him to advance someway on it. Another man came up behind him and started to cross too. They let fly their arrows simultaneously and two hit the first man, one in the leg and the other the chest. He fell onto the footway. At least three other arrows hit the hapless man. Moreover, his colleague sustained a wound in the shoulder as he scrambled backward upon realizing that it was an ambush. The other side fired several arrows but had little hope of hitting anyone within the dense vegetation. They dared not venture onto the bridge to help their relative. Meanwhile Pes and Nap started to chop through the anchorage of one of the vine handrails, causing the bridge to twist over and drop the body into the churning water below. If the man was not dead before he hit the river, he was within seconds of falling, smashed rag-doll-like against large boulders. They never recovered his body. Ongol and his companions were ecstatic and struck up the *ol sowaebay* chant as they withdrew. They had no fear of pursuit with the bridge damaged.

* * * * * * * * * * * * * * *

After about three "moons" of hostilities, people started to tire of the conflict, which seriously disrupted both everyday activities (for example, armed men having to accompany women to gardens) and the interaction between relatives who were on opposite sides. The occurrence of violent encounters declined as increasing numbers of men lost their appetite for continuing the fight. It reflected the pattern of recruitment to any conflict. Not all of the residents occupying the territory of the *semonda* connected to the original *saend tay* [fight originators] take part in all the hostilities. They get on with their own lives—as long as they were not disrupted by the conflict—cultivating gardens, arranging exchange transactions, and so on. While kin recognize an obligation to support one another in violent confrontations and to seek revenge, it is up to men to decide when to do so; no one can force others to fight against their will. Some only take up arms a few times during several months of hostilities. Similarly, kin of the *saend tay* party who live elsewhere may lend their support on some occasions and not others. The numbers involved in any encounter depend in some part on how it unfolds. If several men rally noisily on one side, in a determined effort to even the revenge score for instance, many may mobilize on the other side in defense, and a large, possibly day-long, skirmish may ensue. Whereas, if a small party sets out to ambush someone and is detected, there may be an exchange of some arrows before the attackers flee and the encounter fizzles out. Likewise, if an ambush is successful, the attacking party will hastily withdraw before the enemy can retaliate.

The will to continue the fight ebbs away after two or three months, particularly if the losses on either side are thought to balance. As long as several
men on one side remain determined to wreak vengeance on the other, the
hostilities are likely to continue. The decline in violent encounters gradually
leads to a realization that the armed conflict is probably ending, especially as
increasing numbers of people are likely to be voicing the opinion that it is
time to stop, notably those with kinsfolk on both sides whose social lives have
been seriously disrupted by the conflict. The Wola refer to this process as
saend pol the [fight goes-to-sleep]. It is gradual. There is no declaration of
peace; it is more that a consensus becomes apparent, until it is evident that
further armed aggression is unlikely. Both sides know the opinion on the
other. Individuals with relatives on both remain in contact; for example, a
man whose wife comes from the other side will be in touch with affinal relatives, and such people relay views back and forth.

Ongol was not happy when he sensed that opinion was for the *saend pol*,
as he reckoned that they still had a revenge score to settle. His side had killed
only five individuals, he pointed out, counting them on his fingers as he
named them, while losing seven. The last, he bitterly reminded everyone, was
his *hay*, Pes, who had taken part in the successful ambush. But revenge
account-reckoning is a subjective business. Others pointed out that two of the
fatalities on their side were women ambushed and raped in a remote garden,
whereas they had killed an *ol howma* [a man of renown] of particularly high
standing. There was also the original sorcery victim, who brought their
account up to six deaths. If you counted sorcery deaths, Ongol argued, there
was Korobol, and even Kot's unavenged death, too. Nevertheless, he could
not continue the armed conflict single-handedly with only a few relatives'
half-hearted support; such behavior would be suicidal. He might try to even
the score, he told himself, by resorting to sorcery again or surreptitiously poisoning someone. Alternatively, he might nurse his wish for revenge until further hostilities gave him an opportunity to balance the account. When former
enemies become embroiled in new conflicts, some take the opportunity to
ally themselves with the opposition to have another crack, and if they succeed
in killing someone, they will rejoice in having finally secured revenge,
although the death will count in the tally for the new conflict, too. Such
revenge-score opacity is necessary if hostilities are to "go to sleep," as it is
unlikely that those killed will ever equally balance; otherwise conflicts would
become interminable feuds.

The longer the *saend pol* endures, the less likely open conflict is to recur.
After several months, people talk about *saend pa biy* the [fight being over], but
the resumption of normal relations can take years. After a conflict, there is a
long period before enemies start interacting socially again. They slowly
resume relations on a limited scale at first. Persons related to both sides first
make tentative open contact and gauge the social climate. During the conflict, their social interaction will have been curtailed because, although
unlikely to molest each other, their respective kin might do so. If they have

complete trust in one another (i.e., have no fear of an assassination arrangement), they may arrange to meet quietly during the hostilities. The extent of the danger depends on how closely they are related to the *saend tay* parties to the conflict. If they are only distantly related and arrange to meet somewhere away from the conflict zone, they have little to fear; indeed to assault someone in this situation is likely to start a new *saend*. Close kin of the *saend tay* parties, on the other hand, find their relations disrupted more; for example, a man whose agnatic kin are one party and whose affines are the other will find open contact with his father-in-law and wife's close relatives difficult for many years, the strained relations and distrust interfering with normal interaction and transactions between them.

Relations between *saend tay* parties may remain tense for years and interaction be marked by precautions; for example men only visit the other *semonda* territory in armed groups in case old animosities lead to a fight. Furthermore, it is common for men to fight as allies against old enemies in new conflicts, perpetuating their personal animosity, but the tangled nature of kin networks prevents the emergence of permanent enemy blocs. Unrequited revenge wishes slowly slip into abeyance and are eventually forgotten, albeit possibly not in the lifetimes of those involved in conflicts. It is unusual for persons to harp on about blood debts from long ago, as Ongol went on about Kot, for these are "matters in the past." It is unlikely that relatives would openly take revenge. Over time relations are fluid, disputes occur and fights break out, and are forgotten. People do not nurse revenge obligations for generations—unlike obligations to pay reparation to the relatives of those killed fighting. The resumption of intermarriage between two previous enemy *sem* groups, after some years of curtailed interaction, marks a return to more or less normal social relations. And it was to marriage, not revenge, that Ongol's mind slowly turned as the conflict "went to sleep."

Chapter 5

Marriage, In-Laws, and Sex

*M*arriage is a significant event for any couple. It is both thrilling and disconcerting, with the disquieting aspect perhaps especially apparent in the New Guinea Highlands. After active hostilities stopped, Ongol hesitantly resumed everyday life. Talk among his peers sometimes turned to the merits or otherwise of eligible girls in the region, and he attended a couple of *turmaen* [courting sessions], singing to different young women at each event. One day on a visit to the neighboring Nembi valley, he met a girl called Mindiy of whom he had heard some boys speak warmly. He could see why. She was the epitome of vitality and attractiveness with her firm breasts, wide hips, sparkling eyes, and smooth, clear skin. She also had a reputation for having a bouncy personality but was diligent, not frivolous, like many of that temperament. Although he was strongly attracted to her, Ongol was cautious after the searing Kombaem episode.

When he returned home, he mentioned her to his father and uncles, and they carefully went over the history of connections between his and Mindiy's relatives. As far as they knew, he had no rights to claim access to land on Mindiy's father's *sem* territory, where she lived or that of any of her other relatives such as her mother's or her father's mother's kin, and so on, which, as a rough rule of thumb, defines the extent of marriage prohibitions, since kinship connections delimit land rights. Likewise, he did not use consanguineous kin terms when addressing any of her relatives; if he had, it would have been an indicator that marriage is disallowed. But then they had not known of any in Kombaem's case. They went over all previous interaction with Mindiy's kin and could find no connections that would preclude marriage— that would make it a sibling "climbing" offense. Reassured on that point, Ongol urged his kinsmen to start collecting the wealth necessary for a marriage. Meanwhile, he opened up courting exchanges with Mindiy, which she reciprocated generously, showing that she was interested in the union too.

After Ongol's relatives had opened up negotiations with her kin over the *injiykab*, Mindiy agreed to visit the Was valley for a few days and stay with Wasnonk, helping her to till and plant a newly cleared garden. Such visits not only start the process of building relations between the prospective bride and her husband-to-be's relatives but also ensure that the young woman will have some sweet potato mounds from which to harvest tubers soon after her marriage. She arrived with a friend for company and support, at what was a nerve-racking encounter, her first visit to Ongol's community. The two girls initially stood some distance from the garden, and after half an hour, they approached it coyly. They paced up and down outside the fence for a while, talking to some of the women, including Wasnonk, working inside. When they finally plucked up the courage to climb the fence, they stood on the edge of the garden fidgeting nervously. When they entered, Ongol, who was working there, went hurriedly to the other side and stood hiding behind a tree. The young women started, in a piecemeal way, to turn over the drying vegetation and built some fires to burn it. Later in the day, Wasnonk indicated an area where they could till and mound, and plant sweet potato vines. Ongol did not approach Mindiy or her companion any nearer than five yards or speak to them once all day. They studiously avoided one another, typical behavior for a courting couple, who experience acute embarrassment in one another's company in front of others.

Marriage signals a change in status, frequently marked by a ceremony of the genre that anthropologists call a "rite of passage." It symbolizes the assumption of adult responsibilities, which can be both exciting and intimidating. It is arguably particularly daunting in the New Guinea Highlands. It marks not only the beginning of a new household and subsequent nuclear family, with all the responsibilities entailed, but the couple also has to adjust to one another's personalities and behavior, which can be difficult as they may scarcely know one another. Also, one of them, usually the woman, has to move from one territory to another, which probably means moving in with strangers, increasing the sense of stress. The fears that men entertain of female pollution add to the anxiety and heighten further the embarrassment the couple feels if entering upon sexual relations for the first time, being unsure what to expect, even what is safe. The *injiykab* [bridewealth] negotiations signal the tensions from the start.

* * * * * * * * * * * * * * *

The *injiykab* exchange legitimates a marriage. It may take a groom and his close kin some time to muster sufficient wealth. Ongol had been accumulating wealth for his anticipated *injiykab* and had several valuables stored in the men's house together with two large pigs in his mother's care. He had further pledges from kin, some of whom had shown him the valuables they intended to contribute to his marriage. After discussions with Mindiy's father and brothers as to what they were expecting, Ongol realized that he would need to muster more wealth to be sure of the marriage going ahead, and his father and uncles would have to secure it. Some of them entered into debt and borrowed valuables from friends, while others called in outstanding loans. Meanwhile, Haebay hurried along an *ol bay* mortuary exchange, in which he and Ongol had invested in his sister's deceased son's name. This is a favorable exchange for the investors, as it customarily repays threefold, and Ongol's father's sister's husband, who was responsible for the mortuary sequence, was keen to support his marriage and came through with the wealth.

When Ongol and Haebay judged that they had sufficient wealth accumulated and pledged, they arranged to gather it all together for display, and invited Mindiy's relatives to come and view it. They arranged the shells, plumes, salt bundle, and axes on a bed of casuarina fronds under the eaves of their men's house, and tethered the pigs to a line of stakes in the house yard, in descending size, the largest first. This is a tense time for the groom, the stress heightened by the fact that he takes no part in the ensuing discussions. It is customary for him to sit to one side and act as if he has no interest in the negotiations. A close relative takes the lead; for Ongol this was Haebay. After inspecting the displayed wealth closely, Mindiy's relatives entered into earnest discussions among themselves. They were trying to sort out who should receive what. The negotiations dragged on over several days.

Some of the bride's relatives were unhappy at the wealth being offered. In particular, two more distant kinsmen were disgruntled. They had shown a particular interest in Mindiy's welfare as a girl, creating a "food giver" rela-

Pearl shells for bridewealth displayed under eaves of a men's house.

tionship with her by giving her choice cuts of pork and pandan nuts as she grew up. It is customary to recognize the generosity of such benefactors at a girl's marriage with a suitable valuable. There was also the son of a man who had contributed handsomely to Mindiy's mother's *injiykab*, who was demanding substantial recompense for his father's liberality, it being recognized practice for a man to reciprocate those who contribute to his marriage from the *injiykab* of his daughters when they marry. After some days of coming and going, and hard negotiations both at home and at Ongol's men's house, and on the path in between, Mindiy's father declared that he could not satisfy the expectations of his kin with the wealth offered, and he feared the marriage was off unless Ongol's side could come up with some more. He pointed out that they had been party to the negotiations and could see that he was in an impossible position because whichever way he suggested they divide up the wealth some persons were disgruntled and maintained that they would accept nothing from the *injiykab* rather than be humiliated by accepting what was offered. Such action is tantamount to refusing to recognize the marriage.

Ongol and Haebay had been anticipating such an impasse, common in marriage negotiations (and indeed many exchanges), as the bride's kin push for the best deal possible. They had heard the conversations, sometimes heated, between Mindiy's relatives and knew the problems that her father faced in achieving agreement to the marriage. Ongol's side judged that the demands were no mere bluff but, nonetheless, argued that they had nothing more to offer. They pointed out that the wealth offered was generous and that the kin of many other young women would be glad to accept it in marriage. This, again, is a standard ploy in such negotiations, the subtext being that "we can soon find another girl to marry with this *injiykab*." Mindiy's father regretted that they could not go ahead with the marriage and left with those who had accompanied him to the "final" negotiations. Ongol and Haebay waited for a few days to see if the decline was a pretense and Mindiy's relatives would return, but when they heard from some distant kin with relatives in Mindiy's community that they considered the marriage to be off, Ongol and Haebay decided to take action. They had been keeping some valuables back for this eventuality, again common practice.

They sent a message to Mindiy's father to tell him that they had secured additional wealth to make up the shortfall, inviting him and his kin back to conclude the marriage. A few days later, they displayed the wealth, and after some further discussions, Mindiy's relatives agreed to the marriage. One of her kinsmen was still unhappy with the cowry shell necklace offered to him, and stormed off in a huff, declaring that he would accept nothing. However, he was alone and his behavior did not derail the proceedings, unlike previously when several persons had signaled dissatisfaction. They had to agree that the *injiykab* was a generous one. Mindiy's father took the necklace, and a few weeks later, when the marriage looked secure, the dissenter begrudgingly accepted it rather than receive nothing (if a marriage is going to fail, it is most likely to do so in the first few weeks). It was obvious they would agree to the marriage as

A bride watches as her father and husband-to-be's brother arrange pigs for a bridewealth exchange.

Mindiy had come along wearing a new skirt, carrying a net bag, and wearing *timak tenj* hood—her body glistening with a liberal coating of tree sap *wombok* and a small bamboo knife sticking out of either woven armband, which would feature in the ritual performed after the marriage to protect her husband.

The bride plays a central role in the distribution of the *injiykab*, unlike the groom who continues to maintain a disinterested stance. Once her kin have determined the distribution of the bridewealth, one of them—Mindiy's father at her marriage—indicates to one of the groom's kin—Haebay in this event— who is to receive which things. The groom's kinsman hands these to the bride; with pigs, he hands her the rope securing the animal's front trotter and tells her to which of her kin she is to present them. This act formalizes the union. It symbolizes the woman's linking position in the newly established affinal relationship, and subsequent transactions between affines follow the same pattern, men passing wealth to one another through the woman, until children born to the union—the next generation's blood ties—are sufficiently adult to participate in transactions. Ongol and Mindiy did not exchange a word, even a glance, throughout. After the distribution, she returned to the Nembi valley with her relatives, who were chatting happily about the past few days' events, taking the wealth they had accepted. She led a large pig that her father had received from the *injiykab*. She would return to the Was valley the next day.

It is customary for new brides in the Wola region to wear black, and the following afternoon when Mindiy turned up at Tombem she had smeared herself with a mixture of tree-sap oil and powdered charcoal, giving her a striking, shiny black appearance. On her face she had painted three vertical lines in

The bride wears black: the body decoration of a newly married woman.

yellow clay. Nevertheless, what interested Ongol and his kin were the two large pigs that she and her companion led on tethers. These comprised the *hogol* [groomwealth], together with two shells in her net bag. They came up to the standard that Mindiy's father had led them to expect during the earlier negotiations. One of the pigs was earmarked for Haebay and the other wealth to other relatives who had contributed generously to the *injiykab*. They had already factored in the *hogol* return in their contributions, and Ongol was relieved to see that it met expectations; for if it had not, it would have led to the termination of the previous day's transaction, as his irate kin, not receiving what they had anticipated in return for their open-handed support, would demand the return of their contributions. When Mindiy and her cousin companion had handed over the wealth, they retired to Wasnonk's women's house, for they were thoroughly tired after making the trip between the Nembi and Was valleys several times in the last few weeks and twice in the past two days leading pigs, which made the journey considerably more wearisome. After eating some freshly baked sweet potato tubers they fell soundly asleep.

* * * * * * * *

The cousin companion would stay with Mindiy for the first "moon" of her marriage, acting as a familiar face and confidante during the first stressful weeks, as she settled down to life with her husband's relatives. Not that Mindiy had any large problems; her sparkly disposition and capacity for hard work soon won her friends among the womenfolk, and even Wasnonk found herself warming toward the girl. Nonetheless, those first weeks and months were not easy. The woman is the partner who usually moves from her natal place to that of her spouse, increasing the stress of the change of status for her. She probably finds herself, like Mindiy did, moving in with comparative strangers with whom she has to make new relationships. And she has to familiarize herself with the geography of a new territory, learning her way around a strange place.

The in-law avoidance taboos that married persons have to observe illustrate the tensions inherent in the new affinal relationships. A bride has to remember not to mention the names of any of the men who contributed to her *injiykab*—except for her husband. She will invent nicknames for those in her husband's generation, which she will use when talking about them any time. Those in senior generations she will refer to as *shumb* [elder-in-law] or by circumlocutions such as "so-and-so's" husband. She will observe these "name avoidances" for the rest of her life. This taboo on the use of the personal names of *injiykab* contributors extends to all of the bride's kin who received valuables at the marriage, who should also avoid using their names, although the taboo is not particularly strong and those concerned may only observe it sporadically, such as when in the company of a person whose name is taboo and using it could cause offense. But her father and his close kin should under no circumstances utter her husband's name.

The taboo on the bride is stronger, to such an extent that if the prohibited names are synonyms for common words, she will invent new words for these things. For example, one of the men who contributed to Mindiy's *injiykab* was called Em, and *em* is the word for garden, which now she could no longer use, so she made up her own. Likewise, if one of the bride's relatives has the same name as someone on the groom's side, which she and her parents and their siblings should avoid, they will change their kinsperson's name. Therefore, Mindiy's relatives stopped calling her father's father's brother's son's son's son Sab because this was the name of Haebay's half brother, and they renamed him Huwng. When, as a young girl, Mindiy had asked what would happen if her mother had used her paternal grandfather's name, she was told that not only would he be angry but also her mother's daughters' children (including hers) would all die as infants, a prospect that worried Mindiy for some time afterward. Nevertheless, she need not have fretted, as her mother, like most women, was careful to follow the name taboos incumbent upon her.

Ongol also had to observe a series of name avoidances. He had to reciprocate the taboos observed by Mindiy's kin, namely avoid using the names of all those who received something from the *injiykab*. The onus on him to do so was less strong than the one on his wife, although he would studiously avoid using her father's name and those of close kin in the same generation such as her father's brothers and sisters, and those of her mother's siblings. He would feel acute embarrassment doing so, and they would be offended. A man also observes a strong taboo on mentioning the name of his wife's mother, for to do so is particularly shameful. The mother-in-law reciprocates. Indeed her observance of affinal etiquette goes beyond name avoidance. After her daughter's marriage, a woman dons a *shumba tenj* [elder-in-law hood], which she will use when in her son-in-law's company to hide her face from him. While they may converse with one another, under no circumstances should a mother-in-law look into the face of her daughter's husband, for to do so would be embarrassing to both. If a man wrongs his wife, her mother may in anger look at her son-in-law, and if the consensus is that she was justified in doing so, he is obliged to give her a valuable to cover her face again, thus symbolizing the repair of their disrupted personal relations.

A woman sitting with her granddaughter, wearing a *shumba* mother-in-law hood.

The name avoidances observed by the Wola can make it difficult for a stranger not to cause offense inadvertently, although people turn a blind eye if the person is genuinely ignorant of relations, which was just as well for the anthropologist who arrived in the Was valley some decades later, whose blunders caused considerable embarrassment. Even when in the company of a person who has the same name as an affine of someone present (for example, the same one as his father-in-law) everyone should avoid addressing that person by his name so as not to cause embarrassment, which can lead to some convoluted conversation. In some regards, the strength of name avoidances relates to the amount of wealth that persons contribute, or should contribute, to a *injiykab*, as evident when a more distant kinsperson contributes generously, for such a person's name may become strongly tabooed, whereas on the basis of genealogical closeness it should only be avoided occasionally.

It is not only another occasion for name changes but is also considerable in extent—a practice that was to drive the anthropologist to distraction. In order to anticipate name switches and so follow many conversations, it is necessary to know how people are related to one another. And many are related in more than one way and may draw on one relationship in one context and another elsewhere. There are also the neologisms that persons invent for everyday words, so as not to say names that they have to avoid, which can further make conversations difficult to understand without knowledge of the code, familiar to all those who interact regularly with one another. There were fun and games trying to identify people when the name avoidance taboos observed by those present implied that no one should mention certain persons' names. In this event, a man would sometimes lean over and whisper a name quietly in the anthropologist's ear; other times, the anthropologist had to make a note to check on it again later, when no one observing the name taboo was present, to fill in the gap.

* * * * * * * * * * * * * * *

While adjusting to in-law name avoidance was a challenge for Mindiy, she had anticipated it. Thus, if asked what was difficult about the first months of her marriage, she would not have mentioned it particularly. Far more difficult were her relations with her new husband. The first months are stressful for any couple as they adjust to cooperating as partners, working out the terms of their relationship, and adapting to one another's personalities. However, for Ongol and Mindiy it was a markedly turbulent period and sometimes comical to their relatives, who were not unduly worried that the marriage would founder during the initial collision of these characters, for experience showed that those who fought at first like "carnivorous marsupials," later established secure relationships. Ongol did not feel the same affinity of spirit with Mindiy as he had for tragic Kombaem, due in part to them being so similar temperamentally. He admired her qualities as an energetic and industrious person, the sort of partner who appeals to ambitious young men. And she was attracted to him as a go-getter. But as a pair of forceful characters, they clashed a number of times early on.

On one occasion, when Wasnonk was away for a few days visiting relatives elsewhere, they had a furious argument over the management of a pig that had wandered off and would have done serious damage to a garden if another woman had not seen it. Mindiy maintained that Ongol should have tethered the pig to a stake, knowing its unruly temperament, whereas he thought that she should have taken the animal into the forest and released it to forage far from any gardens. They almost came to blows and Mindiy stormed off, while Ongol shouted to her to clear out and go back to her parents—as he was finished with her. In order to make his point, he cut some wedges and hammered them between the door frame and wooden slats that secured the crawl-through entrance into his mother's house, effectively fastening it tight. When Mindiy returned in the rain later that afternoon and tried to slide the slats to one side and enter, she was puzzled why they were stuck fast until she noticed the wedges. Perplexed for a minute, and standing there shivering under her pandan-leaf rain cape, she made a sound like a growl and took her digging stick and proceeded to make a hole in the thatch in the front corner of the roof at the eaves. She pushed in her net bag of tubers and the firewood that she had carried home, and then squeezed in herself. The wayward pig was already stalled inside, and when their other pigs returned home in the evening, she fed them outside and tethered them to pegs in the house yard for the night. The next day, Haebay was not pleased to see the hole in the roof of his wife's house, although he was somewhat amused when he heard what had happened. He insisted that Ongol help him repair the dam-

A *tenda* women's house with a grove of pandans behind, the door is closed with wooden slats (note firewood stacked under eaves).

age, as he had been a party to it. This did nothing to endear Mindiy to him, and they avoided one another for a few days afterward.

On another occasion, Ongol cuffed Mindiy round the ear, only to receive a painful blow across the shins from her digging stick. They were rowing over firewood. It was some days since Ongol or Haebay had collected and cut any firewood for the women's house, and returning late one afternoon from the gardens to find they were almost out of wood, Mindiy went over to the men's house to find it empty and helped herself to some split lengths of casuarina, prized for its fierce burning qualities. "How dare she?" shouted Ongol, while Mindiy defiantly asked what he expected her to do, if he was going to act like the ne'er-do-well. It was then he cuffed her round the head. The business was to surface again the next day, to Ongol's embarrassment. It was the day of the *ongor goiz* stage of the marriage exchange sequence. This customarily occurs a month or so after the *injiykab* transaction and includes late contributions to it, often comprising wealth pledged by the groom's relatives during the earlier negotiations. When Mindiy's relatives saw the wealth being offered, they expressed disappointment and earnest discussions started in the men's house yard. She sat to one side listening with a group of women but eventually she could not resist making a quip to her kin along the lines of, "What else would you expect of a man who could not be bothered to supply his wife and mother with firewood?"

Ongol glowered at his wife. She stood up and went to leave the house yard, turning to him as she did so and addressing him as Wolmaip, to the amusement of everyone, making an allusion to the *wolmaip* fungus,[1] that somewhat resembles a soft penis. Freely translated, she tossed across her shoulder, "Hey 'limp dick' I'm off to the Tombem garden." While he would have dearly liked to teach her a lesson, Ongol could hardly molest her in front of her kin. Stung, he dived into the sleeping room of the men's house and came out with a sizeable cowry shell necklace to add to the *ongor goiz* payment, to the satisfaction of Mindiy's relatives, who silently applauded her intervention, albeit being somewhat anxious about the apparently hostile state of marital relations. The humor with which her husband's kin reacted to their behavior was reassuring, suggesting that they were not overly troubled. Her kin had heard that relations were stormy between the couple, and her parents were rather worried, knowing how headstrong she could be on occasion. They need not have been, for once the pair had smoothed the edges off one another, their marriage settled down to become a stable, secure, and fruitful one, for a decade or so anyway.

* * * * * * * * * * * * * *

The first few months of a marriage are equally stressful for the man. Not only has he to adjust to life with his new partner, but he also is anxious about the health implications of marital relations. These anxieties focus on fears of female pollution. The sexual act is dangerous for him because of associations with poisonous menstrual blood. It would be lethal to copulate with a menstruating woman or, as we have seen, come into contact with the effluvia of birth. A man undertakes a series of rites with his new wife designed to protect him from these dangers.

The rites last until the girl's oil and charcoal decoration has rubbed off (she is not allowed to wash it off); this takes a month or longer. When she blackened herself, Mindiy prepared a small parcel of the charcoal and oil mixture that she gave to her husband. He used it to paint a vertical line down his sternum, and as he did so, she recited an incantation. It was the first in a series and spoke of her husband's sound physique and sweet smell after performing the rituals—implicitly contrasting with the rotten stink of an unprotected man who indulges in sexual intercourse and is "eaten." The newly married girl's decoration also symbolizes the couple's well-being, relating to physical fitness as highlighted on such occasions as dances when men decorate their torsos with the same glistening oil and charcoal mixture to accentuate their strong bodies and rippling muscles.

The couple rose every morning at dawn throughout this period and stood under a *huwmb* tree[2] to perform the "bird calls early get up" rite. While the novelty lasted, that is for the first few days, Ongol willingly met Mindiy under the *huwmb* tree on the other side of the *howma*. Soon, though, he was complaining about having to leave the warm men's house at daybreak, when he normally would be crawling into the open-fronted foyer, building a large fire to heat some tubers, and looking out at the chilly morning across the mist-filled valley. When he protested about the irksomeness of it—standing there shivering gently, his legs wet from the cold dew on the grass—he imagined the sharp and infuriating remark that Mindiy would probably throw at him if he failed to show up, although truth be told, she found the regime tiresome too. One morning as he muttered about his discomfort, his father quipped that he was the one who wanted to show transactional prowess, "who wished to have a name." He was referring to the belief that the rite improves the husband's exchange success, reflecting his health and vigor, epitomized in keeping up good relations with his new affinal relatives. The red berries of the *huwmb* tree, and the birds these attract to feed, symbolize pearl shells and pigs. The couple continued the allusions to wealth and amicable relations in the spell they recited under the tree:

Ya	*maenday*	*ba*	*bahamay*	*na*	*biya*
We(2)	bridal beads	dawn	nothing	not	do.

Waiphaegap			*bahamay*	*sebayga.*	*Oliy*	*boliy*
Dawn light along horizon			nothing	become.	Husband	husband's brother

bor bilor. Ema		*shumba*	*ba bila.*	*Kariy*		*na*
dawn. All		husband's family	dawn.	Broken pearl shell		not

kariy	*ba bila.*	*Tombay*	*na*	*tombay*	*ba bila.*
broken pearl shell	dawn.	Hole	not	hole	dawn.

The reference to the dawn is an elliptical reference to wealth and success in exchange. As he stood there while the sun rose, Ongol reminisced about his experience as a *sor kem* youth. At least then, he had to wait shivering only once! (When the anthropologist subsequently learned about it, he thought this parallel most interesting, although he was unable to make much headway with it, as there was no evidence of sun worship.) The red crescent of the rising sun symbolizes red ochered pearl shells. The husband will, by implication, transact quality wealth, pleasing everyone and ensuring smooth relationships. The dawn of a new day also symbolizes the start of the new relationship that will grow; just as the sun rises in the sky, the chilly relations of early morning giving way to the warm ones of midday.

While the bride wears black, the couple observes certain taboos. If they eat sugarcane, for example, they should only suck it because to chew and extract all the juice until the pith is dry mimics the consequences of a wife polluting her husband, "sucking" the juices from his body and making his skin sickly—dry and flaky. Also, the girl must not blow on a fire but can only fan it with her rain cape. If she blows on it, the disturbed ash, which drifts about, would be like the wealth her relatives hope to receive in the follow-up *ongor goiz* payment, drifting all over the place and not coming to them. The couple should not engage in sexual relations until the bride's black decoration has worn off, another subject of stress for the newly married couple. The constrained and hesitant attitudes to sexual behavior, underlined in the series of protective rites undertaken following marriage, makes the initiation of relations an anxious prospect for newlyweds, particularly if entering into sexual relations for the first time. It is embarrassing for the pair because while they will have heard hearsay comments and probably smutty talk, they are likely to be naïve about coitus, and find it difficult and awkward to initiate relations.

The prospect so spooked Ongol that when Mindiy's black cosmetic had worn off and they agreed to end their early morning assignations under the *huwmb* tree, he departed for several days with a few relatives to hunt in the distant forest around Mount Waenmaep. It was this period of absence, known to all, that made the "limp dick" jibe so timely and hilarious, such that it really hit home. The pretext was to catch animals to present to her relatives in a *ten sab liy* payment, which the groom's kin may give to the bride's kin as part of the *injiykab* series. They reply with a "dew wiper" payment[3] of one or two valuables, depending on the game they receive. Two of those who accompanied Ongol were married men, and he took the opportunity to discuss with them, often obliquely, his apprehensions about starting marital relations and worries for his well-being. It proved an altogether scary hunting trip. On one of the days, there was a violent wind and they spent several hours huddled together under the shelter of a rock face on the mountainside, fearful of falling trees and branches. They heard the crash of the occasional heavy branch, probably of dead wood falling through the canopy to the forest floor. It was one way that the fearful bush spirits, those ambulant heaps of anthropomorphic foliage, harm people deep in the forest, striking them down with heavy falling timber. The crack of breaking timber is interpreted as the frightful twang of a bush spirit's bow, which will prove fatal if you do not hear it.

A few day's after Ongol's return, the couple contrived an awkward assignation. They carried short lengths of bamboo internode, from which they drank water afterwards. This act is called the "water chest drink," and as they did so, they recited the following spell:

Ya	*ya*	*hwinya,*	*ya*	*belay*	*Bela,*	*ya*	*ya*	*Mondalaha,*
We(2)	we(2)		we(2)	help	help,	we(2)	we(2)	

ya	*belay*	*belay,*	*ya*	*ya*	*pabuwta,*	*ya*	*belay*	*belay.*
we(2)	help	help,	we(2)	we(2)		we(2)	help	help.

Setting a trap in a grassy clearing in the forest.

Ya	*ya*	*giyama,*	*ya*	*belay*	*belay,*	*ya*	*ya*	*ginaela,*	*ya*
We(2)	we(2)		we(2)	help	help,	we(2)	we(2)		we(2)

belay	*belay,*	*pindiy*	*pindiy*	*waen*	*pela*	*pela.*	*Tuwba*	*tuwba*
help	help,			type of tree	branch	branch.		

kolay	*isiy*	*waenay*	*lab*	*mond.*	*Tuwba*	*tuwba*	*ol*	*isiy*
parents	son	daughter	two	one.			man	son

waenay	*lab*	*mond.*	*Nay*	*biduwa*	*ha wabiy*	*layliyma.*	*Nay*
daughter	two	one.	Eat	sexual wasting	standing	say.	Eat

biybiyla	*wabiy*	*laylivma.*	*Nay*	*tigiyla*	*wabiy*	*layliyma.*
sexual wasting	standing	say.	Eat	sexual wasting	standing	say.

Some of the words used in this chant have no specific meaning, although people believe that in some mystical way they improve its protective efficacy. Nevertheless, regardless of these meaningless words, the intention is clear. The spell refers to the dangers of pollution and wasting away, and it assures the husband that contact with his wife to procreate will not expose his body to the ravages of sexual wasting. He will remain strong with glossy skin like the smooth bark of the *waen* [woolly cedar] tree. The drinking of water repeats this theme. It "flushes out the chest," which is where sexual pollution strikes, "eating away" at the vital organs. Clear and glistening, the water also washes dust off the body, showing the skin's natural shine.

After engaging in sexual relations a few times, the couple performed the final "gourd baking" rite. Mindiy gave Ongol a green gourd she had baked in hot ashes, together with one of the short bamboo knives tucked under her woven armband. He cut the gourd in half, while reciting another chant. The rite continued the theme of well-being and strength. Gourds and cucumbers are apt symbols as firm vegetables with glossy skins and moist, juicy flesh when cut open. Therefore, Ongol's skin would be firm and shiny as if moist, and not wrinkled, dry and ash-like. After they had eaten the gourd, Ongol took some yellow clay and smeared a line down his wife's and his chests, harking back to the theme of decoration enhancing a healthy body, uttering a further spell as he did so, which, like the others, he had learned from his father.

Over the next few months Ongol and Mindiy settled down to married life and their days, particularly Mindiy's, took on a certain routine. While marriage marked the start of a new household founded on a productive partnership between the couple, its independence was some way off. Newlyweds usually become gradually independent of one of their parents' households, typically the husband's. It was just as well that Mindiy got on with Wasnonk, as she continued to share her house for over a year, until her husband got around to constructing her own. She was also allocated further areas to cultivate in established gardens, of her father- and brothers-in-law, and Ongol subsequently cleared more new gardens, in which he allocated her sizeable plots to cultivate. As they assumed the responsibilities of married life, so their lives took on a certain regularity and even predictability.

Chapter 6

Everyday Life, Subsistence, and Famine

When couples marry, the expectation is that they will soon settle down and assume adult roles, particularly when they start a family and assume parental responsibilities. No longer free to indulge their youthful fancies, life takes on a certain steadiness, even daily uniformity. So far, this book has somewhat misrepresented Wola everyday life, giving the impression of one stirring event following another with colorful rituals, armed hostilities, and competitive sociopolitical exchanges. In truth, those living in the Was valley would describe daily life as pretty humdrum, as it is in many places when it is familiar to its inhabitants. Everyday existence features a certain steady rhythm, punctuated by occasional exciting events. The routine varies for women and men. They are responsible for different tasks, featuring a societal arrangement that anthropologists call a "sexual division of labor." A married couple comprise a partnership, central to the subsistence economy, where the household is the basic productive unit. They count on one another, as do their dependents, to undertake the mundane tasks and duties of day-to-day life.

Mindiy's daily routine, like that of all women, usually featured a visit to her gardens. Some were an hour or more walk from her homestead, and she spent much time traveling back and forth. Not that she considered this onerous. Sometimes she met others en route and they would gossip. Occasionally she undertook tasks in the company of Wasnonk, her mother-in-law, or other relatives, but gardening was mostly a solitary activity, until that is, she had the twins. That was a surprise, having a boy and a girl as her firstborn. She would not have managed them without Wasnonk's help. Her mother also came to stay for several months when the twins were babies. The five of them would set off for the gardens together, and Mindiy spent much of her time sitting in the shade with a baby at her breast, and sometimes both together, chatting with

Part of a woman's daily routine: harvesting sweet potato tubers.

the other two women. When the babies slept, slung nearby in net bags, she would join her mother and Wasnonk in whatever task they were doing.

The tasks undertaken in gardens vary with the stage of cultivation. If bringing a newly cleared area under cultivation, women's first task is to burn the dried vegetation cut down by male relatives in clearing the site, heaping it onto smoky bonfires. When they have cleared the surface refuse, they proceed to plant crops. This is largely women's responsibility; women cultivate sweet potato, the staple in their diet. They collect planting stock from established gardens, pulling up sweet potato vines and carrying them to the new area as tangled heaps atop their heads. They use sharpened poles to drive holes into the earth, into which they firm sweet potato vines. They may break up the soil in some places to produce beds planted with a variety of crops such as green leafed vegetables, shoots, gourds, cucumbers, bean, and taro.

If they are recultivating an established garden, women will start by pulling up the weeds and grass[1] that have colonized the area and any remaining crops, using their meter-long digging sticks to loosen the soil. They leave the pulled-up vegetation strewn across the surface, usually for several days to dry out in the sun. Next, they break up the soil as necessary into a fine tillage, heap it up into mounds, and plant it with crops, mainly sweet potato vines. They heap some of the up-rooted vegetation as compost into the middle of mounds as they build them, sometimes burning it. Women frequently work their way systematically across an area, preparing a line of square depressions bounded by four-sided ridges of earth, into which they heap compost before scooping the soil over it to build up a mound, two to three meters or so in diameter. The use of composted mounds, characteristic of subsistence agriculture throughout the Highlands of New Guinea, is central to soil fertility management with the nearly continuous production of sweet potato in some gardens, which may remain under cultivation for decades. Finally, they plant the mounds by pushing several sweet potato slips into the surface.

Women subsequently tend gardens, weeding them of invading wild plants. They also harvest most of the crops. It was an almost daily feature of Mindiy's adult life to return home in the late afternoon, carrying a string bag of sweet potato tubers to feed her family and the pigs in her charge. When she returned to her house, she would give a characteristic guttural call, like Ongol as an infant heard his mother cry, to summon her pigs back for their daily ration of stringy tubers, if they were not already there awaiting her return. After housing them in the stalls at the rear of her house, she would rekindle her fire and set to cooking the evening meal, which largely comprised sweet potato tubers that she put to bake in the hot ashes after scraping off their skins with a bamboo knife. Sometimes she cooked some tubers for Ongol but more often than not, she would stop by the men's house on her way back home and drop off a pile of raw tubers for him, together with a share of any other crops she had harvested, such as a parcel of greens or a gourd. She spent the evenings with her young children and sometimes chatting with other adults such as her mother-in-law.

She occupied some of her time making things, mainly rolling string and netting objects from it, notably bags of varying sizes, large for herself and smaller for male relatives, and aprons worn by men. After collecting saplings with bark fiber suitable for string, she would sit stripping it off, separating the inner fiber from the outer bark and sun-drying it before shredding it into strands and rolling these into string between her palm and thigh. If asked about her daily life, Mindiy would have mentioned it, together with gardening, as quintessential female activities. The task that she objected to was collecting firewood, which she deemed to be her husband's responsibility; without an axe, which only men may handle, all that she could collect was small wood that she could break up by hand and dry cane grass stems that did not burn for long or give much heat. After darkness fell and they had finished eating, Mindiy and the children would soon settle down for the night, lying around the central fire, the door slats jammed shut to

A woman rolling string from bark fiber on her knee.

build up a cozy fug. They would wake at first light with the dawn chorus, when they did little more than build up the fire and sit talking, before putting further tubers to bake or reheating some of those cooked the previous evening. There was rarely any sense of haste, and Mindiy might stay until mid-morning or later before setting off for her gardens, particularly if the weather was rainy.

* * * * * * * * * * * * * * *

Ongol also spent a considerable part of his time engaged in cultivation tasks, although not as much as Mindiy, women spending over twice as long on gardening activities as men. The heavy work of pioneering new areas falls to men. The vegetation cleared will be either secondary regrowth, of soft-wood trees and cane grass, or primary montane forest, with its associated understory tangle. Using polished stone axes, men pushed cane over using their body weight and employed a pole as a chopping block, against which they cut the broken stems. Similarly, they cut through the forest understory, ring-barking (stripping the bark from around the diameter of a section of the tree) and lighting fires around large hardwood trees, too big to fell. When dead and dry, such trees supply firewood. Today, using steel axes and machetes, men can fell such forest giants and slash down vegetation. The popular image of shifting cultivators chopping down swathes of forest for gardens is erroneous in the Was valley, where men more often clear fallow vegetation—understandable given the hard work involved in clearing forest.

Following clearance, men enclose areas with fences and ditches, where necessary, to keep pigs out. This is heavy work, particularly before the arrival of steel tools. It involves splitting and dressing stakes from hard timber such as *pel*, sharpening and driving them into the ground, and lashing a sapling runner along the top edge to give added strength. They try to situate gardens in localities where they can exploit natural features as barriers (such as rivers, limestone bluffs, and steep-sided gullies). Many long-term gardens are in such locations, where men have only to maintain limited fencing that secures weak points. Following the creation of an enclosure, they prepare the site for planting. They may lop the branches off any trees left standing and pull up roots. Men often arrange small work parties to help with the tedious and hard work of levering out tree roots and cane clumps, using heavy pointed sticks. They scatter the cut vegetation around the site to dry in the sun and subsequently heap it into large bonfires. Following this, women enter the garden to help with the last of the burning off, giving an important fertility boost by releasing nutrients into the soil in a form available for crop uptake.

Men are responsible for the planting and up-keep of some crops, such as taro, bananas, sugarcane, pandans, and some green-leafed vegetables. They sometimes clear special gardens for taro, in swampy locations favored by this crop, and observe certain taboos to ensure a good harvest of corms, which they may formally distribute to relatives. Newly cleared gardens resemble classic swiddens with a variety of crops planted in scarcely tilled soil, inter-cropped among a jumble of partially fired tree stumps, roots, and logs. The

Throwing cut and dried vegetation on a fire in clearing a garden.

duration of the mixed cropping period depends on yields, but it rarely exceeds two or three crops. Later cultivations, involving more soil tillage by women, are dominated by sweet potato planted in circular mounds.

Another category of heavy physical work that falls to men is house construction. They have again to split and dress hardwood stakes for the walls, beat sheets of pandan bark lining, and gather substantial poles for roof rafters. Sometimes they build houses alone, and other times two or three relatives help, as when Ongol built Mindiy's first house. When they have constructed the walls and the rafters are lashed in place, female relatives help collect the grass for the thatch. A house builder will often arrange to cook vegetables in an earth oven to reward the thatching party.

Ongol also spent some time, like all men, making various things. The production of arrows was a fairly regular pursuit, particularly palm-wood pointed ones, while he kept the same black palm bow inherited from a relative all his life. He also regularly made tethers to secure pigs, plaiting these from tough bark fiber. He learned to weave armbands, using fine rattan strands, from his *ab* Lem who was locally known for his delicate work. Occasionally he had to hone his axe blade after chipping it and would sometimes sit astride one of the sandstone boulders on the banks of the Was River adding to the pocks made by generations of men whetting blades. Other times he sat grinding his axe on a block of sandstone in the men's house living room, which turned an otherwise tedious task into a tolerable one, by combining it with convivial chatter, particularly during an evening or early morning.

The start and finish of Ongol's day were similar to Mindiy's, waking at dawn and retiring not long after nightfall. He usually cooked his main meal

Thatching a house with cane grass.

of baked sweet potato tubers in the ashes of the men's house fire in the evening, and left some tubers to reheat in the morning. He also spent a considerable part of each day walking to places, not only distant gardens but also communities elsewhere, sometimes a day's walk away, to attend public events, notably exchange transactions. Participation in such sociopolitical events took up a great deal of Ongol's time, as an aspiring *ol howma* of renown, as did disputes over wrongdoings and, when informal procedures failed, armed hostilities. Even when not actively taking part in a conflict, men have to keep a constant guard in times of hostilities against potential attacks on their families, which can be stressful and time-consuming.

* * * * * * * * * * * * * * *

Something else that Ongol had realized of late was the scale of the liability that he and his close kin had incurred acting as the *saend tay* in the recent armed hostilities. This was something that was to engage his attention for the rest of his life. He and Haebay were concerned that the debts would burden their descendants, as direct kin are ultimately responsible for clearing all reparation payments. Furthermore, Ongol would be even more concerned at the reparation obligations that he was bequeathing to his descendants when the demon of Kot returned yet again later.

The logic of the reparation exchange series is that the two parties to the original dispute that led to the armed conflict, namely the *saend tay*, are responsible for reparations to the kin of all those who died fighting on their behalf. They do not expect the enemy killers to pay compensation, but their allies to pay it. The responsibility ultimately devolves to the individuals involved in the original dispute. Nevertheless, the volume of reparation payments resulting from hostilities where several deaths occur will be beyond one person's capacity to meet in his lifetime, and so responsibility tends to fall

Arranging pearl shells in groups during an *ol bay* mortuary exchange.

on kin at the *semgᵉnk* level, namely those closely related to the disputants, notably those living on the same territory as the *saend tay*. The identity of those responsible is relative, depending on claimants' whereabouts in their social universe and connection to them. Those who live elsewhere will think of the *semonda* where the original disputants reside as the responsible party, and if they come to fight and lose one of their number, they will look to their nearest kin in this larger grouping to pay them reparation.

The system works with intermediary kin making the initial reparation payments for relatives to whom they are closely related, who came to fight because they are related through them to the *saend tay*. These intermediaries then expect reimbursement, in transactions called *haypuw*, either directly from the *saend tay*, or from kin more closely related to them than they are themselves, who will in turn look directly to the *saend tay* for reimbursement. Those who pay reparation on behalf of other relatives are called *moraret*, which is the same term as used for allies from elsewhere. The receipt of reparation absolves relatives of having a revenge obligation. Otherwise, hostilities would spiral out of control, each new death drawing in evermore kin to fight. While the close relatives of anyone killed may join in with a view to exacting personal revenge, kin that are more distant are not so affected and observe no such obligation. It is up to those who started the hostilities to see that revenge is exacted, as signaled by the obligation on them to take ultimate responsibility for the reparation series of exchanges after the conflict.

It was just as well that Ongol was ambitious to achieve *ol howma* status, given the tangle of transactions that followed the armed conflict with Huwniy's relatives. As the one ultimately responsible for these, he had plenty of opportunities to engage in exchange. In addition to arranging the reparation transactions for close kin, such as his *hay* Pes, Ongol found himself attending a number of other transactions elsewhere, as relatives took it upon themselves to compensate kin for losses. Often Ongol would contribute to these payments, too; he wanted to signal his good intentions to reimburse those who assisted in subsequent exchanges and show the esteem he had for his relationships with these allies. Furthermore, Ongol wished to be present when any opportunity arose—such as reparation transactions afforded—to shout insulting *mogol liy* challenges at the enemy, as a way to vent his anger. Following hostilities, during the "fight sleeps" interval (during which relations remain strained between the two sides), when one side displays much wealth for an exchange, it may shout out challenges to its enemies to match it, or barge in and take it, as the sort that starts *saend* through unreasonable behavior. The implication is "are you as big as us in the valuables that you can amass for exchange," and by insinuation, demonstrate sound social relations, as opposed to the disrupted ones that you have caused between us?

The first months following the cessation of hostilities saw several *ol komb* payments, the first in the reparation series. They followed the same format as the *ol sond*, described earlier. Ongol, Haebay, and their close kin were regularly present, often to be seen in the group of men running along with sides of pork draped across their shoulders, yodeling the characteristic *"wor, wor"* cry. The second payment in the series is the *showmay enjay* [live pigs] exchange, which takes place two or three years later. In this transaction, as the name suggests, men present live pigs, together with some other valuables. On the day of the exchange they display the pigs in a line tethered to stakes, their backs decorated with white clay stripes, and again dance in a circle making the *"wor, wor"* cry. The relatives of the deceased, recipients of the pigs, lead the animals away on their tethers, after agreeing to the distribution among themselves. The third payment in the series is

Men line up with sides of pork across their shoulders in an *ol komb* exchange.

the *ol bay* [man maker] investment exchange sequence, which follows the same pattern as the mortuary transaction described earlier of the same name. It may follow any death, not only violent fatalities like the previous two transactions. It customarily features pearl shells and may occur several years after a death, such that the reparation series extends over a decade or so. It could go on considerably longer, even over generations, if, as we have seen, others are obligated to reimburse those who have made the payments.

* * * * * * * * * * * * * *

The sexual division of labor arrangements have prompted some commentators to argue that relations between the sexes in the New Guinea Highlands are exploitative. Women make regular daily visits to their gardens to work, whereas men's heavy cultivation work is more spasmodic. Households depend on their adult female members to supply them every day with food. It seems that men do not undertake their fair share of labor, if we define work as undertaking physical activities that result in the production of something tangible, such as food. This is not the men's view, who point out that sociopolitical activities, notably meeting exchange obligations and negotiating in disputes, are stressful and demand considerable effort, as do armed conflicts when they occur. While men are more prominent at public events, notably spending much time on exchange activities and negotiating community relations, and traveling back and forth between places to do so, this does not signify that they rule social life.

Women's lives may revolve more around the domestic sphere but the implication is not that they have no say in affairs, as Mindiy's relationship with Ongol shows clearly. As a strong character, she made sure that he knew her views, particularly in matters where she had an interest, such as transactions with her relatives. She was keen to see that her fathers and brothers received their fair share in the periodic payments that occur between affines. One day, she allegedly remarked to Wasnonk, "Men might like to think they are the 'head' of households, but women are the neck and we can turn the head in whatever direction suits us." While overexaggerated, the statement reflects the influence that she could exert over Ongol's thoughts. He soon realized that she gave sound advice and that he was a fool to ignore it, or the consequences were not worth it if he angered her. This was evident if he did not listen to her views on deciding where to locate new gardens.

A first consideration in selecting a new garden site is access to land. Kinship connections to custodian *sem* groups structure rights. They give families a potentially wide choice. They can claim rights to cultivate on the land of any group to which they have acknowledged kin connections, validated contemporarily by participation in exchange transactions. It is not feasible, however, to cultivate anywhere on such a territory. Physical geography sets limits on the location of gardens, although families cultivate surprisingly steep slopes. The country is rugged and precipitous, with turbulent rivers flowing along valleys. The geologically recent folding explains the steep relief, characterized by sharp-crested mountain ridges, together with limestone features such as basins and potholes and scattered pinnacles. Contemporary geomorphological processes maintain the raw and youthful topography, with vigorous erosion and occasional landslides. The small houses of the population are scattered along the valley sides, while the intervening watersheds are left largely unpopulated.

Several criteria besides tenure rights influence families when choosing a new site to clear and cultivate. Among them are aspect, convenience, topography, and so on. There is no point in establishing a garden on a slope that, given its orientation, sees little of the sun. And women in particular are interested in the distance to and between their gardens, as Ongol was reminded when he proposed clearing a cultivation at Boriya, which was some four hours' walk from his Tombem homestead. "Go ahead," Mindiy told him, "if you are willing to do much of the tillage and planting," signaling her unwillingness to make regular visits to such a distant garden. When she reminded Ongol of the taro garden that he had cultivated there in a waterlogged hollow, and the effort required to maintain it, he saw the good sense in her view.

The sexual division of labor results in women and men having different responsibilities that only sometimes overlap and bring them together. Family life is consequently not what we might expect. A husband and wife, occupying separate houses, may go for some days without seeing one another. Family dynamics vary widely depending on personalities. Not all women are as strong-minded and sharp as Mindiy, nor are men as energetic and ambitious as Ongol. Some overbearing and aggressive men seek to impose their wishes on their female relatives. But they have to be careful not to push them too far and make them resentful, such that they cooperate half-heartedly in gardening and herding, mischievously creating problems. A wife may walk out altogether if pushed beyond certain limits, knowing that her natal kin will take her in if they agree that her husband has abused her rights. Such action can seriously embarrass a man, particularly if he has no other female kin to help him out and he has to fend for himself. The settlement of such differences may cost him further if he has to offer her relatives compensation for his ill-advised behavior before she will agree to return.

At the other end of the spectrum are households where the woman habitually scolds her husband and the man is lackadaisical. She may push him into complying with her wishes, and he may largely comply for the sake of a peaceful life. This type of woman is likely to press her relatives' interests over other responsibilities, but she has to beware of overstepping the mark. She must be careful that her husband's relatives not become annoyed, say, if he patently fails to meet obligations to, and through, them. The man may comply with her wishes as far as he thinks he can before his relatives will intervene and make his life even more difficult, possibly stepping in to curb his wife's domineering behavior. Between these two extremes are a range of households, from those who reach most decisions amicably, with the occasional argument, to those where both partners are forceful, as with Mindiy and Ongol, and heated differences of opinion are common and physical confrontations sometimes occur. It is not always the man who assaults the woman, although more often than not, she is the one physically hurt, perhaps decamping with her children to her natal place.

* * * * * * * * * * * * * * *

Life has a way of upsetting regular daily rhythms. After about two years of marriage, a famine disrupted the everyday routine of Ongol's household, and all those in the region. He heard that recent earth tremors had heralded it and supposed that parents had also failed to tell children not to touch the *dayngeltay* [hungry-time-origin] grass,[2] which according to custom leads to food scarcity. Irregular periods of food shortage are a feature of the New Guinea Highlands. They are associated by scientists with the occasional reversal of the El Niño current in the Pacific Ocean, which affects rainfall patterns.

The climate of the Was valley is generally uniform, many days featuring sunny mornings and rainy afternoons. The region usually enjoys high rainfall (annual average 300 cm) and cool temperatures (mean daily 18°C) due to the moderating effect of altitude. There are no notable seasons sufficient to affect crop cultivation, although people distinguish two times of year, which equate with the Southern Hemisphere's summer and winter. But unpredictable perturbations occur, upsetting this moderate regime and bringing hardship. The Wola say that these come in the winter, and associate severe food shortages with clear blue skies and low night temperatures, and sometimes devastating frosts. Staple sweet potato is particularly susceptible.

Those living in the Was valley associate these hard times with the spirit of a fair-skinned woman called Horwar Saliyn, who used to live in the forest. They tell a myth about her exploits killing men who had sexual relations with her, until one day she propositioned a man who was heating some stones for an earth oven, and he thrust a hot stone into her terrifying man-killing vagina when she spread her legs. The woman staggered off in agony, collapsing every so often, and wherever she fell writhing in torment, she left a pool of water, all of which remain at these places to this day. When crops fail and famine threatens, people resort to rituals at such places to appease the fair-skinned woman's spirit.

Ongol attended such a rite at Ngoltimaenda on a neighboring *semonda* territory downriver, situated on a ridge above a pool of water that wells up from a pothole. They say that Horwar Saliyn had a house there. One side falls away vertically and is where the hero in the myth found the corpses of his "brothers." There is a large stone at the site called Henja Hab. According to local lore, it was the one thrust into Saliyn's vagina, which has subsequently grown greatly in size. The large circular earth oven pit on the ridgetop resulted from her writhing with the hot stone inside her. The ritual requires marsupials as offerings, and Ongol spent several days hunting in the forest on the far side of the Ak valley, as did others at this time as garden yields dwindled.

The hunting strategy Ongol favored was setting spring traps, either on branches where spoor indicated animal pathways or the ground adjacent to possible den sites. However, he often innovated in response to circumstances and terrain, sometimes rapidly in the heat of the chase, anticipating the behavior of pursued game and using whatever came to hand. He sometimes hunted with a dog that would run game down, or he used bow and arrows, stalking animals, particularly by moonlight when he could spot nocturnal species feeding in trees. He bagged one of the mountain cuscus[3] that he took to the rite by climbing a tree and snatching it by hand from the hole in which it nested. If the season had been right, he would have liked to set spring traps for cassowary, which frequent the remote Ak valley forest, for the large flightless bird would have supplied much valued meat for his family. He knew, however, that it was pointless during winter when the bird migrates out of the mountains and into the sky, according to legend. So, he had to content himself with a couple of mountain cuscus.

When the participants congregated on the Ngoltimaenda ridgetop, women and children remained quietly at home; there must be no noise in the neighborhood. The participants rubbed the Henja Hab stone with the charred fur and blood of the animals they had caught, said to "please" the white woman's spirit. Ongol dashed the head of the live animal taken from its nest on the stone to kill it. They cracked all the animals' bones on the Henja Hab stone and on another one called Henja Homok—unmarried men doing so on Hab and married men on Homok. Married and unmarried men also sat in separate groups during the ritual. Some men had brought along pigs to offer and smeared blood from the clubbed animals' bleeding snouts over the Henja Hab stone. When administering pigs' blood or singed marsupial fur and blood to the stones, the men chanted the following:

> *Hokay   njiybiy, ma njiybiy,   sab   diy   njiybiy.*
> Sweet potato give, taro give, marsupials and   give.
>
> *Showmay diy njiybiy,   ten   nonknais kab diy   ma   ebay   sha*
> Pigs   and give   women children two and cause good become
>
> *bay. Suw diy   ma   ebay   sha   bay, showmay diy njibiy.*
> do.   Land and cause good become do,   pigs   and give.

The spell's intent is self-evident, relating to the calamitous conditions that prompted the rite's performance. It appeals for adequate food supplies, mentioning sweet potato, taro, pigs, and marsupials as particularly valued foods. It also asks that women and children should enjoy good health and have enough food to eat. It urges the land, which includes the weather, too, to remain fertile and fair. Other than reciting the incantation, those present spoke little during the ritual. The custodians of the site told them not to talk until they had eaten the entrails of the marsupials, which they cooked in a separate small earth oven; the other meat they cooked in the large spirit-made hole. While the entrails cooked, they communicated by miming and pointing only, with the occasional whisper, which Ongol found mildly amusing. Only those present consumed the meat. They heard that communities further down river were staging the "tree throat make see" ritual, which took place at Horwar, the place where Saliyn originated.

* * * * * * * * * * * * * * *

Several communities coordinated their efforts in the "tree throat make see" ritual, each sending two representatives called *moray nais* (similar to the two *kem* boys) to Horwar to participate. After a large rite there, they returned to locations near their communities where Saliyn's seared vaginal secretions left water pools, to stage further local rites. They built a longhouse at Horwar. It was said that men decorated the gable ends with many pearl shells during the ritual. The *moray nais* withdrew from everyday life and observed a range of food taboos; others should not see them as they prepared to intercede with the pale-skinned spirit on behalf of all—their close association with her made them dangerous.

The rite featured a girl leading a red-bristled pig on a tether to the *moray nais* who, it was said, killed and burned the animal as an offering to Saliyn's spirit (one of them subsequently told the anthropologist that they actually cooked and ate it). They also engaged in mysterious activities in the longhouse, reciting spells that recall the presentation of vast amounts of wealth to the spirit long ago to promote an agreeable relationship with her and to persuade her not to behave malevolently, causing hunger and hardship. The climax is a dance attended by people from surrounding communities at which the *moray nais* wear majestic bird-of-paradise plume headdresses set in wigs, stomping in a circle, chanting and clapping pandan leaf strips together.

Next, the *moray nais* visited some of the sites where the wounded Saliyn rested, staying the number of nights the white woman rested in the vicinity nursing her injury, usually one or two. The adjacent communities built a house and three-sided leafy screen there, where men again displayed pearl shells on the day of the rite. Again a girl handed over a red bristled pig, walking through a tunnel formed by the outstretched arms of those present holding a length of vine aloft, leading up to the doorway in the screen's rear wall. The *moray nais* slaughtered and ate the animal, its blood and smell of singeing bristles appeasing Saliyn's spirit—a pig offering made in good faith.

After visiting these places associated with Saliyn's agonized flight, the *moray nais* resumed normal life. It was believed that their intercession would assuage her spirit and persuade her to relent, ending the food shortage and warding off further disaster. A social scientist might point out that whatever the psychological implications, the demands of the ritual cycle that several communities cooperate could reduce the chances of intercommunal violence by concentrating hunger-sapped energies on negotiating with supernatural forces, thereby deterring attacks on others who lived elsewhere, in order to get food. This is significant in a stateless society, with no authoritative offices to enforce order, when severe privation could tempt people to attack each other anarchically to grab what little food there was.

According to hearsay, some communities further up the valley performed another ritual to ward off abnormal weather and food shortage. It involved a pig kill, the pork cooked—after display on horizontal poles—in a large earth oven hole made by some unknown force and not humans. A month or so before this, they cooked marsupials and vegetables in the same oven. Only men should eat the food. The characteristic feature of the rite, widely known to those elsewhere such as Ongol who have not seen it, was a ladder-like construction, up which climbed two boys wearing grass skirts, followed by several men in bewigged bird-of-paradise headdress finery and face paint. He had no idea what else occurred or why.

* * * * * * * * * * * * * * *

Regardless of these ritual endeavors, the famine worsened. It was a nightmare, as Ongol subsequently recalled. People sought to supplement dwindling garden yields by collecting any uncultivated foods they could find, such as the new leaves and fruits of some trees and vines, wild yam and Pueraria tubers, the edible leaves of some grasses, and the immature inflorescence of wild sugarcane. Contrary to popular imagination, the forest is not rich in such wild foods or game, few animals being larger than the domestic cat. Nonetheless, men hunted for what they could find, and women and children sought rodents and edible insects, such as crickets, caterpillars, and wasp and beetle larvae.

Some families were clearing small new swiddens with what strength they could muster and planting a variety of crops in a desperate attempt to increase food supplies, because staple sweet potato yields were badly hit. There were problems with fires, too, as if the food shortage was not enough to contend with; fires lit to burn garden refuse could get out of control and spread into the surrounding vegetation, which was drier than usual. One fire spread uncontrollably from a garden adjacent to the homesteads at Tombem destroying a women's house. Fortunately, no lives were lost. The person who lit the fire without due care (to clear dry vegetation that he had ironically cut down from around the garden edge to give a fire break) was held responsible for the damage and, after a brief dispute, paid compensation to the family, in addition to assisting with the rebuilding of the house.

The population showed the stoic resignation of people familiar with periodic empty bellies. Ongol stuffed a pad comprising a flexible bamboo frame wrapped in an old string bag down the front of his bark girdle to press against his stomach, "so my belly feels like it is pushing against the girdle when full of food." Pigs were the first to die of starvation. When sweet potato tubers are in short supply, humans and pigs come into direct competition for what there are, and people stop feeding their animals. When they died, their owners shared the pork in informal exchanges, so long as the animal showed no signs of "bad blood," that is thick and turgid blood indicative of disease. Some they slaughtered beforehand for food. The small animals succumbed first. Families lost their entire herds. People recalled that the famine was so bad that there were no pigs in their region afterward, and they had to rebuild their herds with animals received through exchange and trade from the north, where they supposed the drought had been less serious.

After the pigs, humans started to pass away. The elderly and sick succumbed first, and then some healthy and young persons followed. There was great suffering and distress as people died for want of food. Ongol and Mindiy lost one of the twins, their firstborn son. Mindiy was hardly able to supplement what the pair received beyond their share of the family's paltry food supplies, as she was lactating less and less. She felt badly that she could not have offered her son more and grieved deeply. They arranged his pathetic little funeral with what strength they could muster. Paradoxically enough however, Ongol's family grew in size due to the famine.

Haebay's brother's daughter—Ongol's *mboliy* [sister]—passed away at this time, as did her husband, leaving behind a daughter and a son. The pair initially attached themselves to a neighboring relative's homestead. One day they were wandering with an adolescent cousin who had befriended them, foraging for any food they could find, when she said that she was too weak to go any further and told them to go on without her. She subsequently died by the path where she lay down exhausted. They felt abandoned and were at a loss for what to do next. Fortunately, someone who knew Haebay took pity on them and led the pair to his homestead up the valley. The girl, who shuffled along holding the hand of her little brother, was a pitiful sight that moved Mindiy greatly, suffering from her recent loss. She took the pair in and, with Wasnonk, fended for them. The drought was over by then and the food shortage soon ended.

The pair of orphans found Ongol's homestead welcoming and opted to stay there. He was firm but fair, and Mindiy gave them a sense of security, and the couple were willing to act in a way that did not give the children any sense that adopting them into their family was a nuisance. It is up to orphans, and the relatives they wish to live with, to decide where they reside, be they paternal kin or maternal (a parent's siblings are a common choice as are older married brothers or sisters). Some orphans adopt an itinerant lifestyle moving between the homesteads of two or more relatives, never entirely at home in any one. The two orphans remained members of Ongol's household until adulthood. The only problem occurred when the time came for the girl to marry many years later. Her father's brother's sons, supported by their relatives, made a fuss at the distribution of the *injiykab*, insisting that they should oversee it. Ongol agreed, but some of his relatives, who had interacted with the girl almost daily, giving her food and so on, were offered what they considered inadequate wealth for having "cared for" the girl. There was a dispute that almost erupted into violence—the offended men refusing to accept the valuables offered to them, thereby not acknowledging the marriage. The wrangling went on for weeks and reminded Ongol of his own painful and embarrassing experiences of marriage negotiations as a would-be groom. Eventually everyone managed to sort out their differences.

Chapter 7

Some Ghostly Encounters and Perils of Polygamy

$\mathcal{T}$here are some events in life that impose themselves indelibly on the memory such that we can remember them in detail years later, even recalling small things like the smell in the air at the time. The valley breeze brought the scent of burning grass up to Ongol from the gardens below when the strange news arrived. He was balancing 15 meters above in a large ring-barked tree chopping off branches for firewood. It all started with someone yodeling across the valley. The message did not make much sense; it seemed to be saying something about seeing ghosts. It sounded alarming, but Ongol continued with what he was doing, pollarding the tree. After all, the shades of ancestors and spirits were everywhere, causing problems for the living; although you never saw them, the evidence of their malicious handiwork was obvious. This was clear from the recent famine and from Haebay's current sickness, which everyone attributed to ghostly attack.

The grueling famine had weakened Haebay, but unlike younger men he did not regain his strength when gardens started to yield again. Instead, he became chronically unwell. He spent his days sitting listlessly in the foyer of the men's house, rubbing himself with painful stinging nettle[1] leaves. This is a common practice when someone is unwell. People say that the nettle pain "fights" the pain of the malady and cancels it. They also believe that the stinging pain "hurts" the attacking *towmow* [ghost] that is causing the illness and drives it out. A ghost causes sickness, they say, by "eating the insides of a person." Haebay's kin, increasingly concerned, arranged a rite to divine the cause of his sickness. They assumed that it was the malicious spirit of a deceased relative and they needed to find out the *sem* of the attacking ghost and its current abode.

A person may be attacked by the ghost of any deceased relative— whether father's father's kin, mother's father's kin, father's mother's kin, and so forth (as far back as genealogical memory goes)—and it is necessary to work out the ghost's *sem* affiliation, so that offerings can be made at the right place to placate it. Ghosts, it is believed, frequent certain locales on the territories of their *sem*. These places include shelters in which people keep prehistoric stone objects, such as mortars and pestles that they occasionally find (particularly after earth tremors); deep pools of water in some potholes; the skulls of ancestors housed in specially built structures; the ground beneath the fireplace in house foyers; or other refuges erected to accommodate them. It is necessary to pinpoint which one the ghost is currently frequenting in order to make an offering there to persuade it to desist.

Haebay endured the "nettle blow" divination to establish the whereabouts of the *towmow* "eating away" at him. The operator used a cordyline leaf to hold some stinging nettle leaves, which he rubbed on Haebay's body several times. Each time, before rubbing him, he whispered over the leaves the name of a *sem* and then blew on them. Anxious kin watched as he did so. When a sick person writhes in pain from the nettles it indicates that the ghost is from the named *sem*. The operator repeats the process to identify the place where the ghost is currently, listing various locations. He also recites the following spell in the Huli language over the nettles:

> *Pibiy ala, pibiy ala,   taebaenda   nigiy,   towmow   aenda.*
> Blow say, blow say, bamboo knife nettle, ancestor house.
>
> *Nigiy,   pubuw nigiy,   popu   nigiy.*
> Nettle,   pain nettle, chert blade nettle.

It seeks to frighten off the attacking *towmow* with threats of pain. It mentions, in addition to nettles, bamboo knife and chert blade—cutting implements that can inflict pain. In this event, Haebay's response indicated that a paternal ghost was to blame and that it was frequenting both the nearby *hungnaip* [prehistoric objects] and a distant water pool.

* * * * * * * * * * * * * * *

The following day, Wasnonk, who was worried about her husband's condition, led one of their pigs to the *muwnaenda* lean-to structure housing the family's *hungnaip*. Haebay's relatives clubbed and butchered the animal and heated stones to cook the meat in the earth oven pit there. Before laying the fire to heat the stones, Ongol put a small piece of pork on a leaf and placed it in the bottom of the oven hole, chewing on a *kongol* [Piper] leaf[2] and spitting on it as he did so. This was for the attacking *towmow*, which "eats" the aroma of the burning meat. Ongol called on deceased relatives to come and partake of it, blowing on the meat to attract their attention and saying:

> Blow. *Ora   shumb   njay   ngo   njuruk   nabay.   Howa   njay   nenyin*
> Blow. Father ancestor you   there (I) give eat. Ancestor you   eat
>
> *ko.* Blow. *Ora   haeraekow.* Blow. *Hul   gunk   ngo   haeraekow.*
> say. Blow. Father (I) cook. Blow. Meat small there (I) cook.

While they sat waiting for the pork to cook, some of his relatives took the prehistoric stone objects from their resting place at the rear of the shelter and rubbed them over with some *wombok* from a gourd and then smeared powdered charcoal on parts (such as the outside of the mortars) and painted the remainder with red ocher. This black and red decoration "pleased" the residing ghosts. The prehistoric objects belonging to Haebay's *sem* included "penises" (pestles), "vaginas" (stone club heads), and "hats" (mortars). People say that their ancestors made and continue to shape them by "walking around on them."

Meanwhile, Ongol took a frond of *hongok* [tree fern][3] left over from those used to cook with the pork and went up to the men's house where Haebay sat, too listless to come to the *hungnaip aenda* [prehistoric objects house]. He went to perform *pogom biyay* on his sick father, which involved talking into the leaf and then rubbing it gently on the patient's body, muttering such phrases as, "Don't hurt, we are killing a pig, don't do that, don't 'eat' [the sick person]." The purpose is to inform the molesting spirit of the offering and ask it to stop its attack. Ongol used a frond from the fern cooked with the pork to show the attacking ghost that they had killed a pig for it. While he made sure his father received a choice neck cut of pork, Haebay only nibbled at it for he had no appetite even for meat. The nettle diviner received prime neck meat and the large intestines for his services. The others present shared the remaining pork among themselves.

The next, day Ongol, Lem, and his son took the strip of belly pork and kidneys, which they had kept back, to the pothole water pool in the forest beyond Homal, to offer to the spirit residing there. When they arrived, they heated the stones of the earth oven in the adjacent lean-to shelter and put the pork in to cook. Before sharing and eating the meat, Ongol cut off small pieces and wrapped them in a large parcel of *hongok* fronds. "Make it large," said Lem, "that way the ghosts will think that we are giving them a large cut of meat." When ready, Ongol took the parcel and shouting out "*Weeeeeeeeeeeee*" to attract the attention of spirits in the locality, threw it into the pool. He also called out the names of various dead kin, such as "Kot, it's yours, eat," repeating the names of several kinsmen not knowing which ghost was responsible for the sickness. They looked for the size of the ripples on the water as indicating the number of ghosts present that had come to catch the meat parcel. Ongol and the others ate the rest of the meat before retracing their steps.

* * * * * * * * * * * * * * *

On the way back, they met someone on the path who told them that he had actually seen some ghosts. At first, they could make little sense of what he told them. They stopped and lit a fire by the side of the path and sat for a smoke while he regaled them with his improbable story. He said that there were many of them, holding up and knocking together his clenched fists to indicate that they numbered more than 10. There were two white-skinned spirits, one of them leading the column. The rest were black-skinned carrying large bundles on their backs and the strangest things in their hands, including some of the weirdest digging sticks that he had ever seen. They had appeared from the northwest and were following the Was valley southeastward. He put his hand in his string bag and pulled out a strange piece of white material similar to the silky cocoon of the Emperor Moth[4] used to wrap pearl shells, only much tougher. "One of them left this where they built their 'houses' of last night," he said. They all handled the material and marvelled at the sort of moth that might have produced it.

Apparently, the column of ghosts had stopped in the afternoon and put up "houses" roofed with the white cloth. Some of them were giving things "like you have never seen before" to those who brought along food, while some in the column helped themselves from nearby gardens, digging up sweet potato tubers. It was said that further up the valley they had taken and killed a pig, too. People were too "shit scared" to do anything, their informant told them. According to him, the ghosts had crossed the Was River below Pinjweshuwt and would be setting up camp somewhere near Boiya that day. He urged them to go and look for themselves. When they returned to Tombem, everyone was talking about the arrival of the spirits; some spoke of the white-skinned sky-being Sabkabyinten, while others were of the opinion that they were lost forest spirits, as some had telltale black teeth. Those who spoke of *towmow* said that some persons had identified returning dead relatives among those carrying cargo. It was getting on in the afternoon when Ongol and his relatives arrived home, and they decided that it was too late to walk on to Boiya, especially as these accounts of ghostly intruders in the vicinity suggested that it would be dangerous to be out at night. They decided that they would go and look tomorrow.

They never did see the ghosts, which was perhaps just as well with the way events turned out next day. They were having a smoke at the place where the ghostly column had spent the night, inspecting some traces of a mysterious white powder left behind, similar to sago flour, when a crowd of frightened people came hurrying onto the grass clearing. "They have turned angry, it is awful," they said. "They have killed many people at Sezinda, and everyone is fleeing from them." Some other men arrived who had been on a path above the one on which the attack occurred and had seen, or at least heard, what had happened. "Those strange digging sticks carried by the two white spirits and some of the black ones, they made a dreadful 'tuw' noise when pointed at people. They fell as if hit in the chest with a spear. They inflicted the most awful wounds—*aaarrgh*—much worse than any arrow. It is terrifying magic." The strangers set up their houses nearby, helped themselves to food from gardens, and shot several pigs to eat, too. No one approached them. They left the next morning and the Wola subsequently heard that they shot more people further down the valley. "Something must have greatly annoyed those ghosts," Lem commented. But no one had any idea what. The name of the place where this dreadful event occurred became the expletive "*sezinda*," which people use to this day as a swear word.

The first patrol to enter the Was valley. Local people watch armed policemen bringing up the rear *(photo from J. Hides 1936:116)*.

The day had featured events like no others they had ever known. It was 9 May 1935 when the world beyond had come blundering into their valleys. Ongol saw at firsthand the dreadful wounds inflicted by the strangers' "digging sticks," because one of Mindiy's relatives was among those hit. When they arrived the next day at his place, he had little time left to live. Hit in the stomach, some of his entrails were protruding out of the nasty wound, and he was desperately thirsty. He passed away that afternoon. At least his shocked family could mourn over his corpse, unlike one man whose mutilated body they gathered up onto an exposed grave platform near where he had fallen. Ongol had brought along a particularly fine pearl shell, anticipating an *ol gwat* funeral exchange, which made Mindiy feel proud as it was handed over to her brothers. During the weeks that followed, there was much discussion about the ghostly apparition. It was probably a once in a lifetime happening, they said, as no one had heard of such a thing previously. It was an apocalyptic event, which some likened to the destruction of the land in their ancestors' "volcanic ash" legend, involving catastrophic pyroclastic fallout across the region, something assumed to have taken place once long ago and thankfully not repeated in living memory. They did not realize how wrong they were, how this ghostly column augured further intrusions—and the unimaginable changes that were to come.

* * * * * * * * * * * * * * *

The passage of the ghostly patrol was particularly disturbing in view of the problems that Haebay was having with some of his ancestors' ghosts.

Unfortunately, he showed no signs of recovery. His kin decided to perform the *showbez ak* divination to confirm the cause of his illness, which people resort to when pig offerings have no effect. They swept clean an area in the house yard and marked out a cross with two cane stems. They designated each quadrant to one of those possibly responsible for the attack: father's, mother's or mother's mother's family ancestors, and sorcery. Ongol held a small pig under his arm and made as if to club it over each quadrant in turn. He used a heavy *pel* club painted with charcoal and ocher stripes, of the sort used when making offerings, the decoration believed to frighten off ghosts. Everyone present watched the swept ground intently in each segment for any foreign thing such as an ant, spider, or other creature walking across it, or a piece of wind blown vegetation such as a leaf or seed and so on. The first quadrant in which they see anything indicates what is responsible for the attack causing the illness.

They spotted an ant in the paternal quadrant, confirming that Haebay's father's ancestors were responsible for his sickness. Ongol clubbed the pig over this segment and held the animal with blood dripping onto the ground there from its smashed snout. They decided to offer the pig in the fireplace of the men's house foyer. Strong spirits reside under it, where they take on the form of frightening snakes. Ongol made the *hobaen*, a pronged implement used during the rite. It was made of three sharpened prongs, 15 or so centimeters long (two of *hobaen*[5] and one of *pel* wood), lashed around a *lomat* puffball[6] fungus wrapped in *hobaen* and *shiyp*[7] tree leaves; the resulting object resembled a large shuttlecock with three filamentless feathers. It was again painted with red and black stripes. The *hobaen* tree has hard wood, particularly suitable for spearing ghosts, whereas the spongy *lomat* fungus shows how "the rite will make the mouths and teeth of ghosts soft and ineffective," unable to attack and eat people.

Someone dug a hole in the ashes with the painted club, and they put the pig's snout into it and piled hot ashes over it. Beforehand, Ongol rammed a sharpened length of *hobaen* wood into the animal's snout to promote blood flow. They also placed a piece cut from its ear on the hot embers. Ongol blew along the animal's snout toward the fire to catch the attention of the "snake ghosts" residing there, and stroking its body muttered phrases such as previously, "Kot, its yours, eat," repeating the names of several kinsmen, inviting them to accept the offering of meat, blood, and singeing snout bristles. He then took the pronged *hobaen* and with a long singsong chant "*pa, pa, pa . . .*" "stop it, stop it, stop it . . ." pushed it over the snout and into the ashes, driving it in with the painted club. The sharpened prongs will enter the eyes of any "snake spirit" residing there and blind it, so making it unable to see and attack any of its descendants further, including its current sick victim. They left the *hobaen* to burn away in the hearth.

The pig was subsequently taken outside for bristle singeing and butchering on a bed of fern leaves. Others present prepared the earth oven in the corner of the house yard to cook the meat. They decided to keep back one side of pork to offer at the *hungnaip* house the next day, and the belly pork and kidneys to offer at the water pool as they had done a few days previously, both also locations where strong ghosts reside. Everyone present, men and women, shared the meat.

* * * * * * * *

Sadly, regardless of his kinsmen's best efforts, Haebay passed away a few nights later. In grief, Wasnonk chopped off a finger phalanx, and she and Mindiy donned widow's weeds of voluminous skirt and Job's tears seed necklace. Before interring the corpse, they decided to perform an autopsy that involved cutting open the chest cavity from neck to abdomen, and breaking through the sternum bone using a club and sharp wooden wedge. They used two hooked sticks to pull

The offering of a pig in a fireplace; the *hobaen* trident raised as driven over the snout.

the rib cage apart and peer at the internal organs. The men looking inside the chest wore a red *ongol* tree leaf in their hair above the forehead to protect them from the ghost. The red leaf "shines like a bright light" into the deceased's staring eyes and dazzles the ghost so that it cannot recognize and attack them. They spat on the ground in revulsion, too, after looking into the chest cavity, a common response to seeing something repulsive.

Relatives look at the lungs and heart to ascertain the reason for death. Stains on the right-hand lung are evidence of paternal ghost attack; on the left, maternal; sooty black deposits indicate menstrual pollution, and any laceration to the heart points to sorcery, while a white sappy substance indicates *mogtomb*. Haebay's right lung showed strange discoloration, taken as evidence of a weird death, and thoughts of Kot striking again as a malicious ghost came to mind, although there was no way of knowing the ghost's identity. When they had finished inspecting the organs, the man who had performed the operation, a distant relative from another *sem*, who received a pig for his services, poured some *wombok* into the chest cavity, using a pandan leaf as a funnel. The oil is very painful if you get any in your eyes, and it is

Preparing to lower a corpse into a grave.

thought to blind the ghost, so preventing it from attacking another relative, effectively putting it out of action.

They buried the corpse following the autopsy. The Wola always bury persons who die from ghost attacks, as part of their strategy of ensuring that the spirit responsible cannot attack again. Two distant kinsmen prepared the grave, digging a hole a meter or so deep, in the bottom of which they constructed a rough wooden platform. They lined it and the sides of the hole with tough pandan leaves, and drove in forked stakes at each corner onto which crossbeams were laid, which would support the plank roof arranged over the corpse. They put long strips of strong bark across the hole to lower the corpse onto the bed below. They then put the plank roof in place before back filling the hole with soil. Finally, they erected a fence of sharpened *pel* stakes around the grave. There was no ceremony. In the afternoon, Ongol arranged the distribution of the *ol gwat* mortuary wealth, conducting the exchange in a way that brought him praise, adding to his growing reputation as a man who showed competence in managing transactions.

Following the funeral, Haebay's kin led a quiet life. They remained in and around their homesteads for the next fortnight or so and did not leave their houses at night for fear of attack. The *towmow* of the recently deceased are particularly strong and vindictive and relatives go in fear of them. As time passes, their strength diminishes until eventually, when dead persons pass from memory, their ghosts go with them. They cease to exist and hence attack. Such spirits do not go elsewhere, such as paradise, they simply fade away. According to some people, they become butterflies. Nevertheless, fol-

Back filling a grave while watched by crying children.

lowing a ghost death, relatives take several steps to put the attacking spirit out of action.

* * * * * * * * * * * * * * * *

One involves a post-inhumation rite, organized by two men who know the necessary spell, who receive selected cuts from pigs slaughtered (such as neck joint, intestines, head) together with other things (such as cowries, *wombok*, net bags). These men give themselves a frightening black appearance to scare the attacking ghost away. They blacken their faces with charcoal, on which they paint designs in white clay, they smear their bodies with a *wombok* and charcoal mixture, wear pompons of wispy black cassowary feathers, and sport the dark maroon leaves of the *kal* variety of cordyline. They arrange three red *shwimb* tree leaves under their forehead bands, again to dazzle any ghosts.

The afternoon before the slaughter of the pigs, one of the spellholders cooks a taro in the flames of a fierce fire, burning the outside. As he scrapes the charred layer off the corm, he mutters a spell, such as:

Ma	*aena*	*nor*	*twenj*	*biyae*	*laeglaeg.*	*Aena*	*nor*	*twenj*
Taro	south-east	eat	beetle[8]	do		. S.E.	eat	beetle

biyae	*laeglaeg.*	*Aena*	*nor*	*bombort*	*biyae*	*laeglaeg.*	*Ol*	*ngon*
do		. S.E.	eat	grub[9]	do		. Man	there

ji	*hul*	*porbok.*	*Ol*	*ngon*	*ongor*	*hul*	*porbok.*
hand	bone	break.	Man	there	foot	bone	break.

Ol	*ngon*	*hiyma*	*hul*	*porbok.*	*Na*	*hul*	*porbok.*
Man	there	tooth	bone	break.	My	bone	break.

The taro symbolizes the deceased person whose internal organs the ghost has eaten away, in the manner that insects eat the inside of taro tubers. The spell refers to the spirit breaking several bones of the victim in eating him (sometimes ghosts only eat limbs, as in leprosy, which may not prove fatal.) The officiant then cuts up the taro and gives it to the deceased's relatives to eat with some *omok* greens[10] and salt. This will protect them from the ghosts that will assemble to share the offering the following day.

Later in the evening, relatives of the deceased drag the crowns of *keret* pandans[11] around the grass clearing adjacent to their houses, shouting loudly. This is to drive all the lurking ghosts toward a stretch of path, across which the two men overseeing the rite have erected a leafy barrier of *hobaen* and *shiyp* branches and *omak* tree fern[12] fronds. The grave is sited on the other side of this makeshift fence to the homesteads; the fence is intended to keep the ghosts away from the living. It is important that there are no holes in the leafy screen; otherwise, the spirits will breach it "like they enter humans through orifices in the body." They leave a gap the middle where they will trap and immobilize any intruding ghost.

The rite has some similarities to that undertaken to drive away fireplace "snake spirits." The officiants will have prepared and decorated *hobaen* tridents beforehand and some pointed spikes of *hobaen* wood, muttering their spell as they did so. The following morning they slaughter the pigs adjacent to the fence where the ghosts linger and consume the spilled blood. (They killed five pigs at Haebay's rite.) They carry them back to the deceased's house, arranging them with their snouts in the fireplace and push spikes into them to stimulate blood flow, while muttering the spell. They follow the same procedure as with the fireplace rite, culminating with the banging in of the *hobaen* trident to blind and frighten off any ghosts.

Next, they carry the pigs back to the leafy barrier and arrange them with their snouts pointing to the gap, their blood (the flow stimulated with further spike jabs and the recitation of the spell) attracting nearby ghosts. The barrier channels the ghosts to the gap. The officiant hammers a three-pronged *hobaen* into the ground in the gap between the snouts, shouting "*pa, pa, pa*"— "stop, stop, stop"—to blind the attracted ghosts. He knocks in a fence of *pel* stakes around the trident to trap them inside and binds a length of *maip ya* vine around it. He then jams two stones on either side of the *hobaen*, fungus and leaf bundle, which are said to be "like a rock face up which a ghost cannot climb and attack living persons." This frightens spirits not trapped and blinded, so that they flee the area. The barrier and fenced-in trident remain on the path, such that persons using it have to step through the gap. Their combined footfall on the spot serves additionally to scare off ghosts.

When the officiants knock the *hobaen* trident into the ground, the ghost that killed the recently deceased person rushes to the grave. The pair conducting the rite go to the grave with two sharpened branches of *hobaen* wood that still have leaves attached; they will have painted their sharpened ends with black and red stripes while muttering their spell. They push these sticks diagonally into the ground at the head of the grave. They believe that these again blind the ghost. Such repeated blinding is necessary to incapacitate it, since it was a strong spirit that recently killed someone. They also throw a charcoal-blackened rock inside the grave fence, saying that the heavy object pins the blinded spirit down in the grave. The officiants return slowly, with their heads bowed, to join the others at the *howma*, not looking around to encourage any ghosts to follow them. When they return, a close relative of the deceased cooks a pig's liver over a fire, and one of them stabs it with a tree fern pin while muttering the spell. The deceased's relatives share the liver to strengthen their insides and resist further ghost attacks. Meanwhile, others have singed and butchered the pigs and prepared the earth oven. The cooked pork is shared, as at any funeral.

* * * * * * * * * * * * * * *

A while later, there were reports of the column of ghosts returning and crossing the Was River to the south, and subsequently some men from the Ak valley visiting Tombem spoke of rumors about these strange visitors staying at Lake Kutubu. They said that the ghosts were not angry like the first time and were not killing people but had returned with seashells that they were giving to those who gave them food. They were extraordinarily generous, for it was unheard of for people to give shells for a pile of tubers. Ongol had plans to visit Kutubu to trade for *wombok*, tapped from a large swamp forest tree there,[13] and decided to combine this with looking at these ghosts for himself and maybe obtaining some shells too. He had Mindiy fill a large string bag with tubers and departed, carrying this slung across his back and leading a pig on a tether.

Some of those living in the Ak valley know the location of longhouses in which the Foi speakers of the lake region live. It is customary for one or two of the Ak residents to accompany a group of men on a trading trip, as their "faces are known" to the lakeside dwellers, even though no one speaks the language or knows anyone there beyond trading acquaintances. The Foi have a frightening reputation as cannibals among the Highlanders, a horrific practice in their eyes, and for practicing diabolical sorcery. When visiting the lake they are careful not to leave anything associated personally with them behind, such as uneaten food or peelings, which a sorcerer could use to attack them. The Highlanders in turn have a hot tempered and violent reputation among the Foi, who treat them with a guarded respect that can come across as devious, inflaming Highlander suspicions. Consequently, meetings between them are tense and difficult. The prospect of encountering the ghost column added considerably to the anxiety of Ongol's party.

After a three-day walk through the forest leading the pigs they intended to trade for oil, they waded across the Mubi River, and their Ak valley associates led them to the nearest longhouse. Ongol negotiated, with much head and arm waving, for a substantial three-meter-long bamboo tube of *wombok*, and was pleased with his trade, having plans to use it in a future transaction. Some Foi signaled to his party to get into nearby dugout canoes, pointing to the bags of sweet potato tubers they had brought, surmizing that they wanted to trade with the newcomers. Ongol was reluctant to do so at first, but the eager and friendly overtures persuaded him. He guessed that the excitement had something to do with the ghosts reportedly camping at the lakeside. After a short canoe ride along a creek and around a small headland, they saw the camp. It was as others had described it, comprising several "bark-cloth houses." A rope cordon suspended from wooden stakes surrounded it, and some of the black-skinned spirits carrying the fearsome digging sticks signaled that they were not to cross it.

Ongol saw, just as others had described, that these strange newcomers wore the most peculiar garb, encasing their bodies in sleeves of material "like the cane-grass-leaf 'sleeves' we put on arrow points." After some further arm waving and mutually incomprehensible exchange of words, he and his party exchanged their sweet potato tubers with the guards for some shells. He was well pleased with the deal, seeing the shells supporting his future transactional plans. His only regret was that the newcomers had set up camp so far away from the Was valley, for he could see here an unprecedented source of wealth. Sometime later, Ongol learned that the strangers were also giving out axes of some shiny new material. When he first saw one of these, he was not impressed; it was much heavier than his polished stone axe and ungainly of swing. But when he subsequently obtained one in a mortuary exchange payment, he soon appreciated that the steel head was more durable than his stone blade. It could cut the hardest wood and even serve as a wedge when splitting logs, either of which actions would have shattered his stone axe.

While Ongol and his party stood gawking at the strange objects in the camp, catching glimpses into the tents, they heard a deep buzzing sound, louder than any hornet. The Foi men became very excited and pulling at their arms pointed up into the sky. What Ongol saw next was the most astonishing thing in his life. It felt as if his jaw hit his toes. Toward them along the lake came the largest and strangest bird imaginable; it seemed to glide, not flapping its outstretched wings at all. It came closer and lower, and it was apparently going to land on the water. Ongol and his friends were going to run off in fear but seeing the Foi men and those in the camp showing no signs of terror, they remained rooted to the spot. The roaring sound made by the bird-like thing as it approached was unimaginable, and it was enormous in size, as large as a forest tree. But the most amazing thing was yet to happen. When the "bird" came to a standstill floating out on the lake, some canoes paddled out to it and some of the strange fair-skinned newcomers climbed out and boarded them. They also unloaded many strange objects from the belly of the bird. Ongol was literally dumbstruck. When, a few days later, he related what he had seen to his *haemay* Hond, his *weray* [wife] Mindiy, and others, they refused to believe him. They thought that some malicious forest spirit must have invaded his *konay* and driven him a little mad, making him imagine things, similar to the temporary hallucinations sometimes experienced by people collecting wild fungi in the forest.

Seaplane unloading cargo on Lake Kutubu *(photo from F. E. Williams' collection, National Archive, Waigani, Papua New Guinea)*.

* * * * * * * * * * * * * *

Ongol's acts over the coming weeks were to convince Mindiy that he had certainly undergone some sort of change, although she should not have been surprised, for what he did was true to character. He had been accumulating wealth to marry a second wife, envisaging the bamboo tube of *wombok* as clinching the *injiykab*. He could expect only token help from his relatives, unlike amassing a first *injiykab* where they rally around to guarantee a marriage. It was part of his striving to achieve transactional renown, as only successful men can afford to marry more than one wife (except for those who encourage women to elope, but for a man to do this is to lose face). Mindiy was furious and made no secret of it.

When his first attempts to find a second wife failed, Ongol started to suspect Mindiy of sabotaging his efforts. He accused her of performing the "women's basalt stone" rite, which men believe women use to influence who they marry (as men employ the frog drying rite), or if married, to deter other women from being attracted to their husbands by making them ugly and undesirable in their eyes, so that they cannot find a second wife. Mindiy laughed in his face when he accused her of such action, denying any knowledge of such a procedure. She told him that it was a figment of men's imaginations. Indeed, it is possible that it more reflects their paranoia of females, as manifest in their fear of menstrual pollution, than anything to do with women's activities. It would certainly be unfortunate for a wife if her husband caught her engaging in such acts, as they would likely provoke him to act violently.

About this time, Ongol became unwell and attributed it to female pollution sickness. He showed the symptoms that a man has when a woman "eats" him. He became weak, lethargic, and could not be bothered with life. The outward signs were a dry and crusty skin, having the appearance of dusty grey ash. He lost some weight and some of his bones, such as his ribs, became more prominent. And he started losing hair. In short, the sickness sapped his vitality. The Wola say that men fall sick like this when they ingest poisonous menstrual "period dirt," *mogtomb,* which collects in the chest cavity, the heart, and lungs, as shown at autopsy by charcoal-like stains.

If menstrual blood infects a man (for example, because he unwittingly takes food from a menstruating woman), it is serious, and he must take steps to purify himself. The *hiyaib hiyay* rite to nullify the effects of pollution requires the slaughter of a pig. The person who officiates, who knows the required spell, takes the tongue attached by the windpipe to the heart and lungs, and wraps it in a parcel with some *piyp* tree[14] bark, an *ongol* tree leaf, and a *kabiyp* tree fern frond. He dips this tongue parcel in some of the pig's blood and rubs it down the center of the sick man's chest and abdomen from throat to bark girdle. He does this several times, repeating an incantation such as the following:

Yuwmenay	*tay*	*Kuwndiy*	*komay.*	*Yumbaelay*	*tay*	*lidiygiy*	*komay.*
Heart	base	Backside	skin.	Spine	base		skin.

Tombow	*tay*	*Kiniy*	*komay.*	*Kuw*	*tay*	*koniyba*	*komay.*
Stomach	base		skin.	Rectum	base		skin.

Hiba	*tay*	*Kindaniy*	*komay.*	*Yumbaelay*	*tay*	*kindaniy*	*komay.*
Liver	base		skin.	Spine	base		skin.

Pondow	*tay*	*Kindaniy*	*komay.*	*Hiba*	*tay*	*kindaniy*	*komay.*
Neck	base		skin.	Liver	base		skin.

Kola	*akaniniy,*	*kola*	*akikiy,*	*kola*	*akikiy,*	*kola*	*akikiy.*
Claw	Fairy Lory,[15]	claw	Fairy Lory,	claw	Fairy Lory,	claw	Fairy Lory.

The spell refers to the different internal organs that the ritual washes clean. The black soot of menstrual *mogtomb* spreads over the internal organs from the throat to the rectum; when a victim's inside is full, he dies. The spell names one organ after another as the rite expels the *mogtomb.* The reference to the lory's claw is an allusion to the reciter's hand holding the medicinal parcel with which he sweeps out the poisonous blood. It also brings to mind the bird's fine colorful plumage, inferring that, following the cure, the man will be admired for his well-being, puffed up like a handsome bird.

The act of rubbing the chest with the bloody bundle symbolizes an internal wash that flushes away the poisonous menstrual blood. The healthy pink organs of the pig "show" what the victim's clean insides will be like following the ritual cleansing, after sweeping away all the festering black smuts caused by the "menstrual dirt." The *ongol* leaf and the *piyp* bark are red like the pig's blood, and the sweeping of these three elements down the chest simulates the internal flow of the menstrual substance out of the victim's system. The *kabiyp* frond has a sweet scent and leaves a wholesome aroma on the chest like the sweet smell of the victim's insides, when the stink of the rotting blood has been "washed out."

There are degrees of pollution. A man may undergo this purification ritual once or more, depending on the seriousness of the pollution, as indicated by his rate of recovery. The person who does the ritual cleaning receives a handsome cut from the slaughtered pig as his reward, and the owner distributes the remaining pork to relatives and friends. A man who is reckless enough to indulge in sexual intercourse out of wedlock, and who subsequently falls ill, may have to resort, with the woman, to the water-drinking and gourd-eating rites described previously. The drawback is that it

Rubbing the pig's tongue parcel, with lungs and heart attached, down a man's chest in the *hiyaib hiyay* rite.

announces their actions and will likely lead to a dispute and demands from the woman's relatives or husband for compensation.

While Mindiy may have privately taken some satisfaction in her husband's plight, she would never have shown it because to do so would be tantamount to admitting that she had deliberately poisoned him, which she certainly had not. Ongol did not blame her directly, even though relations between them were more tense than usual. Everyone recognizes that it sometimes happens that men are careless or unfortunate enough to contract pollution sickness, regardless of the precautions that they take to protect themselves. Traces of toxic menstrual blood can, for example, be transmitted to a man via a woman's bag or rain cape, which then comes into contact with his food. If Mindiy hoped that the brush with "period *mogtomb*" would deter Ongol from his plans to marry a second bride, she was disappointed.

* * * * * * * * * * * * * * *

After some months and several abortive attempts, Ongol finally managed to take Wat as his second wife. They undertook the earlier series of protection rites to safeguard him from pollution when he entered into relations with her, although as a sexually experienced man, he did so less conscientiously than at his first marriage. His new marriage not only enhanced his social standing, but also, by marrying a younger woman, it bolstered his middle-aged male ego. As Ongol was heard to comment in his men's house, he was "penis proud"; he no longer felt that was going over the hill, having a young sexual partner. Whatever the positive effect on his sex life, the marriage had a negative impact on his household, which Ongol would not admit to anyone, even perhaps himself.

In anger, Mindiy walked out and returned to her natal place with her children where one of her brothers allowed them to reside in his women's house. She left behind several pigs that were her responsibility. Mindiy had a reputation as a *ten howma* [grass-clearing woman], the epithet given to those admired for their ability to handle large numbers of pigs. The inexperienced young Wat was unable to manage the animals. Ongol was embarrassed and obliged to approach his *mboliy* Twaen to help him out, who mocked him in sympathizing with Mindiy's sense of indignation. When Mindiy returned, her commitment to their partnership was gone, and as a result, the efficiency of the homestead declined appreciably. She was unwilling to manage the same number of pigs as previously. Indeed, she declined to look after any pigs before Ongol had agreed to give her brothers a good "herding payment." It was embarrassing for him to have to reach an agreement beforehand, as usually women trust their husbands to meet such commitments. She was publicly showing her mistrust of Ongol and her jaundiced view of their partnership.

There were other downsides to a polygynous marriage, as Ongol discovered. He had expected the two women to share the same house divided into two separate rooms, but the interminable arguments that occurred obliged him to build two separate houses some distance from one another, to keep his wives apart. The fragmented arrangement of his homestead reflected the poor cooperation within it and its diminished efficiency. When Ongol married a third young wife some years later, matters worsened even further. Not only did he have to construct and maintain three women's houses, but also one of these was empty for much of the time. The third wife was too much for Mindiy, who took to spending considerable time away with her kin or daughter elsewhere. This is usual behavior in estranged relationships; although divorce is not an option when a woman has reached a certain age and borne several children, she can effectively opt out of her married relationship by living with kin elsewhere.

Even with three wives, the efficiency of Ongol's household did not reach the levels that Mindiy had achieved alone. Nevertheless, he had demonstrated his skill at handling wealth and justified his *ol howma* reputation. For example, he had raised nearly all the wealth for the two subsequent *injiykab* single-handedly, his kin contributing relatively little. Furthermore, the additional affinal relations brought added demands and opportunities to show his transactional prowess, and in consistently meeting these, he earned the admiration of others.

Chapter 8

Making It Big, Poison, and Sorcery

$\mathscr{W}$e all have ambitions in life, be it to lead a quiet self-effacing existence or a hectic headline-grabbing one. Ongol was a headline grabber, which, for a man in his society, meant excelling in the sociopolitical transaction of wealth. By the time he was middle aged, Ongol was secure in his reputation as an *ol howma*, so called because of his prominent participation in exchanges that often took place on the nearest grass clearing, frequently located in front of the men's house. The status approximates to big-men elsewhere. Any man endowed with the required qualities can aspire to such renown. It is an achieved position, not an ascribed position inherited by virtue of birth. Consequently, it is an informal status, not an instituted office. The standing of an *ol howma* declines as his transactional prowess wanes with age: distinction depends on current ability.

While such esteemed individuals may enjoy a degree of influence locally in certain contexts—people pay more heed to their thoughts and advice than they do those of others—they cannot be said to achieve, or create for themselves, positions of political leadership. The value placed on equality ensures that while they are respected and admired as persons of transactional repute, they have neither political authority nor power to direct the actions of others. They are first among equals. People talk of such characters as strong, which catches something of the meaning of the *howma* epithet, which is not a political status as such but more an acknowledgement of vigorous individuals who are doing well in life. They are the energetic doers who achieve things—for men this means participating in many exchange transactions and for women it means managing efficient homesteads.

A good deal of Ongol's transactional energies went toward arranging reparation exchanges arising from the earlier armed hostilities. He was

A men's house and *howma* "grass clearing" behind a defensive palisade, viewed through a stile entrance.

engaged in several *ol bay* transactions with the relatives of those allies to whom he and his kin had made the *ol komb* and *showmay enjay* payments. He was simultaneously planning the first in the series of outstanding *haypuw* reimbursement exchanges that they owed to relatives who had taken responsibility for the reparation series for individuals killed fighting on their behalf. Unfortunately, not all was going well with respect to the earlier conflict. While open fighting had ceased, covert bad feelings continued and had recently burst forth into the open with *mogtomb* accusations.

* * * * * * * * * * * * * * *

In addition to attacking enemies on a supernatural plane through sorcery, people sometimes resort to surreptitiously administering what they consider toxic substances. While no one will admit to knowing the ingredients, because to do so would invite accusation for any suspected *mogtomb* deaths, they speculate that menstrual blood and squashed earthworm are among them, as two substances widely believed to be deadly. Someone wishing to kill this way will likely try to purchase *mogtomb*, probably from the Foi at Kutubu who are believed to have the most dangerous concoctions. *Mogtomb* is usually slow working, taking a month or more to kill. The symptoms include pain all over the body, as it causes the victim to rot inside and turn bad.

The firefly[1] is a sign of *mogtomb*. If a man sees fireflies on his cordyline leaf buttock-covering when he wakes in the morning and goes to collect it from the roof of his house where he left it for the night to keep fresh, he will fear that someone has poisoned him. He has the same fear if he sees fireflies on a banana skin that he has discarded or on the leaves lining an earth oven from which he has eaten food. A person who believes that someone has poisoned him will seek out a relative who knows the recipe for the necessary emetic and associated spell. This is likely to include some greasy pig fat mixed with ginger root, uncooked fungi known to cause vomiting, and tar scraped from the inside of a tobacco pipe. When ingested, these cause the victim to vomit, "throwing" the *mogtomb* out of his body. The supplier of the medicine receives a generous cut of pork from the pig killed to supply the fat.

There are several ways to administer *mogtomb*. It can be introduced into food that is ready to eat or into a gourd of drinking water. It may be blown slyly into a victim's nose and eyes, or it can be mixed with some of his personal leavings (e.g., piece of cordyline leaf buttock-covering, leftover food remains, nail or hair clippings) and then thrown away. A pointed needle may be dipped in *mogtomb* and poked through the wall of the victim's house at night to lightly inject him. If relatives suspect *mogtomb* for a death, they look out for fireflies on the corpse or telltale "white sap" on the heart if they perform an autopsy. It is usually difficult to identify the poisoner, unless the victim gives a clue, such as telling relatives that he fell sick after so-and-so gave him some food. If it is a person known to have a revenge score to settle, this will confirm relatives' suspicions, and they will likely confront him—the confrontation possibly leading to violence.

The *mogtomb* that reawakened hostilities in the Was valley concerned a woman related through her mother to Ongol's *sem*. She had married an ally of Huwniy's relatives who was closely related to the man who had fired the fatal arrow that had killed his *hay* Pes. Some of Pes' kinsmen came up with the idea of using her to poison her husband in revenge. He was a weak character and she was unhappy in her marriage, so it was easy for her mother to persuade her. She thought that the best way to avoid detection was for her daughter to put the *mogtomb* (which she thought toxic to men only) inside her vagina, so that when they engaged in intercourse she would poison her husband. Unfortunately, for her, the husband did not approach her for several days after she had inserted the *mogtomb*. It was inside her for too long. She subsequently died, and he had a lucky escape. No one on her husband's side need have known anything about the plot but at her daughter's funeral her distraught and guilty mother told others what had happened.

* * * * * * * * * * * * * * *

Angry at the news, some of the husband's relatives showed up at the funeral and demanded the return of the wealth they had contributed a couple of days earlier to the *ol gwat* mortuary exchange. This unprecedented act of disrespect, effectively repudiating recognition of any relations through the deceased woman, started a heated argument, her kin refusing to give the wealth back. As one of them put it when the demand was made, holding his index finger up vertically toward the sky in a rude gesture, "you can go and sit" [with such a prong up your ass]. During the ensuing dispute, one of the deceased's brothers went further and picked up a pearl shell donated by one of her husband's relatives and said provocatively, "OK, by *sezinda*, if you want this come and take it," and when someone came forward to take it, he sneered and passed the shell between his legs. This is a grossly insulting act. People should always avoid stepping over others and their possessions. It equates with "showing one's genitals" and is distinctly offensive because of its associations with sexual pollution, which is particularly evident with women who at all costs will avoid stepping over men and their possessions or risk accusations of threatening their well-being. The "crotching" of the shell was too much for some of the husband's kin and one of them swung an axe and caught the man a glancing blow to the head. In the ensuing mêlée, someone took a fatal arrow in the neck.

The armed hostilities that followed lasted for three months. The connection with the earlier conflict is common, disputes and fights frequently relating chain-like to one another. If Kot had known, he would probably have taken an evil pleasure in seeing how his unruly behavior had rolled on, fuelling ongoing disputes and hostilities. In any conflict, it is necessary to consider the history of the relationship between the parties and previous interactions between them to understand their current behavior and expectations. If they already have strained and difficult relations, a dispute between them will exacerbate these and increase the chances of violence. We have to see disputes as episodes in a series of interrelated, probably life-long, encounters where disputants and would-be arbiters are related, or at least certainly not strangers.

In any "new" dispute, both parties, supported by their relatives, will argue over the matter. They do so, keeping their tempers in check to varying extents, until they come to some agreement and settle it to both their satisfactions, until one admits to being in the wrong and makes good, or until the plaintiff lets the matter drop or resorts to some action to redress his rights. This last may cause the disputation to spiral and occasionally boil over into open violence, as we have seen, with the other party interpreting any unilateral revengeful act as an unjust wrong. Apparent wrongdoers and their kin may consider their actions as justified because they even the score for some wrong suffered previously, which itself may have been action that sought to redress an even earlier misdeed, and so on—one dispute leading to another. It is not necessarily clear who is right or wrong, or who has suffered the greater damage.

It is inappropriate in some respects to think in terms of a final settlement of disputes. It is more appropriate to consider their occurrence and resolution as incidents in a life-long tit-for-tat. That we cannot treat any conflict as an isolated event that demands arbitration and settlement relates to the absence of state-informed ideas of laws and justice. People have some clear, and some not so clear, conceptions of what is right and wrong behavior and expectations of one another founded on mutually recognized claims and duties, but transgressions of these are not infringements of codified laws that carry stipulated punishments; instead, they are trespasses against flexibly interpreted customary responsibilities. The informality of judicial concepts in this state-less context allows a degree of adaptability that makes settlement arrangements considerably fairer, allowing that every dispute is the result of a unique coming together of historical events and working out of social relationships.

No premium is put on justice. While we may assume that there are certain judicial assumptions applicable to all humankind, these are culturally relative and may be irrelevant, even distorting, in such contexts. All those who live in the same locality in the Was valley will have some vested interests in a dispute and its outcome, being related in some way to one or both parties, living in a face-to-face society where social networks intermesh. The way relatives of disputants customarily unite and support them reflects their partisan attitudes. The idea of an impartial judge who can mete out justice fairly according to the law is clearly inappropriate. Situational factors determine the outcome of disputes, in addition to people's ideas about what ought or ought not to be done over any dereliction. The process is more just in some ways, as it allows for the consideration of the specific social circumstances surrounding any dispute. A cardinal principle regulating settlement is equivalence; the aim of the parties is to balance the score between them. Handing over valuables in compensation makes good the loss suffered by the plaintiff and simultaneously signals and re-establishes amicable relations. If the wrongdoer obdurately refuses to give compensation, the plaintiff may redress the balance by taking retributive action. The reverse of compensation, it is socially negative. Taking retributive action against someone who refuses to pay compensation is not meant to be punishment only; it is also an act aimed at securing an equivalence of losses.

* * * * * * * * * * * * * * *

After the armed conflict "went to sleep," Ongol did not think that they had achieved a balance and again sought to even the score on the occult plane. This time he turned to *hul tort* sorcery, believed to be the most powerful. It originated in the Huli region and is only known to persons with connections there. After some months of surreptitious inquiries, Ongol found a man with the knowledge to the north who lived near Kapenda and had extensive connections with Huli speakers; he was a distant maternal relative who indicated that he would perform the sorcery for a fee.

The payments were considerable, and Ongol called on a few close kin to contribute, too. First, in order to induce the sorcerer to perform the rite, they had to make *taz iysh* [pig wood] payments to him that included seashells, *wombok*, and net bags. Second, the day he undertook the procedure they made the *habuwk* payment, which included more of these things together with pigs and a side pork from the animal slaughtered in the process. Third, periodically after the rite, they had to make further *taz iysh* payments to him to keep the *tort* [an unseen malicious force] "happy," particularly as the attack proved devastatingly effective. The descendants of those who commissioned the attack were expected, it was said, to keep up these payments occasionally to ensure that the *tort* did not turn on them. This responsibility on future generations theoretically links together all those who have performed *tort* sorcery, men paying those who taught them, who in turn pay their teachers and their descendants, and so on, back to the ritual's originators.

The sorcery was again performed at the secluded rock face on Ebera Mountain. The day before the sorcerer prepared the site. He made a *sor tor* ladder-like construction, the top pointing in the direction in which they wished the *tort* to travel, that is, toward the settlement of those on whom they sought revenge. At the top of the ladder, on the two tree stumps against which it leaned, he built a small platform using lengths of split wood. He covered this with a thick bed of moss and decaying leaf litter. He erected a sapling wall around the construction, on which he arranged *kabiyp* tree fern[2] fronds and *baerel* tree[3] leaves. About two meters away from the bottom of the ladder, the sorcerer excavated a small 50-centimeter-deep hole that he again covered over with *kabiyp* tree fern fronds and *baerel* tree leaves.

The following night Ongol led a pig to the site. He followed a devious route to throw anyone who saw him off, for those performing sorcery go to great pains to keep it secret. Other than those who had contributed to the payment, only Mindiy was aware as the pig's keeper, and she knew how to keep a secret. Men perform the rite at dead of night not only to ensure secrecy but also because this is the time, as we have seen, when the *wezow* of sleeping persons roam around, the target of *tort* attacks. The *tort* waits in ambush outside the unsuspecting victim's house; when his *wezow* appears, as he dreams, the *tort* strikes and kills it.

While Ongol held the pig, the sorcerer killed it by winding a length of *maip ya* vine round its snout, and up around its neck to strangle it. He had heard that others killed the pig by hoisting it up a tree with the vine round its neck and shooting the animal in the neck with a broad-blade arrow. The strangling simulates the victim's death, involving terrible pains in the throat and neck, which swells

The "ladder" construction erected in *hul tort* sorcery.

with blood after death. When the gagged animal fell, the sorcerer held both hands up to his face and spat on them, reciting the following spell in the Huli language:

Haywa	*ndabay.*	*Haywabay*	*ndabay.*	*Haywa*	*ndabay.*	*Haywabay*
Kutubu	there.	Kutubu people	there.	Kutubu	there.	Kutubu people

ndabay.	*Hay*	*waenda.*	*Guwguwaenkay,*	*guwguwluwminiy.*	*Giybiy*
there.	Kutubu	there.	Forked stick rake	forked stick rake.	Frightened

gaybiy.	*Paeraendiyoliy, Paerawayoliy.*	*Giybiy*	*gaybiy*	*lara.*
ceaseless pain.	Two mountains toward Tari.	Frightened	ceaseless pain	say.

At the end, he muttered the names of places where the *tort* was to strike, and the names of potential victims living there.

The spell is loaded with allusions believed to make the rite efficacious. It opens by referring to the Kutubu region where the diabolical *howaytok* sorcery and most potent *mogtomb* imaginable occur. The *hul tort* rite gains power by association with this place of powerful nefarious activity. Some think that the *hul tort* sorcery itself originated from Kutubu, the Huli learning it from there and passing it on to the Wola region; in this event, the spell commemorates its origin. The forked stick alludes to the ritual raking up and catching victims and to the forked sticks used in the rite. The spell refers to the fear and ceaseless pain the attacked will experience, with no prospect of recovery. The twin peaks mentioned in the Tari region are where the *hort leb* "sweet flag" plant originates that features in the rite. This is a frightening place. The leaf of this sweet flag variety has a thin red line down one edge likened to a fine streak of blood. The sorcerer cultivates the plant in a secret, small, fenced garden about one meter in diameter. Every time he performs the sorcery, he collects a container of blood from the snout of the killed pig and pours it over the plants, also rubbing some over the leaves. He has to care for the garden and give it blood or the *tort* will attack him and his relatives in anger. Someone known to Ongol lost two young sons because he failed to care adequately for his sweet flag garden.

After strangling the pig, the sorcerer slapped both the animal's ears simultaneously to send the intended victim soundly to sleep, so that he will not hear any sounds during the night, and the *tort* can approach and kill his unsuspecting *wezow.* He then pushed a cassowary bone dagger up into the animal's snout to make the blood flow copiously, followed by a blade of sweet flag poked up each nostril. Next, he took a fork made from two *tagen* "bare-backed fruit bat"[4] leg bones tied together at one end and pushed the two blades of flag leaf right up into the snout. This causes the victim's nose to block up, with bleeding and considerable pain, and difficulty with breathing, leading to death. The symbolism of the bat bone fork is unclear. Next, the sorcerer repeated the spell, holding to his mouth a 50-centimeter length of *baerel* wood, one end of which he had painted with red ocher. He used this to club the remaining life from the pig; this final clubbing enacted the beating of the life out of the victim, hastening death. He tossed the club away and it hit a nearby tree with a thump, foretelling the success of the ritual—that it would similarly "hit" its victim.

Next, they singed the bristles and butchered the pig. The sorcerer took the *kwiyba* "kidneys" and *aeraelow* "belly fat strip,"[5] and using the cassowary bone dagger to make a hole, he pushed a blade of sweet flag into them. He then used the bat bone fork to stab the kidneys repeatedly. This destroyed the victim's kidneys, causing acute renal pain. Ongol lit fires both in the hole at the foot of the ladder and on the platform at the top, using *baerel* wood that burns with a fierce heat. Meanwhile, the sorcerer prepared two forked sticks, 50 centimeters or so long, spearing both kidneys onto the prong of one stick and pieces of *aeraelow* fat onto the other prongs. He took the kidney and fat stick and some blades of sweet flag and climbed the ladder to the platform fire where he burned them while repeating the spell, blowing on the embers to send the *tort* like the "wind to hit the victim." He gave the forked stick with only the fat to Ongol together with some blades of sweet flag and told him to incinerate these over the fire in the hole at the bottom of the ladder. The two fires burning meat transmitted the *tort* from top and bottom of the ladder "like a blast from head to foot," such that it cannot fail to strike a victim. At this time, strong winds and heavy rain occurred at the victim's place of residence as the *tort* swept in.

Finally, Ongol and the sorcerer cooked the slaughtered pig and ate some of the pork. They destroyed the ladder and all evidence of the sorcery. Ongol parceled up the remainder of the meat to share with his kinsmen. No woman or child may eat the pork. Indeed no man who eats the pork should accept food from a woman for three "moons" after the ritual or he would risk his children ailing, even dying. During the fourth month, he may accept food from old women or girls only. In addition, no pork-eater should indulge in sexual intercourse during this period for fear of his wife bearing sickly children.

* * * * * * * * * * * * * * *

The *tort* is an unseen malicious force originating from somewhere in the Huli-speaking region or possibly Lake Kutubu. No one knows for sure where it resides. Some think that it may on occasion occupy a sorcerer's wig. It haunts sweet flag gardens expecting periodically to consume blood from pigs, particularly those killed in sorcery activity. In addition, it sometimes manifests itself in various guises to the sorcerer or its victims when it attacks, for instance as a *kuwntok* "skink,"[6] or *winzinziy* "blossom bat,"[7] or a bird. Some say that it uses the sorcerer's *wezow* as a vehicle to attack its victims.

The problem with *hul tort* is that while it may be the most effective and lethal form of occult revenge attack, it is unpredictable in its outcomes. While those who know the ritual manipulations can direct the malicious *tort* at others and kill them, and deflect the attacks of others, they cannot aim it accurately at particular homesteads let alone individuals. They can only determine its general trajectory, and it can inadvertently strike down an innocent person living in the direction in which it is aimed, someone uninvolved in the revenge cycle. It can go wrong, even run amok and kill several people, which is a constant fear of those who manipulate this force. Indeed, they have to be careful that the *tort* does not attack them in anger, their mismanagement rousing it to strike them in spite. They have to "look after" it properly. The *taz iysh* payments made to the sorcerer after the rite's performance by those on whose behalf he staged it, are necessary to keep the force content. If omitted, it will become angry and turn on the remiss party, just as it will turn on the sorcerer for neglecting it. No one messes with the *tort* lightly.

While the sorcerer is responsible for directing the *tort* in an attack, neither he nor any of his relatives are liable for the deaths that ensue; instead, those who seek revenge and hire him are held responsible. The victim's relatives will seek in turn to wreak vengeance on the revenge seekers, if they can identify them. Those who commission sorcery seek to keep it a secret for this reason, taking private pleasure in deaths they attribute to their nefarious activities. They limit those in the know to only a few people to avoid information slipping out—to admit to sorcery is tantamount to admit to killing someone. Only occasionally do people intimate sorcery, more as a threat than as a deed.

In Ongol's mind, the *tort* sorcery would square the account for all the outstanding deaths stemming from Kot's fatality. When his *ab* Lem learned about the sorcery, he was disturbed. They had tried to keep him out of the loop because he was an elderly man, but it is difficult to keep such a secret from those living in the same men's house. He became aware of it when someone asked him if he could lend him some wealth for the *taz iysh* payment that was due. One evening, as Ongol and Lem sat alone, he started to talk

A Foi longhouse adjacent to Lake Kutubu.

about Kot's death. He hesitated and busied himself with digging some sweet potato tubers out of the ashes of the fire with wooden tongs, squeezing them with experienced hands to see if the tubers were baked through. Satisfied that they were, he patted off the ash in a white cloud, broke some of the tubers in two, and handed some steaming pieces to Ongol, who sensed his awkwardness. Lem said that he wanted to see the ongoing violent confrontation "put to sleep for good" and be assured that Ongol and his accomplices kept secret the recent sorcery, which would likely lead to armed hostilities breaking out again if any deaths were attributed to it. He muttered something about being old and sick; he sensed that he would die soon, and so had nothing to lose. His words and grave tone of voice made Ongol both uneasy and curious.

Lem went on to recount some of Kot's misdemeanors, of which Ongol was ignorant, including the final rape, pointing out how Kot's unruly acts made life difficult for his kinsmen. Lem reminded Ongol how he and Ongol's father had sought unsuccessfully to disabuse him of the idea that Huwniy's relatives had killed Kot, and mumbled something about not being able to bring themselves for shame to tell him the whole truth. "What truth?" asked Ongol, somewhat apprehensively. Lem sighed loudly and started to tell him what had happened three days after the rape. He and his brother, together with Haebay, had encountered Kot in the Ak valley wading across the river. The water was high, and wading waist deep they had to use poles to brace themselves against the strong current and keep their balance. Ongol could imagine the scene, having waded across the Ak River many times. They waylaid Kot near the far bank of the river, and he was unable to flee.

They remonstrated with him but he only sneered and laughed, refusing to see the seriousness of the situation for all of them, and they lost their tempers. In a rage, Lem and his brother made a move to grab Kot while, exasperated, Haebay threw a punch in his face. Kot lost his footing on the stony riverbed as the pole he held slipped sideways, and he fell headlong into the water. Before they knew it, the strong current swept his body over a nearby waterfall and away down the river. Ongol could visualize it, he knew the place well and the churning water. They rushed after him along the bank but soon realized the futility of trying to catch up, as Kot was quickly swept away downstream through the rocky gorges that mark the river's course. They could not even follow along the riverbank, as there is no path.

They walked to the nearest house to sit down, stunned by the implications of their actions. After all, fratricide is unheard of outside myths. Many people knew that Haebay and his cousins were looking for Kot in the Ak valley, but none apparently made the connection with his death. For their part, they could not admit to having killed their *haemay*, which is an unthinkable offense. The shame was too great. It is a cardinal value that brothers always support one another. They agreed that afternoon that no one could know what had happened, that the terrible knowledge must die with them. Now Lem was the only one of the three still alive and felt a responsibility to Ongol and his kinsmen to "bring out" the *tay* "origin" of the ongoing conflicts.

"The truth," Lem said, looking sadly into Ongol's eyes, "is that your father and I murdered his brother." Ongol was shocked into silence. At first, he could not believe it, but when he asked himself why Lem should lie to him and confess his part in such an awful act, he saw that he must have been telling the truth. Knowing what happened to Kot did not, to his mind, make up for the inadequately revenged deaths of such kin as his *hay* Pes and his *mai* [nephew] Naway, but it threw an entirely new light on the ongoing conflict and its current occult phase. He could appreciate why Lem was so anxious that they keep the recent sorcery a closely guarded secret, to see an end to the chain of violence for which he felt a certain guilty responsibility. Keeping such nefarious activities secret is difficult, however, in a society where people readily look for evidence of such goings-on—as when unexplained, sudden deaths occur.

* * * * * * * * * * * * * * *

The sudden death of a man across the valley followed by that of a nubile young woman started a spate of sorcery accusations. The violent death of the middle-aged man, who was well liked and of *ol howma* status, caused great grief. He and a distant relative had been hunting on the slopes of Waenmaep Mountain when they saw an inaccessible hole in a tree that they suspected was a marsupial den. When they felled the tree it suddenly swung backwards on vines attached to a nearby branch and hit him, plowing his body into the soil from where his kin had to dig his mangled corpse. While there was no reason for him to have been the target of a sorcery attack, there was for his associate, who was a party to the slaying of a man in recent armed hostilities. Opinion was that the *tort* had been inside the tree, causing it to swing backwards, but that it had missed its intended target. The survivor was further held responsible for the death because he had "not looked out properly" for the victim. It is customary for those accompanying persons who suffer accidents to be held liable, and he and his relatives duly entered into *ol sond* with the deceased's kin. The subsequent death of the healthy young woman, who was a popular and jovial character, made people determined to find out the source of the sorcery and have those responsible pay. She died within two days of contracting a mysterious illness, her neck badly swollen. Her death also caused much grief in her family, even causing her father to pull out his beard.

It was inevitable that suspicion should fall on those living across the valley, with whom relations were tense and hostile. The result was a challenge to a *komay* [retributive divination] believed to find out a wrongdoer in sorcery. Initially, Ongol and his relatives refused to consider it, not wishing to entertain the idea that the sorcery had missed its target, and also fearful that such a rite could reveal their recent nefarious activities. But they found themselves in an increasingly difficult position. The other side continually kept up the *komay* challenges and their refusal to participate looked more and more like fear of the consequences and hence guilt of sorcery. In the end, they had to capitulate and agree to take part.

For a few days beforehand, the accusers and plaintiffs chanted accusations and denials. They stood at locales on their territories facing toward the
other side so that they could hear them. These are framed as invitations, featuring the characteristic yodel cry of *haelaiba* [anyone there?]. They were
addressed to both the living and to *towmow* to attend and witness the event,
the latter to mete out supernatural punishment to the party in the wrong.
These chants announce each party's position, one accusing and the other
denying sorcery. While one man yodels the phrases, all those present join in
the *wor* chorus. The following is the chant shouted by the accusers:

Yuw	Sebiyba	*haelaiba.*	*Wor.*	Hobaenk	*haelaiba.*
Up there	Place name	anyone there?	Chorus.	Place name	anyone there?

Wor.	Hiyt	*haelaiba.*	*Wor.*	Ak	Pel-a.
Chorus.	Place name	anyone there?	Chorus.	*Sem* name	Deceased's name.

Wor.	Ak	Kem-a	*Wor.*	Kend
Chorus.	*Sem* name	Deceased's name.	Chorus.	*Sem* name

Pis-a	*Wor.*	Kend	Wol-a.	*Wor.*
Deceased's name.	Chorus.	*Sem* name	Deceased's name.	Chorus.

Ak	Hond-a.	*Wor.*	Hobaenk	Sab-a.
Sem name	Deceased's name.	Chorus.	Place name	Deceased's name.

Wor.	Lusimb-a.	*Wor.*	*Niy lay*	*hendelba.*	*Wor.*
Chorus.	Come gather here.	Chorus.	Me struck	look.	Chorus.

Ak	Waenil-a.	*Wor.*	*Lubtuw kay-a.*	*Wor.*	*Nobtuw kay-a.*
Sem name	Victim's name.	Chorus.	Struck say.	Chorus.	Ate say.

Wor.	*Bubtuw kay-a.*	*Wor.*	*Uwt-waeb*	*shuwai*
Chorus.	Did for say.	Chorus.	Black palm bow	chant word

buruk iyb-a.	*Wor.*	*Kongliyp*	*buruk iyb-a.*	*Wor.*
sit come.	Chorus.	Decorative bush[8]	sit come.	Chorus.

The denying chant shouted by the other side comprises a similar list of
places, and associated *sem* names and the names of deceased relatives, until
the last part, when it denies the accusations, as follows:

Lusimb-a.	*Wor.*	Ak	Waenil-a.	*Wor.*	*Niy Na*
Come gather here.	Chorus.	*Sem* name	Victim's name.	Chorus.	I not

Hondowa.	*Wor.*	*Niy na luwa.*	*Wor.*	*Nim na buwa.*
know.	Chorus.	I not struck.	Chorus.	I not did.

Wor.	*buwa.*	*Wor.*	*Niy kelobtuw kay-a.*	*Wor.*	*Niy*
Chorus.	did.	Chorus.	Me falsely accuse say.	Chorus.	Me

showmay-a.	*Wor.*	*Uwt-waeb*	*shuwai*	*buruk iyb-a.*
falsely accuse.	Chorus.	Black palm bow	chant word	sit come.

Wor.	*Kongliyp*	*buruk iyb-a.*	*Wor.*
Chorus.	Decorative bush	sit come.	Chorus.

The chants open by naming various places where *towmow* may be residing, to attract their attention. They then call out the *sem* affiliation and names of deceased relatives,[9] who are now ghosts, to invite them to the upcoming divination. In effect, they are calling out, "Hey ghosts at such-and-such place, listen to what we are doing." It is unusual behavior because the living do not usually wish to attract the attention of ghosts for fear of inviting their attacks. The accusing chant then goes on to tell the *towmow* "look, they've struck one of us down, they've killed Waenil, eaten him, done for him." It invites the ghosts to come and "sit" on the bows of their living relatives, infuse them with their presence, so that if a fight erupts they will convey their deadly supernatural power to their arrows and so ensure enemy fatalities. It also intimates the "ghosts'" coming attack on the challenged party for not telling the truth. Finally, it calls the ghosts to the homestead where they are staging the divination, inviting them to come and sit among the ornamental *kongliyp* bushes cultivated around house yards. The denying chant is similar, except that it tells the *towmow* of those yodeling that they are falsely accused, that they know nothing about the death and were not party to it.

Both chants inform the *towmow* about the issue and invite them to come and witness and judge the coming retributive divination. It is believed that they will "see the truth" of the accusations and denials made against their kin during the divination, and if the accusations are false, the *towmow* will be empowered to attack the liars. It is as dangerous to make false accusations as it is to make denials, because the ghosts of the wrongly accused will attack and "eat" whoever is not telling the truth. This is one of the few occasions when the *towmow* of one *sem* may attack and kill members of another, sanctioned and activated by the *komay*. It was small wonder that Ongol, and his kin in the know, were reluctant to participate in such an event.

* * * * * * * * * * * * * *

On the agreed day, both sides met on a neighboring *sem* territory where they had relatives. Only men attended, no women and children were allowed because of the danger. They had blackened their faces and painted on white clay designs and wore black cassowary pompom feather headdresses. They stopped several times en route to shout out their chants, and when they arrived at the appointed grass clearing, they stood on opposite sides, calling out their chants of accusation and denial, punctuated with a shuffling dance in which they threateningly cried, "*Uw-uw-uw*" and "*Brrrr*" at one another. The atmosphere was fraught with tension. It felt as if physical violence could erupt at any time. They yelled accusations and denials back and forth. "We didn't hit him," shouted Ongol and his kin.

Finally, both sides converged on a screen of leafy saplings running out from the trunk of a large tree on the clearing, which the accusers had erected the day before. It was of a construction familiar to several rituals, lined with the pale leaves of *bat*[10] and *shiyp* trees pushed behind strips of wood lashed lengthways. In front of it, they had made a raised oven from the crown of a

Clubbing a pig.

tree fern driven into the ground with a sheet of bark lashed around it, producing a container. These structures are the *komay*, which give their name to the retributive divination. In an adjacent place, they had dug a standard earth oven pit. Two men, one from either side, clubbed a pig as both sides advanced toward the leafy wall, chanting menacingly and waving and banging their bows and arrows together in threat gestures. The advance was intended not only to intimidate the other side but also to drive the summoned *towmow* toward the wall and up into the crown of the tree where they will "see" the events and judge them.

It was said that the innocent side would be the first to

Butchering a pig, cutting flesh away from ribs.

land a blow on the pig but in their excitement the two men's clubs collided and neither was first. They used legs from the raised coffin of the sorcery victim as clubs. Putrid juices from his rotting corpse had run down and impregnated them with his essence, which they transferred to the pig. They effected further transference of his being by burning the blood-stained pole to which they had lashed his corpse to bring it back from the forest, together with his old, soiled apron, on the fire over which they singed off the animal's bristles. It "infected the meat" so that those lying about the sorcery would be struck down. It also carried the "smell" of the deceased along the leaf wall and up into the tree, enraging the *towmow* there to take revenge. While some men heated the stones for the ovens, others butchered the pig. They set the heart, lungs, liver, head, and belly pork strip on one side to cook in the raised tree-fern-crown oven, with *henk* [tree fern fronds],[11] *omok* [acanth greens], and *shombiy* [ginger root],[12] and prepared the remainder of the meat to cook in the earth oven.

Finally, when the contents of the raised oven were cooked, the time came to perform the divination. The men cut the oven's contents in half so that each side had equal shares, and those subjecting themselves to the *komay* test received a piece to eat. Before doing so, they took the jawbone of the deceased, retrieved from his raised grave, and rubbed their meat on it to imbue it further with his essence, so promoting the efficacy of the rite to identify and punish the liars. They swore an oath declaring the truth of their accusations or denials before consuming the potentially lethal piece of meat. "I didn't do anything, so I'll eat it," said Ongol defiantly. He chewed the meat

The jawbone of a man believed killed in sorcery is kept by relatives in anticipation of a *komay* challenge.

for a long time and found it like a stone to swallow, fearful as he was of the consequences of the *komay* rite. For it is not only those who eat the raised oven's contents who are at risk if telling untruths but also their kin; the avenging *towmow* may attack and kill any of them. The tension eased afterward. Later on that afternoon all the men present shared the rest of the pig cooked in the earth oven.

Chapter 9

Rituals of Well-Being

*E*very so often in life we have reason to look back and reflect on what we have done and look forward, considering what we might do. Ongol had good reason to do so in view of the armed and supernatural conflicts in which he had become embroiled, knowing about the dreadful and tragic events involving his *ab* Kot that had preceded them. Although he would never admit it to himself, Ongol felt guilty about his hotheaded actions as a young man and the burden of extensive *haypuw* commitments with which he had saddled his descendants. While he was in such a reflective mood, it was suggested that the community should stage the *saybel* ritual to promote well-being. People were ready to cooperate in such an undertaking after the harrowing events of the recent past, notably the famine. There was also the disconcerting appearance of the "ghost" column. After one or two more patrols had passed through their territory, the strange newcomers had disappeared again—back to wherever they had come from, as suddenly as they had appeared. But everyone feared that they would return, and their worries were well-founded, as it turned out, for the "ghost" column would reappear in force a decade later and change their lives irrevocably.

Ongol took up the suggestion of a *saybel* festival with alacrity. He had a strong urge to promote community prosperity after learning of his fathers' actions and being disturbed at what had followed—and after realizing how his ignorance and misinterpretation of what had happened contributed to events. Communities stage the *saybel* festival only once a generation. It is believed to please the *towmow* and dissuade them from attacking their kin; it also promotes participants' success in upcoming exchange transactions. The first stage in the festival involves building a new *muwnaenda* to accommodate the sponsoring family's prehistoric *hungnaip haen*. They may also refurbish the adjacent *masho-raenda* [taro-leaf house]—a small, open-ended, ridge structure—where they cook certain cuts from pig offerings including back, belly, and stomach pieces.

When they had completed the construction work, they killed some pigs for the resident *towmow.* This offering followed the same procedure as others made when kin are sick. While some men singed and butchered the animals, an individual sanctioned to do so placed a small cut of fatty meat in the earth-oven pit. After spraying it with chewed *kongol* juice, he put a hot ember on it to inciner-ate it, while blowing on the meat and inviting *towmow* to come and eat it: "Ancestors, it is yours, eat it." He also recited the names of the large *hungnaip haen* kept in the *muwnaenda*. While a side of pork cooked in the *muwnaenda* oven, some men decorated the *hungnaip haen* by rubbing over the outside of the bowls with a mixture of charcoal and *wombok* and the inside with red ocher.

The participants wore their second-best decorations, cassowary pom-poms on clay-whitened net caps together with other feathers, and white clay designs painted on charcoal blackened faces to intimidate the *towmow*. While the pork was cooking in the spirit house, they performed the "pearl shell car-rying" shuffling dance. They formed a single line, and crouching down, they held a pearl shell to their foreheads while they shuffled around the grass clearing adjacent to the spirit house. They did not chant or say anything. This dance and their decoration awed the *towmow*; seeing the shell wealth made them think twice about attacking such successful men's families. In addition, the shell display inclined the spirits to help their descendants in forthcoming exchange transactions by entering the minds of their partners, ensuring that they met their obligations generously so that they achieved *ol howma* status. The men shared and ate the tidbits that were cooked in the *mashoraenda* first, followed by the *muwnaenda* side of pork. Finally, they opened the large com-munal oven in which they had cooked the rest of the pork and shared it with kin, including women and children, as at a pig-kill festival.

* * * * * * * * * * * * * *

Shortly after this first stage of the *saybel* festival, Ongol's eldest son by his second wife Wat fell seriously ill. He was worried that it was the result of the *komay* and that he was powerless to do anything. He resolved to treat it as a sorcery attack and talked about commissioning a "man stakes take" sorcery curing ritual. Wat thought that it was the *komay* punishing Ongol, as she had not believed his denials. She became convinced when she found a small enclosure of *leb* in the forest near their Homal homestead. She pulled it up in fury and waved it in Ongol's face as evidence of his sorcery magic, accusing him of putting their children at risk. He exploded in rage, fearing that the "stupid woman's actions will make the *tort* go berserk" and ensure their son's death. The sorcery-curing rite became a matter of urgency and that afternoon the healer arrived and took a bunch of *niysh* stinging nettle leaves and, after reciting the following spell[1] over them, rubbed them over the boy's body:

Puwpuw	*nigiy,*	*popuw,*	*nigiy,*	*taebaenda*
Pain	stinging leaf,	chert blade,	stinging leaf,	bamboo knife

	nigiy,	*puwpuw*	*nigiy,*	*taebaenda*	*nigiy,*
	stinging leaf,	pain	stinging leaf,	bamboo knife	stinging leaf,

	popuw	*nigiy.*
	chert blade,	stinging leaf.

The leaves are the sort sick persons regularly rub on painful parts of their body, employing the "pain fights off pain" theory. The spell underscores the pain theme, mentioning not only stinging leaves but also chert blades and bamboo knives that can wound. The pain frightens the attacking sorcery force or sorcerer's *wezow,* warning them to desist and depart. If the sick person evidences great agony, he is the casualty of a sorcery attack. In addition, if he recovers some appetite, having been off his food for days previously, this is a further sign of such an attack. The next day the healer arranged the *ol iysh* [man stakes] rite.

The healer decorated himself to frighten and intimidate further the attacking sorcery force. After blackening his face with charcoal and painting a white clay design, he pinned a cassowary feather pompom on his wig and tucked three red leaves into his forehead band. First, he strangled a pig by binding some vine around the animal's snout and then around its neck, while muttering the following spell:[2]

Daela	*Haego*	*nono*	*hauabidow.*	*Daela*	*haega*	*nono*	*hauabidow.*
Snake	Snake	mouth	bind.	Snake	snake	mouth	bind.

Daela	*baero*	*Nono*	*hauabidow.*	*Kuduw*	*oli*	*nono*
Snake	snake	Mouth	bind.	Kutubu	crocodile	mouth

hauabidow.	*Kuduw*	*tonoli*	*nono*	*hauabidow.*	*Kaela*	*ogomow*
bind.	Kutubu	crocodile	mouth	bind.		giant rat

nono	*ngaengo*	*nono*	*ngolngol.*
mouth	snarl	mouth	gnash.

It refers to tying closed the mouths of feared creatures including the *daela, haego,* and *baero* snakes of the Kutubu region and the crocodile, rendering them harmless. Similarly, the attacking sorcery force is feared for its bite and for eating vital organs; the rite ties its mouth closed and stops its attack. The binding of vine around the pig's snout has the same symbolic importance. It also repeats the way the sorcerer kills the pig during the sorcery and so counteracts its effects of "tying up" the victim in the attack.

The healer finished the animal off by clubbing it with a stone smeared with red ocher, causing blood to flow from the snout. He held the animal over a small bowl-shaped hole that he had dug and lined with banana leaves to catch the blood, inducing a copious flow by thrusting a sharpened bat's bone into the animal's nostrils. He topped the bowl with water and added some red ocher to this "pig's blood mirror." He studied the surface intently, as in the previous sorcery-curing rite, while the boy sat by it, searching for his *wezow* [reflection]. When he finally saw it, he said that it suggested the boy might recover. Other relatives present, who might also be sorcery targets, checked for their reflections. While they did this, the man officiating took several short *pel* stakes and rubbed these with ocher and blood from the pool.

Next, the healer twirled together a twist of hair on the boy's head— called, as in the previous rite, an *aenk way*—and smeared it with some of the bloody concoction from the bowl while muttering the spell below. He then twisted and smeared a knot on his own crown and the heads of others in need of protection. After this, he folded the protruding ends of the banana leaves over the top of the hole and drove in three short *pel* stakes around it, tying a length of *maip ya* vine around them to secure the leaves closed over the hole. He used the ochered stone to drive the stakes flush into the ground before scraping earth over the leaf-enclosed hole, securely burying its charged contents. He threw the stone away, calling out the names of possible places from whence the sorcery might have come, thereby directing it back at those who had launched the supernatural attack. It hit a tree to everyone's delight, as this foretells the ritual's success and possible turning of the sorcery back at the attackers.

Then the healer took two more of the short *pel* stakes, called the *ol iysh*, and passed these simultaneously down either side of the victim while reciting the following spell:[3]

> *Kuluw   kuluw. Kuluw kuluw. Ponda   nigiy,   taebaenda*
>   Spell word   Throat nettle,   bamboo knife
>
> *nigiy. Kiniy   lobow, holini   lobow, mbida   lobow,*
>   .   Hand   dry,   eight   dry,   one   dry,
>
> *ayreno lobow,   yo   lobow, haegwano lobow.*
>   tail   dry,   tree trunk   dry,   head   dry.

He pushed the stakes into the ground, between the big and second toes of one foot and behind the heel of the other, hammering them in flush. He did the same for each person who was in danger of becoming a sorcery victim. Banging the *ol iysh* into the ground "spears and kills the attacking sorcery force." It also acts like a fence protecting them from further attack, allowing the victim to recover. The spell continues this theme, starting with the reciter frightening off the attacking force by blowing onto a nettle that causes pain like a bamboo knife. The reference to drying alludes to the sick person ceasing to sweat in illness and discomfort as he recovers. The tree trunk and the numbers eight and one are all metaphors for the convalescing person; eight standing for head, torso, two arms, two thighs, and two shins.

Finally, the healer took a handful of the bloody *pel* stakes and banged them with a stone into the ground around Ongol's homestead as a defense against further sorcery attacks. He repeated the spell as he did so. He drove further pairs of stakes into the ground on either side of all paths approaching the sick boy's house, and a final two stakes on either side of the door into the sleeping room, so fencing out the attacking *tort*. The stakes also "frighten the sorcery force away" when it encounters them. While the healer was busy, Ongol's eldest *iyziy* [son], together with his younger *haemay*, Hond, had butchered the pig and put the meat to cook in an earth oven. Only men could eat the pork, which they shared later in the afternoon. The only downside to this meal is the taboo they must observe not to accept any food from a woman or engage in sexual intercourse for a fortnight or so. The healer received the head, stomach, and neck joint in *habuwk* payment, together with a cowry shell necklace and gourd of *wombok* If the sick person rallies sufficiently to share some of the pork, this is taken as a good omen. Although he nibbled at some meat, the boy had no appetite but lay down exhausted by the fire in the men's house foyer.

* * * * * * * * * * * * * *

The "man stakes" curing rite was to no avail and the boy sadly passed away a few days later. Ongol's relationship with Wat deteriorated further as a result, and she left him to live for several months with one of her brothers' wives. It added to his reputation as someone who had trouble maintaining smooth marital relations. In the circumstances, he thought that it was just as well he had married a third wife. Getting through the funeral was difficult. Ongol carried a heavy personal burden of guilt, although he publicly continued to deny that he had engaged in sorcery. He reflected on the way the twisted course of events followed Kot's character, knowing now from Lem what sort of man he was and the chaos caused by his behavior.

It was inevitable that after the *komay*, healthy persons would fall ill and die and that some people would attribute their deaths to the *komay*. People disagreed over which deaths to accredit to it. While one side might assign a death on the other side to either retributive divination or the assumed sorcery that led to the divination, the other side might put the death down to other reasons. While Ongol and a few close kinsmen knew about the *hul tort* sorcery, the majority of the boy's relatives accepted their denials and concluded that the divination rite could not be responsible for his death. The other side that had issued the *komay* challenge was convinced that it had killed the boy.

There were several other deaths on both sides that each interpreted differently. The result was that they came up with different revenge scores for the hostilities, disagreeing over which deaths to attribute to them. The outcome of these discrepancies over the death score is that both sides can add it up in such a way that it balances for them and makes further revenge action unnecessary. The disagreements and consequent obfuscation are one way, sociologically speaking, that the potentially never-ending round of revenge can end. For actors in the event, however, sociological arguments are beside the point, because what they feel is raw emotion at losing relatives.

* * * * * * * * * * * * * *

One dark night disaster struck at Tombem. It had started to rain heavily late in the afternoon and reached an intensity that no one could recall by the evening, with the rain falling like "arrows." Everyone sat indoors listening to it drumming on the roof. The storm showed no sign of abating after several hours, and people started to become scared during the night because in such conditions landslides are likely. Ongol tried to reassure everyone in his men's house that they would be all right because rocks projected from the ground around their homestead and the adjacent grass clearing. According to local lore avalanches do not occur where there are rock outcrops, as they act to "hold the soil" in place—an observation that accords with geophysical findings. Avalanches happen when the soil is unable to cope with the volume of water arriving in heavy storms. The terrain and soils of the Was valley make it prone to landslides, with steep mountainous slopes combined with relatively thin topsoil over impermeable clay subsoil. Rain percolates through the thin topsoil until it meets the impermeable clay subsoil when it starts to flow downhill, acting lubricant-like between the two soil horizons such that the top one may start to move over the lower. When combined with the large amount of water running down the surface and undermining shallow rooted vegetation, the soil on steep slopes becomes increasingly unstable. If it starts to move, an avalanche will result.

Ongol's attempts at reassurance were only partly successful. No one was able to sleep properly with the noise of the intense rain combined with their worries. Not only was it beating down loudly but it was also finding weak points in the roof thatch and dripping on them. They sat huddled around the fire chatting or curled on the floor away from the leaks. They kept the fire going with cheerful flames to illuminate the room and stay warm through the chilly night. They started to entertain themselves and take their attention off the frightening storm by telling stories, a common pastime of an evening as people prepare to sleep. Storytelling was a time when Lem came into his own as an amusing raconteur whose animated impersonations of characters in stories could be hilarious. He told several stories that night, among them the ones about the kidnapped boy and the cassowary, and the Kutubu cannibals. The story of the kidnapped boy was a favorite.

> Long ago there was this woman who lived with her small son. One day the boy stalked a bird and it led him to a pool of water. When he peered into it, he saw that someone had thrown the guts of butchered pigs into the water. The boy fetched the innards and washed the chyme and feces out of them, as he had seen his mother do previously, and took the offal home to eat. When he returned to the pool again another day, the boy noticed that there was a root growing out of the water and he decided to climb up it. The root came from a large tree that stood on top of the mountain that towered above the pool. When the boy reached the trunk of the tree at the mountain summit, he saw a man there butchering a pig and putting the meat to cook in an earth oven. When the man stood up and threw the intestines into the pool, he spied the boy hiding behind a clump of cane grass.
>
> The lad shook with fear when the man saw him. The man grabbed him and stuffed him into five large string bags. He suspended him in the bags above the fireguard in the roof space of his house. He did not feed the boy and he became very hungry. He left him hanging from the roof for two months. The boy's mother was very upset when he did not return home and she sat crying all the time. One day a small fruit bat came and told the woman that it had seen her son hanging in the man's house. "If you bring my son back to me, you can take as many bananas as you wish

to eat," said the woman pointing to her many banana plants. The bat brought the boy back and sat him on the ridge of her house. The woman was delighted to see her son again and thanked the bat with bananas. But she was sad to see how withered the boy was with hardly any flesh on his bones. And that is the story of the kidnapped boy.

The story of the cassowary and the Kutubu cannibals starts with a brother and a sister living together.

One day a *payawiy* Spotted Honeyeater[4] bird came and told the boy that he had something to show him somewhere. "Are they having a dance in the Mendi region?" he asked. "Yes," answered the bird. The boy told his sister to

Washing chyme from pigs' intestines.

stay indoors while he went and decorated himself, rubbing *wombok* on his body and putting on fresh cordyline buttock leaves. While he was away at the dance, he told his sister to stay inside their house yard and not to venture outside the fence surrounding it. He brought her enough firewood, sweet potato, and drinking water to meet her needs, and he collected pandan leaves for her to make a rain cape and bark fiber to roll string for netting bags. He told her that when she finished making these things she was not to leave and search for more raw materials; instead, she must stay inside the house yard as instructed. "You can collect bananas that ripen inside the house yard but not those that ripen outside," he said.

Nevertheless, she did not listen to him, and she left the house yard to collect more pandan leaves for rain-cape making. While she was in the forest, she found a cassowary egg at the foot of a tree. She collected the egg and took it home with the pandan leaves. She made a round nest out of moss for the egg and placed it in a warm place on top of the pig stalls in her house. While she sat sewing her rain cape, the egg broke open and a fluffy chick emerged to her delight. She fed the bird sweet potato and it grew a little at a time into a large adult. The cassowary called the woman its mother and told her, "You can rest easy because if any Kutubu cannibals come to harm you I shall kill them." They lived together and she brought baked sweet potato tubers and wild raspberries in her net bag for the bird. One day while they were in the garden, two cannibals from Kutubu came by intending to kill the woman, but the cassowary speared them both with its long claws and threw their corpses out of the garden. It did the same with several other cannibals that came from Kutubu to eat the woman.

One day the woman's brother returned with two wives. They stopped at the garden and he cut down some sugarcane for them to eat. When the cassowary saw them it thought that they were stealing from the garden and it quietly crept up on them and stabbed all three to death with its ferocious claws. The bird reported to the woman that it had found three people stealing from their garden. When she went to look, she saw that her brother was one of the corpses tossed out of the garden. "Thanks, you scaly-shinned bird," she said sarcastically. "That is my brother you have killed there." In anger, she told the bird no longer to call her mother but to leave her homestead and go and live in the forest feeding on whole gamboge tree fruits like other wild cassowaries.

After the cassowary had left, a large Kutubu man came to the woman's house and killed her and carried her off to eat at his longhouse by the lake. The cassowary followed the man, and when it knew where he lived, it informed all the cassowaries in the forest and they came and surrounded the longhouse, forming a line all the way around it. One of them looked inside the house and saw that everyone was asleep. Some cassowaries entered and "speared" the sleepers with their claws through the heart. Those who fled terrified outside were ambushed by others and "speared" to death. After the cassowaries had killed all of them, they burned down the longhouse. They returned to the forest where they have kept watch for cannibal raiding parties from Kutubu ever since, defending us Wola speakers by killing them, otherwise there would be nobody living in this valley.

Anthropologists have shown considerable interest in stories such as these and have come up with a range of explanations for them. Some seek to understand their performance by associating them with any related rituals and ceremonies. Others think that they are intellectual in content and purpose, serving as explanations for things in the world and various incidents. The sociologically minded see such stories as promoting social solidarity or serving as charters to substantiate claims to resources and knowledge, notably as origin myths. The psychologically inclined think that they tell us something about human cognition, serving as expressions of unconscious concerns or helping to resolve the paradoxes of life. All of these approaches to myth have some validity.

According to some, they are narratives told for entertainment, akin to fairy tales. This is what Ongol and the others would have said about the stories they told that stormy night. The two stories above, and many others in the Wola corpus, bring to mind such English folktales as "Jack and the Beanstalk" and "Little Red Riding Hood." They are entertaining and can be humorous, particularly when told by a good storyteller. No one necessarily believes them. This is clear in origin myths that have today's *sem* descending from marsupials and birds. These stories are the same genre as the Biblical myth featuring Adam and Eve in the Garden of Eden, which would supplant them when the white "ghosts" returned, and is certainly no less fantastic.

It was in the small hours that disaster struck. Some of the men were dozing fitfully and others were smoking and talking when they heard the deep rumbling, followed by a roar that made the ground tremble. They thought that they heard some terrified shrieks but they could not be certain. Some of them went outside to see what had happened, but it was too dark to see anything. The torrential rain soon doused the flaming brands they had taken from the fire and they dared not venture far. They returned wet and shivering to warm themselves by the fire. It was not until dawn that they saw what had happened; a horrendous sight awaited them as they emerged from their house. A large section of the adjacent hillside and forest had disappeared taking houses and gardens with it. There was an enormous brown gouge in the slope. If they had possessed a rain gauge, it would have shown that 20 centimeters of rain had fallen in 10 hours. Looking out across the valley from Tombem they could see several similar large brown scars torn through the green vegetation on the slopes opposite.

After recovering from their initial shock at the scene, several men started to make their way downhill toward the debris of the landslide, a hillock of churned earth with tree trunks and branches sticking out of it at crazy angles. It was still raining but less heavily than previously. Not that they noticed in their urgency. They started to dig in the vain hope of finding those caught up in the avalanche. They found some, their bodies smashed and limbs akimbo with soil forced into their screaming mouths, noses, and eyes. They did not find all those buried alive that awful night. The landslide had almost wiped out an entire *semgⁿk* carrying off men's and women's houses. There was a large funeral and mortuary exchange the likes of which no one could ever recall. They marked off the hillock with cordyline shrubs like an enormous grave; it would remain in local folklore as a place that people should avoid.

The occurrence of such disasters may make some wonder how people can believe in rites of well-being such as the *saybel*, for they seem so patently ineffective. On the other hand, it is arguable that they offer some hope of protection in the face of such natural catastrophes, against which we humans are otherwise so helpless. The alternative is resigned acceptance that we can do nothing. Such defeatism is not a human trait, no matter how limited available technology. While previous rites may fail, it is possible that another will prove successful in the future. It is possible that such a quest in part feeds the apparent readiness of New Guinea Highlanders to take up new cults when they come along, as occurred in the years that followed the night of the landslides. We can make similar observations with respect to illness. The attitude of the Was valley population in seeking to protect itself through various rituals has parallels with our faith in Western medicine, which is not always successful at curing illness and regularly adopts new therapies as previous ones prove inadequate or even wrong. Similarly, the sick sometimes recovered following rites to cure them from ghost or sorcery attack, such as when Ongol returned to normal health following his illness, and other times not, as with his unfortunate "sorcery victim" son.

* * * * * * * * * * * * * * *

The avalanche disaster delayed by many "moons" the anticipated next stage of the *saybel* ritual. It involved the construction of the "long-neck

house," so called because of its tall spire-like roof. Many of those residing in the community sponsoring the festival cooperated in building this roundhouse. It has a single long pole in the center that supports the grass-thatch roof tapering up it like a steeple. It took some weeks to amass the materials and build the house. No special ritual marked its construction. Inside the builders dug a large earth oven pit that would feature in the ritual's next phase and collected a large pile of cooking stones. Otherwise, the house remained empty. The tall spire "pleases the ghosts." It also "tells them of the coming offering" and encourages them to gather in anticipation for it. The sight of the spire also advertises the coming ritual to others in the region.

A *masolaenda* house erected for a *saybel* rite.

The long-neck house stage features an offering of marsupials. When those sponsoring the event agree on the date, they spend the days before hunting for game. The waxing and waning of the previous full moon was a busy time for Ongol and many others. They ventured into the forest every night with bow and arrows, and dogs. They spent time stalking through areas of secondary regrowth, which supports vegetation particularly attractive to arboreal creatures, listening for them and seeking their silhouettes against the pale sky. It was not an easy time for Ongol's family as he became irritable with lack of sleep and acted bad temperedly when children disturbed him as he dozed during the day. Other men went off for many days to remote forested regions on the other side of the Ak valley, setting traps, climbing trees to inspect any likely den holes, and chasing down game. They returned with many animals. In anticipation of the *saybel* offering, Ongol had obtained a pair of tree kangaroos some weeks previously in trade from someone living in the lower Was valley. The two animals had become family pets. The children fed the docile pair foliage and garden waste daily. When he took them away on the day of the offering at the long-neck house, there were tears and tantrums.

All those taking part in the rite, both those living in the community and relatives from elsewhere, assembled early on the agreed morning at the long-neck house with their animals. They slaughtered any still alive, such as the tree kangaroos. They singed the fur off the animals over a large pyre arranged to heat the earth oven stones. They muttered the names of dead kin as they did so, blowing on the smoldering fur, inviting the spirits to "eat" the

A captive tree kangaroo sitting on the roof of a house.

smell and also the spilled blood. They cooked the butchered animals in the house oven pit, together with a range of vegetables harvested the previous afternoon. They dug a second pit in front of the house to accommodate the excess animals, as their hunting efforts had been so successful. Those who had not contributed much or anything to the construction of the long-neck house cooked their animals outside. When they opened the ovens, they distributed meat and vegetables among kin and friends present; only men were present and consumed the food.

The dramatic part of the festival was yet to come. When the feast was over, some men laid a fire around the central pole supporting the roof of the long-neck house. When they lit it, the house went up in a large conflagration, the tall roof collapsing inward with a huge shower of sparks. They denied any symbolism to the destruction of the house. It is what custom dictated following the sharing of marsupials and vegetables. After the long-neck house feast, life returned again to humdrum normality. The daily routine had scarcely changed for Ongol's wives and other women.

* * * * * * * * * * * * * *

While some of Ongol's sons were now old enough to help him pioneer new gardens, they only did so desultorily. He had to carry most of the burden of ensuring that his large family had sufficient land under cultivation. He was also engaged, as always, in negotiations over a number of forthcoming exchange transactions. He anticipated contributing to a young relative's *injiykab* and was also engrossed in some ongoing mortuary exchanges related to the reparation sequence following the earlier armed conflicts. But his mind was particularly focused on the large pig-kill festival that would take place during the third stage of the *saybel* cycle. While this final stage was some months off, all households intending to participate were occupied with managing and building up their pig herds for it. Ongol had plans to kill several large animals but was concerned about his household's capacity to manage the number that would come to him as he built up the herd. He realized that he would have to come to an agreement with Mindiy to pull out the stops, as she was the only one with the necessary pig management skills.

In anticipation, he approached her and she agreed that both of them might meet and negotiate a herding payment with her brothers. After some considerable wrangling, Ongol found himself offering her brothers a prized "bone" pearl shell "with a name" and cowry necklaces, public affirmation of Mindiy's *ten howma* status. Predictably, given their strong evenly matched characters and personal history, Ongol overstepped the mark one day and they argued loudly, and turning on her heel, she told him that he could look after the pigs himself. By now, the herd included some large beasts and realizing how catastrophic it would be to have her walk off in fury, he found himself promising to give handsome joints of pork to her relatives, which would further reflect well on her. She knew that he would have to keep his word, making the promise in front of several men, or lose face, which was the last thing that someone of *ol howma* status like him would risk. Anyway, whatever else she might have to say about her husband, Mindiy would agree that he was always fair in his dealings with her.

It was just as well that Ongol made up his differences with Mindiy, as he was going to depend on her well-known *ten howma* pig managing abilities more than he knew. She was widely admired for her skills, which she attributed in part to the pig welfare spell that she had learned from her mother, together with the small glassy white stone that she had inherited from her, which she rubbed occasionally on the backs of animals together with white ash from her fireplace. These "showed" pigs how to grow thick layers of desirable subcutaneous-fat and encouraged their rapid development into valuable large beasts. The spell was as follows:

Amim	*tuwgol,*	*hobom*	*tuwgol.*
Adipose-fat	grow- rapidly,	subcutaneous-fat	grow- rapidly.

Laek amim	*tuwgol,*	*laek hobom*	*tuwgol.*
Cucumber fat	grow- rapidly,	cucumber fat	grow- rapidly.

Heb	*maem*	*berayzol,*	*senim*	*maem*
Cucumber	vine-growing-tip	turnover,	gourd	vine-growing-tip

berayzol,	*laek*	*maem*	*berayzol.*	*Amim*
turnover,	cucumber	vine-growing-tip	turnover.	Adipose-fat

tuwgol,	*hobom*	*tuwgol.*
grow- rapidly,	subcutaneous-fat	grow- rapidly.

It likens the fat of pigs to the pale soft flesh of cucumbers and gourds, which swell up quickly following pollination, and urges animals similarly to grow rapidly. It emphasizes the quick growth theme in referring to the growing tips of cucumber and gourd vines, which spread prolifically across the soil, bearing fruits each time they flower, which "turnover," that is, swell up within days. Gardeners also turn over the foliage to find the fruit, and a disturbed vine is one that has recently yielded a juicy fat fruit.

During the herd buildup, one of the animals fell ill with swine influenza, developing a bad cough and losing its appetite. Mindiy's quick reactions saved the herd. She soon realized that the pig was unwell, and, concerned about contagion, she quarantined it away from the others, which she moved to her cowife's house. She watched the animals closely, and when another showed signs of listlessness, she promptly removed it from the herd. She strengthened the animals by feeding them blades of the medicinal *leb* pushed into holes made in sweet potato tubers. Ongol was lucky to lose only two animals, which annoyed him, and not more.

The pig sickness episode led to further problems between Ongol's wives. Wat made a fuss about Mindiy moving her pigs into her house, fearing that they would infect the ones in her charge, too. While she acknowledged Mindiy's pig keeping talents, she resented her receiving conspicuously better

A woman strokes a pair of her pigs.

wealth in the herding transaction, public affirmation by their husband of his high regard for her. Wat saw the pig sickness episode as an opportunity to score one over her senior cowife. But Ongol realized that Mindiy's swift action had probably saved several animals and all Wat got for her troubles was verbal abuse, which she reciprocated, arguing that he should reward her equally in the forthcoming herding transactions. When Ongol duly gave Mindiy the prize "bone" pearl shell to hand on to her relatives, Wat made a scene publicly and decamped the next day to her brother's place with her children.

* * * * * * * * * * * * * * *

The third stage of the *saybel* cycle extended over two days. On the first day, Ongol cut a fine figure. Like other participants he donned his finest bewigged decorations with headdress topped by enamelled bird-of-paradise plumes, prize pearl shell around his neck, face blackened with charcoal and painted with designs in white clay, and body glistening with powdered charcoal in *wombok*. He wore the deep red leaves of the *haezaegow* cordyline over his buttocks, necklace and chest bandolier made of *orol* tree[5] berries threaded on string, and new red-hued *kuwliy* tree[6] leaves as hair and beard decoration. He was up before dawn excitedly dressing in finery, having prepared his wig in the days before. They assembled at the site of the demolished long-neck house, where the Ak valley man officiating had laid a length of vine across the clearing. The men arranged themselves alternately on either side of the vine and, facing one another, picked it up in both hands. They then "danced" the *saybel ishmenay*, the "*saybel* tree-lift," raising the vine up and down, repeating each phrase of the following chant after the Ak valley man:

Luwinjtenj.	*Poriyneben.*	*Ngon*	*yabim.*	*Ngon*	*ebem.*	*Pinj*	*pinj.*
Place.	Stone mortar.	That	rub.	That	good.	Plenty	plenty.

Golgol.	*Dukduk.*	*Ngon*	*yabim.*	*Ngon*	*ebem.*	*Ngon*
Spread.	Thread on string.	That	rub.	That	good.	That

bukom.	*Pinj*	*pinj.*	*Golgol.*	*Dukduk.*	*Ngon*	*yabim.*
stone dish.	Plenty	plenty.	Spread.	Thread on string.	That	rub.

Ngon	*ebem.*	*Pinj*	*pinj.*	*Golgol.*	*Pa*	*pa.*
That	good.	Plenty	plenty.	Spread.	Stop	stop.

When quizzed years later by an anthropologist, some men said that holding the vine joined the participants together and was "like them all shaking hands with their ancestors' spirits," gathered for the rite. The chant captures the dual health and prosperity aims of the ritual: to ensure a healthy future, free from ghostly attack, for participants and their families and to secure for them increased wealth in future transactions. They refer to their largest and best prehistoric ritual stones, pointing out how well they are curating them for their *towmow*. They ask for much wealth to pass through their hands in exchange transactions, comparable to the many cowries threaded on a necklace. In the last phrase, they prevail upon the ghosts not to attack and "eat" any of their kin, as they are looking out so well for their interests. During the vine-lifting dance, two decorated adolescent boys wearing long mourning skirts ran around the line of men holding the vine, brandishing rattles of hard pangi seed cases and bow and arrows to keep the crowds of spectators back from the dancers.

The dancers and the crowd subsequently made their way to the nearby large grass clearing to continue with a regular dance. The Ak valley man took the vine and hid it in the nearby forest, so "putting the *towmow* the men had shaken hands with out of harm's way" where they could not attack people. When he arrived at the edge of the grass clearing, he snatched a small pig belonging to Ongol that was tethered there. He was accused of stealing the pig and a mock dispute started, whereas Mindiy had left the animal there under her husband's instructions for the man to take. The argument was staged to show the ghosts how angry their living relatives could be when they have to offer pigs in times of sickness. It was intended to persuade the *towmow* to refrain from "eating" them. The show of anger, they said, "frightens the ghosts." The man also received some seashells, salt, and a net bag and grass skirt in a *towmow habuwk bay* transaction for his services. It included the women's goods because the *saybel* rite is intended equally to ensure their well-being and their children's, too.

The majestically decorated men paraded in a large circle around the grass clearing, chanting and performing a stomping dance, holding bow and arrows upright in one hand and a ceremonial stone axe in the other. The two decorated adolescents wearing long mourning skirts preceded the phalanx of dancers, waving rattles and bow and arrows to keep the crowds back and clear

A twirling girl dancer leads a phalanx of decorated men in a *tomp* dance.

a path. One man present had dressed as a woman in a grass skirt with a net bag hanging down his back. He was signaling his grief at the death of his sister, which occurred during a fight with her husband, and his intention to take revenge. The dancers paraded around until early afternoon when the rain came and broke the dance up, men hurriedly removing feather headdresses for fear of damage to the valuable plumes. It was just as well the dance ended; men needed to remove their decorations and make the final preparations for the next day's pig-kill festival, the transactional climax of the *saybel* sequence. They had been preparing for the event for many weeks, collecting stones for the large earth oven, erecting poles to display the sides of pork, and collecting bundles of banana leaves and tree fern fronds.

A man wears a woman's skirt during a dance, with his face painted in the female style.

Early the following morning some men gathered at the site of the long-neck house, each *sem* represented with a pig. They slaughtered and butchered the animals, calling on the *towmow* to partake of the spilled blood and the smell of singeing bristles. They put the internal organs, neck joint, and belly pork to cook in the *mashoraenda* oven. The sides of pork they took to cook in a large earth oven in the *muwnaenda* that housed the prehistoric *hungnaip haen*. Before putting the pork to cook, they placed a small cut in the oven hole and again spat on it while chewing a piper leaf, incinerating it for the spirits to enjoy, calling on them to come and do so. It was a large version of the sickness offering, except it featured the following spell:

Kongon	*Ebera*	*kabonow.*	*Puga*	*Siybim*	*Kabonow.*
Place name	Place name	both.	Place name	Place name	both.

Poriya	*Momiya*	*kabonow.*	*Saeborton*	*kombow*	*maem*
Place name	Place name	both.	Rain cape		take

powa	*tomb*	*na*	*aenda*	*taiyo.*	*O. O. O.*
[I] went	when	my	house	burnt down.	O. O. O.

The spell relates how, while wandering in the forest and collecting pandan leaves at the places named to make a rain cape, their house burned down—a reference to the previous destruction of the long-neck house. Their intention is to "trick" the *towmow* into thinking that they were not responsible for destroying the spirit house, but it happened when they were away in the forest. While the meat was cooking, some men curated the *hungnaip haen*, rubbing them over with *wombok*, charcoal mixture, and red ocher. Only men consumed the meat that was shared at the site of the *saybel* long-neck house.

Others killed and butchered pigs on the nearby grass clearing where they slaughtered most of the animals for the festival. It followed the same format as other pig-kill festivals—pork cooked in long communal earth ovens after being displayed on horizontal poles. Those dealing with the spirits at the long-neck house site moved back and forth during the day, everyone congregating on the clearing for the large distribution of pork when they opened the ovens. This was the climax of the event; men's reputations were on the line, the ambitious seeking to bolster their renown by their generosity. They put on a big show.

Ongol excelled in the number of large pigs he slaughtered, thanks to Mindiy's management of the herd, which swelled alarmingly in size just before the event. Everyone was impressed with what she had accomplished with the large pig herd, but not surprised, for after all she was a woman known to suckle the runt of a litter at her own breast to ensure that it grew into a healthy animal. Following the pork distribution, people returned home and the *saybel* cycle ended. Its aim of promoting prosperity was to surpass their wildest imaginings, as they were about to become wealthier than they could have thought possible. It was also to bring new and unheard of problems in its wake.

Chapter 10

Encounters with New Cults

*O*ngol was busy pushing in cane poles for beans to climb when he heard the yodel. He was almost at the same place as last time. The tree that he was pollarding before had fallen over and he had reduced it to firewood. Whereas previously, the message had made little sense, now he knew what was meant by the news that a column of ghosts had been seen again. It was approaching from the Kutubu direction. Ongol was unsure which path it was on but decided to take no chances. He called to his two wives working in the garden and the children playing nearby to follow him, and they went and hid in a thick brake of cane grass.

This was the pattern of early encounters with the newcomers. The Wola sought to avoid them, scurrying off into the surrounding bush to hide when they heard that a patrol was coming, and watching it from a distance hidden from view. Men were particularly anxious to get women and children out of the way and where possible, pigs, because the newcomers were known to use their fearsome "digging sticks" to spit "small arrows" into animals. "When we heard a loud bang we said that someone's pig had been killed and taken for meat." Bold men would sometimes approach a patrol out of curiosity, particularly when it set up camp, for word spread that the pale-skinned newcomers paid handsomely for food with seashells.

The actions of these returned newcomers were deeply puzzling, as demonstrated by their stealing and eating pigs while paying exorbitantly for tubers. After a patrol had passed through and people returned to their houses, they sometimes discovered that the intruders had entered and taken things such as bird-of-paradise plumes. They often found bow staves and arrows broken or put on the fire to burn. "To tell us not to fight, eh?" opinion had it later. Sometimes they found that the intruders had defecated in fireplaces, an indication of the contempt in which they held these bush people. Other times the newcomers would seek to talk to people, particularly when they camped, when the pale-skinned ones would address any assembled onlookers.

They spoke to them through an Ak valley man who had disappeared with the "ghosts" when they had come and gone many years before. His relatives were astonished and delighted to see him return. They had assumed that he had died, and they had long ago arranged a funeral and a mortuary exchange in his name, mourning over a few of his personal possessions. While away, he had learned to communicate with the newcomers and so served as an interpreter, but given the odd things that he was telling them about what the newcomers said, people doubted that he really understood what they were saying, although anything was possible with these "ghosts." One of their strange announcements, for example, was that people were to dig holes as deep as a man and that they were to defecate in them and not in the surrounding bush as was their custom. Who could possibly want people to collect their feces in a hole? It was not only a crazy suggestion but a disgusting one too.

All manner of astonishing stories started to circulate about the pale-skinned newcomers, such as how they made no gardens but secured their food from various containers, notably tin cans, which originated from no one knew where. When the newcomers discarded empty cans, the Wola picked them up, as they found them useful. The colorful labels made good decoration too, for instance pinned on wigs. The Was valley population soon realized that the returned newcomers were not spirits at all but humans. "They eat and pee like us," people observed, and to top it all, some of them sought to satisfy their sexual appetites by preying on women, offering tantalizing gifts in return for favors. Rumor had it that they had appropriated some land on the edge of Lake Kutubu and built strange houses there, suggesting that they planned to stay longer this time. Other than the occasional patrol into the Was, Nembi, and Ak valleys, which people could avoid, the Europeans had little impact on everyday existence. Life went on much as before, which was just as well, people having various activities and events to attend to, notably the arrival of a new cult from the southeast moving up the Nembi valley.

* * * * * * * * * * * * * *

The stress of his son's death and the landslide disaster took its toll on Ongol's health. He suffered from stomach upsets, diarrhea, and bad headaches. One evening they decided to make an offering at the *bomboraenda*, a leafy bower of saplings and cane grass behind the men's house where the *towmow* sometimes reside. They are said to be "weak" when there and cause minor illnesses. The relative officiating placed a piece of banana leaf in front of him on the floor of the men's house foyer with two fern tree fronds side by side on it. Someone fetched two handfuls of moss that he put under the ferns, and he sprinkled some red ocher on these, which he took from his string bag. Next, he took a cassowary quill that he had through his pierced nose and cut it in two; he hollowed out one half and put the other half back through his septum.

When he had completed these preparations, the man went outside into the darkness and recited a short spell in a singsong voice. On his return, he took some nettles that he had placed outside on the roof and, leaning over the short front wall of the house foyer, hit Ongol while shouting at him. Ongol, who had been lying down by the fire, writhed about clutching himself. The healer then took the small pig brought along for the offering and, holding the animal firmly under one arm, pushed another cassowary quill into a nostril, the two pangi seed cases hanging from the proximal end rattling together as he rammed it up and down with rapid repeated jerks. Ongol's *haemay*, Hond, helped, hitting the pig on the snout with an axe. They held the struggling creature over the banana and fern leaves and allowed blood to flow freely on to them,

Smoke streams from *bombortaenda* as fire is kindled inside for offering.

while Hond delivered more axe blows on its snout to kill it.

The healer took the pig and rushed outside again for several minutes and they could hear his low whistles, here and there. When he returned, he held the pig's snout on the sick man's chest, and on others present, too. He repeated this with the bloody fern, banana leaf, and moss bundle, pushing it with deliberation against their chests in turn. Next, he reached for a small bamboo internode container from the wall behind him and, taking the hollowed cassowary quill stuck in his hair, proceeded to suck from it. He went outside into the darkness again sucking and whistling, and when he returned put the hollow quill on Ongol's chest and sucked his flesh up the tube. Someone held a leaf onto which the healer spat out saliva, which he and others inspected closely. He repeated this half a dozen times on different parts of the Ongol's chest. They did not find anything in the spittle, which was a good sign. When the quill slipped, the man exclaimed that the ghost had departed. He did the same perfunctorily on the chests of the others there that night.

Some of them singed the pig's bristles, the barely alive animal writhing feebly. Then they butchered it. They wrapped the liver in some leaves and cooked it in the ashes of the fire to eat as a snack while the pork cooked in an earth oven dug in the men's house foyer. They passed the animal's head to the healer who took it outside to the *bomboraenda* bower with a pile of faggots.

A *wesaembow aend* "skull house."

The healer kindled a fire inside the bower and offered the singeing smell of the remaining bristles and a small piece of meat to lurking *towmow*, whistling to attract their attention. The others sat quietly, resuming their chatter when he returned after 10 minutes or so. He took the pig's head as payment for his services and Ongol cut two cowries from his necklace and gave them to him, too.

Ongol kept the pig's innards and strip of belly pork to use the next morning in an offering at the "skull house" adjacent to his men's house yard. This is another place where the residing *towmow* are thought to be less strong and to cause the sort of sickness from which he was suffering. It was an act of insurance, covering all bases so to speak. But it failed.

* * * * * * * * * * * * * *

A fortnight later, Ongol was still unwell. He was worried that it was the start of a fatal *komay*-induced illness, but he refused to feel helpless. After some deliberation, he decided that he needed to take some further, stronger action. He would offer a pig at another location frequented by *towmow*: a flooded earth oven pit in the waterlogged cane grass below his house. The pit featured a small, fist-sized tunnel excavated on the downhill side. It was during a dry spell that Ongol visited the hole and he added water using a bamboo container before making his offering there. There was an old club standing in the ground in the hole with some pig tethers wound around it. After clubbing the pig, and catching the blood on a bed of banana and tree fern leaves, he thrust its snout into the pit of water. The water turned bloody red and displaced, flooded out through the tunnel, spreading across the ground below. Ongol called gently to the ghosts in the vicinity to come and "eat, eat" of the bloody water.

He took the tether off the animal's front trotter and wound it around the club with the others. The sight of all these "pleased the ghosts," reminding them of the offerings made there for them. He would thrust it stake-like into the pit when he was finished. For good measure, Ongol carried the pig to his house and thrust its snout into the ashes of the foyer fireplace, to placate any ghosts lurking there too, calling on them to come and share in the offering. After singeing off the pig's bristles, calling again on the ghosts to come and "eat the smell," he proceeded to butcher the animal and arranged to cook the meat with hot stones in the oven pit, lining it with banana leaves, covering what remained of the bloody water in the bottom. When he removed the cooked pork to carve and share with relatives, they blocked off the hole in the side of the pit with a wide flat stone, damming it so that it would again fill with water and be ready for the next offering there. A week or so later, Ongol started to feel much better.

* * * * * * * * * * * * * *

The *timp* ritual also arrived at this time. It was a new ritual. Men from several *semonda* in a locality would agree to sponsor it, four of them agreeing to become spell owners. Ongol was keen to act in this role, one that would afford him a further opportunity to demonstrate his prowess in managing wealth, for those wishing to stage the cult had to give valuables to their neighbors, who had hosted it and knew the procedure and spells, in exchange for the ritual knowledge. These transactions occurred in installments stretched out over several months as the new hosts prepared to take on the cult; various men contributed to the payments, handing over seashells, *wombok*, and bundles of salt—but not pigs, which they needed for the cult.

The participants joined forces to build the *timp* cult house. This had a characteristic sloping ridge, from being some six meters high at the front gable to two meters at the rear, with sidewalls of *pel* stakes similar to a standard house. It was roofed with a mixture of kunai grass thatch and bark sheets. The high front end had two entrances, one on either side of the pole supporting the central ridge. Internally the house was divided in two, a small room at the rear low end, entered by a small crawl-through doorway, and a large room, entered by the two doors in the high front wall. In the small room, they dug a circular earth-oven hole and constructed a slat-top table. And down the center of the large room they excavated a long earth-oven pit.

Some of those taking part made the *timp* "cover-up," a large circular plate-like object of entwined rattan with a hole in the center. They did this secretly inside the cult house, so that others, particularly women and children, could not see what they were doing. Some of those sponsoring the ritual painted a design on the entwined disc in white and orange clay and charcoal comprising a black cross on a white background and concentric black and orange circles. During *timp* events, they suspended the disc from the high gable end of the cult house, on the outside in full view of everyone. When questioned, no one could explain the meaning of the disc, saying that it "came with the *timp*, so we do it."

When they had completed the house, the sponsors slaughtered some pigs to inaugurate the *timp* cult. Those who contributed animals were inducted into the cult. There was much excitement on this first day as the spellholders studiously undertook their allotted tasks. One of them had overseen the previous days' preparations for killing the pigs, which largely involved readying the ovens. When splitting the firewood to heat the stones over the cult house pit, he muttered the following spell:

Yaeliyp	tegiy.	Hot	tegiy.	Mo	tegiy.	Kwin	tegiy.
Cuscus	stock.	Tree	stock.	Tree	stock.	Forest plant	stock.

Kaylayp	tegiy.	Hoten	non.	Kupom.	Puwai	buwawo.	Puwai	buwawo.
Tree	stock.	Tree	there.	Sap.	Chop	does.	Chop	does.

No one could explain the meaning of the spell, which refers to various trees and chopping up wood, because "it came from somewhere else where they did the *timp* before us." Its use elsewhere ensured its efficacy in their eyes.

Ongol was responsible for overseeing the pig slaughter. During the house construction he had supervised the digging of a two-meter-deep hole, out of view in the adjacent cane grass, in the center of which he had driven in a *pel* stake and over which he had arranged a roof of casuarina and cinnamon tree[1] bark. All pigs killed in the *timp* would be clubbed over this hole and their blood would drip into it. Occasionally he would pour some *wombok* in the hole, too. This was for the *towmow* to "eat." Both blood and *wombok* are "soft food," which make the "ghosts'" mouths soft, so that they cannot "bite" their victims and cause sickness and death. They heard that in some places men killed pigs over *hungnaip haen* arranged outside the cult house so that the spilled blood fell on them, but they did not do this in the Was valley. Ongol had learned the following spell from the person from whom he purchased it in the neighboring community, to mutter as they slaughtered pigs over the hole:

Hulom	kolkol.	Hulom	kolkol.	Pokolom	kolkol.	Paebiya	hulom
Bones	bare.	Bones	bare.	Thigh bone	bare.	Sternum	bone

kolkol.	Iy	hulom	kolkol.	Wesaembow	hulom	kolkol	Mesow
bare.	Coccyx	bone	bare.	Skull	bone	bare.	Mid-spine

Hulom	kolkol.	Paebiya	hulom	kolkol.	Mesow	hulom	kolkol.
bone	bare.	Sternum	bone	bare.	Mid-spine	bone	bare.

Iy	hulom	kolkol.	Porol	hulom	kolkol.
Coccyx	bone	bare.	Rib	bone	bare.

He was not sure what the spell meant, as it originated elsewhere, from the Poroma direction. It refers to the bones of pigs offered, which played an important part throughout the cult cycle. It alludes to the subsequent parcelling up of the bones, which mimics the immobilizing of "ancestral ghosts" so they cannot attack people. Ongol made sure that the hole was covered with its roof of bark when not in use. Only he, and the man who "carried" the spell said when singeing bristles off offered pigs, should carry the slaughtered animals into the *timp* house.

Singeing the bristles off a pig (notice the *tok* pole for pork display in background).

They were also responsible for lighting the fire inside the *timp* house to singe the bristles and heat the stones for the earth oven. Ongol could recall the tension that he felt holding the friction firelighter on a bed of dry tinder as his partner sawed a length of split cane back and forth to ignite an ember. They had prepared to light the fire with unusual care because if they failed at the first attempt this would indicate the *towmow* were not satisfied with the offering so far and they would have to find another pig to slaughter. They need not have worried, they soon had a roaring fire going over which men singed the pigs' bristles, and as they did so the spellholder recited the following, all the men present joining in the *kiya* [he says] chorus at the end of each phrase:

> *Wesaembow   hulom   kiya.   Shongo   hulom   kiya.   Habuw   hulom   kiya.*
> Skull   bone   say.   Jaw   bone   say.   Tooth   bone   say.
>
> *Hogol   hulom   kiya.   Pokoltor   hulom   kiya.   Wesaembow   hulom   kiya.*
> Sternum   bone   say.   Thigh   bone   say.   Skull   bone   say.
>
> *Porol   hulom   kiya.   Paebiya   hulom   kiya.   Wesaembow   hulom   kiya.*
> Rib   bone   say.   Sternum   bone   say.   Skull   bone   say.
>
> *Shongo   hulom   kiya.   Ero   hulom   Kiya.   Mesow   hulom   kiya.*
> Jaw   bone   say.   Coccyx   bone   say.   Mid-spine   bone   say.
>
> *Kiya - a*
> Say - ay.

The spell's symbolism is the same as the previous one. While those participating in the rite (those who had contributed pigs) butchered the animals on beds of banana leaves in the large room of the cult house, the spell "carriers" entered the rear room to prepare the small earth oven there. They took the stomach, intestines, and strips of fat trimmed from the edge of the pork belly and put these to cook in the circular oven. These are traditionally the parts of the animal claimed by women to distribute and consume, prompting this special treatment in *timp* kills. It relates to the exclusion of women from the cult.

When the contents of the small oven were cooked, the spellholders cut these up, and all those participating took turns approaching the rear outside door of the small room to receive a share. They did not take it into the large room but ate it outside. Some of the men staged a small stomping dance around the house, wearing their second-best finery of cassowary feather pompoms and cockatoo feather headdresses, white clay designs painted on charcoal blackened faces, and carrying bow and arrows, which they rattled as they chanted. It was done with some exuberance in celebration of the initiation of the *timp* cult.

Others sat around talking and smoking while the contents of the main oven cooked. They subsequently emptied the oven and cut the meat up for distribution. Unlike other pig-kill festivals, only those inducted into the cult could share it. This included both those from the sponsoring community who had contributed pigs to the kill and those who had participated previously in the *timp* elsewhere, such as those who had passed on the spells and procedure to the hosts. These restrictions prevented women and children from eating the pork. Furthermore, they should never see inside the cult house or know

Putting pork and hot stones into an earth oven.

what men did there. During offerings, they should remain in their houses with the doors closed. The secrecy surrounding the cult also extended to men who had not been initiated into it, notably those from places that had not purchased and performed the cult.

After eating the pork, the spellholders arranged for everyone to collect all the bones, which they took to the small rear room. They placed them on a large, tough, leather-like *goiz* palm[2] spathe and tied them up in a bundle. While they did so, one of them recited a version of the above spell, listing various bones. They kept the bundle on the slat table. The parceling up of the bones, they said, mimicked tying up the bones of deceased kin, immobilizing their *towmow* so that they were unable to attack, being "too weak to do so."

* * * * * * * * * * * * * * *

Once a community has initiated the *timp* sequence, it continues for many months, men periodically killing pigs. All those living in the area aim to contribute at least one pig on occasion and be inducted into the cult, while more successful men such as Ongol contribute several beasts during the cult's lifetime. Besides these periodic collective pig offerings, when persons fell sick while their community was hosting the cult, the stinging nettle divination might indicate that the *towmow* responsible was residing in the *timp* house, calling for relatives to offer a pig there to fight off the attack and aid recovery.

All pig offerings, both those undertaken as part of the cult and those for sick persons, follow the same routine as at the cult's opening—animals clubbed over the hole, guts and fat cooked in the small-room oven, and bones added to the parcel. Nevertheless, after the excitement of the cult opening, men started to lose interest and increasingly undertook tasks in a perfunctory way, treating the slaughter and distribution of pork as any other pig kill, having more interest in the transactional side than the ritual one. Unless, that is, someone was particularly sick, in which event relatives might engage earnestly in the ritual, anxious not to do anything wrong and jeopardize their sick relative's recovery by annoying the spirits.

Eventually communities tired of the *timp* and its demands, and they ended it. The participants arranged a two-day event to mark the cult's close. It required considerable preparation, featuring a two-day feast of wild game and pork. Not only did participants have to collect firewood and bundles of leaves for the ovens, but they also had to clear their transactional obligations so they could take animals out of circulation at the pig-kill festival. The weeks before saw a burst of frenetic exchange activity as men sought to settle their accounts. Ongol found it particularly stressful, as he was keen to bolster his successful transactional reputation but found it difficult to manage his affairs as effectively as previously. Men become increasingly reluctant to enter into long-term investment transactions with older individuals, fearing that they could lose out if the older person should die in the interval. In addition, Ongol's domestic problems were, if anything, greater, as Mindiy now focused her efforts on her sons, living with her eldest son's wife in her women's house.

The first day of the *timp* finale involved the cooking and distribution of wild animal meat, mainly marsupial. Before the event, men spent much time hunting in the forest, as they did previously for the *saybel* rite. On the agreed day, they met on the clearing before the cult house with the game they had caught and prepared a large earth oven. While the meat was cooking, the man who had learned the necessary closing spell led all those present in chanting it, calling out each phrase with everyone repeating it after him:

Winj	*kobow*	*koba*	*biya.*	*Kolem*	*kobow*	*koba*	*biya.*	*Engelai*
Place	cuscus	cuscus	do [catch].	Place	cuscus	cuscus	do.	Place

kobow	*koba*	*biya.*	*Kolem*	*kob*	*izi*	*pum*
cuscus	cuscus	do.	Mountain	cuscus	son	heart & lungs

kombowa	*amum*	*kombowa.*	*Engelai*	*kob*	*izi*
cut carcass across	heart & lungs	cut carcass across.	Place	cuscus	son

pum	*kombowa*	*amum*	*kombowa.*
heart & lungs	cut carcass across	heart & lungs	cut carcass across.

Kolem	*kobow*	*koba*	*biya.*	*Winj*	*kobow*	*koba*	*biya.*	*Engelai*
Mountain	cuscus	cuscus	do.	Place	cuscus	cuscus	do.	Place

kobow	*koba*	*biya.*	*Tit*	*kobow*	*koba*	*biya.*	*Kolem*	*kob*
cuscus	cuscus	do.	Mountain	cuscus	cuscus	do.	Mountain	cuscus

izi	*pum*	*kombowa*	*amum*	*kombowa*
son	heart & lungs	cut carcass across	heart & lungs	cut carcass across.

Bort	*paipow*	*aendonow.*	*Gonkliypow*	*aendonow.*	*Po*	*paipow*
There	fence	inside.	Shrub	inside.	Beech	fence

aendonow.	*Tuluwo.*	*Kagluwo.*
inside.	First club blow.	Subsequent club blow.

The spell alludes to the participants' efforts to catch animals to please the *towmow*, who have enjoyed the spilled blood and singeing fur aroma. It names the distant forest places to which hunters travel to catch game such as mountain cuscus. The *pel* fence, with red-berried *gonkliyp* shrubs planted to fill the gaps between pales, suggests to participants an impenetrable barrier, like the kind erected for defending homesteads. The fence also refers to the secrets of the *timp* remaining hidden from noninductees. The spell closes by referring to the next day's pig-kill festival. It also mentions the unusual way animals are butchered in this *timp* event by cutting them transversely in half, separating the head and front legs from the hindquarters. There was much socializing while people waited for the meat to cook, sitting around the clearing outside the cult house.

The second day featured a pig-kill festival on the clearing in front of the *timp* house. It followed the pattern of any pig kill. Men clubbed animals at dawn, doing so over the pit, collecting the blood for the ghosts to enjoy for the last time. They displayed the sides of butchered pork on a horizontal pole behind the earth oven on the clearing. Ongol and his fellow spellholders had nothing to do with it. Relatives and friends slaughtered and butchered their animals; Ongol's sons dealt with his pigs. They were busy donning their best finery of enameled bird-of-paradise headdresses mounted on fine wigs, faces painted colorfully, and torsos smeared with gleaming *wombok*. When decorated, they remained hidden from view in a nearby house yard, smoking and chatting, until the pork was in the oven. Then they burst forth, chanting and performing a stomp dance around the clearing, holding bow and arrows in one hand and a fine-stone dance axe or a rattle in the other. The dance was the *timp ankway tuway*—throw away the *timp*. In some places the dancers showed themselves off standing on a platform erected on the clearing accompanied by two nervous adolescent girls with distinctive body decoration, the right half of their bodies, legs, and arms painted red and the left blue, but they did not do this in the Was valley. After a while, the dancers went to the small room at the rear of the cult house.

While the spellholders were busy putting on their best finery, another two men were dressing like women in mourning, putting on ankle-length grass skirts and voluminous Job's tears seed necklaces, and smearing their bodies with white clay. They were in the small rear room of the *timp* house where they had securely tied up the amassed pig bones in the *goiz* spathe parcel, and slung this on a pole like a corpse. Later, the decorated spellholders would emerge with the "corpse" and carry it off into the surrounding cane grass accompanied by the two "female" mourners. In some regions, such as Mendi, two additional persons accompanied them wearing white clay-daubed "helmet masks" of coiled vine, but this was unheard of in the Was

Fully decorated men brandishing bows and arrows and rattles parade past the front of a *timp* house.

valley. Some way off, they stopped and dug a "grave" in soft, boggy ground where they buried the bundle of pig bones. They said that this fooled spectators who were uninitiated into the *timp*, particularly women and children attending the pig kill and dance. It maintained the cult's aura of secrecy, such that the next confederation up the valley willingly paid to secure the *timp* mysteries. In addition, by interring the bones they further weakened the *towmow* associated with the offerings, by "burying them so that they could not attack people."

When the burial party returned, the men opened the earth ovens and distributed the meat as at any pig-kill festival. They shared the pork with women and children, too, as they had done with the game the previous day. While the atmosphere was exciting, it was not tense. The initial scary atmosphere had diminished over time, such that the cult finished more like a secular event than a sacred one, some men even dismissing the need for spells. Some even remarked later that it was a good trick to have played on women, saying that only men could eat some of the meat. Finally, in some places, men burned the *timp* house down to mark the cult's end, but in the Was valley they left it to collapse, helped along by men taking some of the wall stakes to use in garden fences.

Before the two-day finale men had started to transfer the cult to the next confederation of *sem* up the Was valley, in exchange for valuables including seashells, axes, and salt bundles. Those who had invested in the cult thus regained their stake, although there was some argument over who should receive which valuables, but that was expectable. It was said that men felt obliged to buy into the cult and promote community well-being by keeping their ancestors' spirits content, otherwise they would be angry and attack their kin. The spirits appreciated their share of spilled blood, the *wombok* libations, and the smell of singeing bristles and fur. The cult also helped the living to incapacitate the ghosts that came to share in these things and served to stop them from "eating" their relatives, causing illness and death. However, like other rites it did not prove particularly effective at preventing the ghosts from attacking their kin, as measured by persons falling ill and dying. This presumably made people receptive to the next cult to come along, on the principle that one day they might come upon a successful formula to protect themselves.

The *timp* was not an aberration. New cults had periodically entered and traveled along the Was valley for as long as anyone could recall. Wola speakers have a history of enthusiastically adopting new cults and subsequently dropping them, as if searching for more effective ways to control their malicious ancestors' spirits and protect themselves from their attacks, only to find them wanting and turning later to something new. They were not peculiar in this behavior, which is reported for large areas of the New Guinea Highlands where cults come and go in fashion, moving around the region. The next cult was about to arrive in the Was region, the largest of them all, like nothing they had experienced before.

* * * * * * * * * * * * * * *

The new cult belonged to the pale-skinned newcomers. It was called Christianity. The readiness of people to adopt new practices and their experience of doing so over generations predisposed them to take up the pale-skinneds' faith when it arrived. They were intellectually prepared to adopt an entirely new religion. The astonishing speed with which they converted to Christianity testifies to their readiness to try something new. Missionaries in the New Guinea Highlands found it easy to convert people to Christianity, at least nominally, compared to their contemporaries elsewhere in the world. While they attributed this to the "will of the Lord" and their evangelizing zeal and abilities, it is evident that the local cultural and historical tradition contributed significantly, too. The population of the entire Was valley and the neighboring Nembi and Ak valleys converted in less than one decade, apparently overturning their previous belief system and associated rituals.

The association of the Christian message with the all-powerful newcomers, particularly their awesome technology, contributed further to its adoption. They were not only irresistible politically but also spiritually. After all, how could people with such remarkable technological capabilities be wrong? They had to have the correct message, the answer to everything. One aspect of this new technology that seemed truly magical in its effects when it became available was Western medicine. The mid-American evangelical church that marked out the Was valley as part of its "parish,"—missions so dividing up tracts of the Highlands—devoted considerable resources to dispensing medical assistance and running clinics, such that people associated their beliefs with this work, which seemed to them supernatural in its effects.

Compared to their attempts previously to fight illness—offering pigs to placate attacking ghostly spirits—Western medicine appeared truly miraculous in its success. Ongol was astonished when he staggered to a patrol clinic with a sore on his thigh, weeping pus, to find it healing within hours of receiving an injection of penicillin in his buttock. "The 'pale-skin' stuck this odd-looking fine 'arrow point' in, it hurt, but that was all and now look at me," he told his kin, walking without the stick that he had been hobbling about on for weeks past. He had a similar experience some time later when he was suffering from severe stomach ache and diarrhea and he received a drug to drink. "I thought that it was *mogtomb* when I smelled it, but I drank it all the same and the next day I was much better," he told everyone. Many others had similar experiences.

While the arrival of another cult may not have been novel, the new Christian one was shockingly radical in its aims. It did not seek to appease *towmow* with some new take on the traditional pig offering approach but proposed instead to banish the spirits from people's lives entirely. This had the appeal of not only promising to rid the region of a major cause of illness and death but also "saving" their pigs, which was attractive, as they resented having to kill animals in times of sickness, depriving them of wealth to use in transactions. The missionaries underscored their intent to drive the ghosts away by going into communities and breaking up *hungnaip haen* and skull houses with hammers. They saw it as a way of convincing locals to convert, by destroying the paraphernalia associated with their "pagan beliefs." When asked how he would respond to persons of another faith demolishing his church in mid-America, a missionary responded that there was no parallel to his mind, as he and his colleagues were converting people to the truth and saving their souls.

The driving away of the ghosts not only appealed to people but also frightened them, particularly the destruction of places they frequented and associated ritual paraphernalia. While it showed that the strangers had the nerve and power to defy the ghosts, it struck fear into people who were terrified of some awful retribution by their *towmow.* When Ongol heard about missionaries destroying *hungnaip haen* further down the Was valley, he was worried and talked of resisting them if they came to do likewise in his settlement, but his sons pointed out that those who defied the powerful pale-skinned newcomers ended up in a bad way. In desperation, he decided to hide some of his family's more valuable stones in a rock crevice. He and his kin subsequently sold these to the anthropologist for safekeeping in the "big school away from our place," and they were deposited in the National Museum of Papua New Guinea.

While missionaries attributed their evangelical success to the power of the Lord's word and their proselytizing zeal, the message fell on fertile ground, to use Biblical phraseology, where it readily took root. The new cult house was the *lotu* [church] in Pidgin. Every settlement built one, a large and airy thatched structure with walls of woven split cane, after the new coastal way of constructing buildings. It became a focus of social gatherings before and after services, particularly among women who regularly met there to talk. A self-selected mission-boy emerged in each community and acted as

Some prehistoric ritual stones hidden in a rock crevice.

caretaker. He went weekly to the mission, when established in the Nembi valley, to receive the message, which he relayed back to the community, at a service in the *lotu*. The mission-boy from Tombem was an amiable but weak character who had taken up the opportunity to bolster his social standing. It was an attractive role, as the missionaries gave their "boys" European shirts and shorts to wear, and on the weekly overnight stay at the mission, they received generous helpings of delicious foreign food, notably boiled rice and oily tinned fish that became a favorite meal in the region.

The mission-boys came back with new stories to tell people, new chants to sing, and powerful new spells called prayers. The missionaries seemed to have an inexhaustible supply of these. The Wola came to understand that the marks on the thin rectangular "leaves" that the missionaries carried in a large bundle communicated the stories, songs, and spells that these pale-skinned *sem* had come to tell them, and the Wola learned to call the bundle the Bible and treat it with great reverence. The missionaries subsequently invested much time and energy in teaching children to make sense of the marks. The stories were about an all-powerful God-person and his son, who were mysteriously the same being and sometimes appeared as an almighty ghost. These ideas were entirely alien to them, as their traditional beliefs did not feature any concept of a god or gods, albeit the idea of the Holy Ghost had some parallel with ancestral ghosts. The stories were fascinating and beyond anything they had imagined previously, including God's son being cruelly killed and coming back to life, the creation of a woman from a man's rib bone, and a flood covering the land and drowning everyone.

In addition to the powerful new medicine, people asked the mission-boy to say "prayer spells" over the sick, as instructed by the missionaries. These new spells, like the stories, were mysterious indeed, which added greatly to their power in people's minds—beyond anything previously chanted in the neighboring Huli tongue, however arcane. The incomprehension was inevitable as they derived from the ancient history and religious ideas of Hebrew tribes in the Middle East translated into a New Guinea Highlands language and categories (via already distorted translations into ancient Greek, Latin, and Old English). It was, to mix cultural images, Chinese whispers with a vengeance. The opening translation of Psalm 23 reads as strangely as any spell in this book, and it is difficult to know what the Wola made of it, as it is not easy for a contemporary English speaker to comprehend:

> *"You the best, look out for me as man stands. I nothing worry about, nor will I search.*
> "The Lord is my shepherd; I shall not want.

> *He tells me to sit in sort of black earth, he tells me to sit lightly.*
> He maketh me to lie down in green pastures.

> *He will lead me to truly good cold water.*
> He leadeth me beside the still waters.

> *My light mind shares do I give it stands."*
> He restoreth my soul."

The New Testament comes off no better, as the following extract from the Sermon on the Mount shows (Matthew 5:13–14):

> *"Like this he spoke, salt causes food to be good, so you [two] women and men stand as salt. If that salt has no taste, is bad, what can you [all] do to make it taste again? If that salt is bad, throw it away, as all women and men do with rubbish, step on it.*
> "Ye are the salt of the earth: but if the salt have lost his savor, wherewith shall it be salted? It is thenceforth good for nothing, but to be cast out, and to be trodden under foot by men.
>
> *All you women and men are like a torch of dry cane grass stems. Somewhere a homestead stands built on a summit, that house they cannot hide."*
> Ye are the light of the world. A city that is on a hill cannot be hid."

It is hard to say what people thought about being likened to torches of dry cane grass, such as they use when out on dark nights, or reflecting on the Lord telling someone to sit on black earth, which brings to mind someone kneeling to till the soil for sweet potato. While the metaphors and poetry of the Bible may have been largely lost on them, or were subject to their own idiosyncratic interpretations, people identified some elements that they could relate to their own beliefs. One was the serpent that tempted Eve to give Adam the fruit of the tree of knowledge. They could see in the missionaries' reviling of the wicked creature their own fear of snakes as manifestations of ghosts. Another aspect of the evangelical message that appealed to them was its millennial tone. The story of Noah and the flood and Revelations' message that the "end of the world is nigh" chimed in with concerns about disaster that feature in Wola folklore, such as accounts of devastating ash falls from volcanic eruptions, and the experience of occasional awful famines.

The new Christian cult had further disconcerting aspects. The missionaries told people that their *wezow* [souls] would no longer become *towmow*, following the banishment of ghosts. They learned that this was an erroneous belief of what happens at death. According to the newcomers' religion, they would either go to heaven, some wonderful place above, and live with God and his angels, or to hell, some terrifying place below, and be burnt in awful fires. It all depended on their behavior in life. They evidently had much to fear still, if not *towmow* then judgement day and hell's fires, and these new and frightening ideas gave missionaries surprising power, people believing almost everything they were told. They heard that the way to ensure a skyward passage was to believe in Jesus and convert to Christianity, and it is perhaps no wonder that large numbers came forward to do so, albeit they differed somewhat from missionaries in their creed, having evolved a unique syncretic view of Christianity informed by traditional beliefs.

After attending a series of classes reminiscent of those that precede initiation rites at which elders divulge ritual secrets in some New Guinea cultures, the missionaries marked peoples' formal entry into their Christian cult with a spectacular public rite, which they called a baptism. It was one of the exotic new ceremonies introduced by the missionaries. It involved dramatic full-body immersion, not the tame marking of a cross on the forehead with holy water. A missionary dressed dazzlingly in all white stood waist deep in a pool of water and, after uttering an incantation about "washing away their sins," dunked converts under the water. It was a frightening experience for people who could not swim. Those being baptized wore white shirts or blouses, given to them by the mission. Large crowds attended these affairs at which there was much singing, chanting, and praying together with the recital of further mysterious gory stories about someone called John whose head was chopped off and put on a plate.

While the power of the pale-skinned newcomers impressed Ongol, he did not formally convert to Christianity and submit to baptism, but he sometimes sat in the *lotu* with his relatives and listened to the puzzling stories. He was too much of a "white beard"—set in his ways—to engage enthusiastically with these strange new ideas. Nevertheless, he would subsequently adopt yet another new name, when it became the fashion to have a Biblical moniker, particularly in mission contexts. There were many exotic names to choose from and he opted for Abraham, while his brothers chose Isaac, Solomon, and Job. Again, this mirrored previous custom and added further to the confusion experienced by people unfamiliar with communities, where individuals reply to several names. It brings to mind those participating in rituals who adopted names that featured as titles, such as Kem and Moray, although to be transported back to the Old Testament in this way in the New Guinea Highlands was strangely incongruous to us.

Chapter 11

New Exchanges in a Changing World

*W*hile it may be possible to get people outwardly to change their beliefs, they are likely to continue holding certain old values in their hearts. The missionaries did a good job of suppressing local supernatural activities, but they scarcely affected the all-important exchange world of the Was valley. This was evident in the arrival of a new exchange cycle called the *sa* from the valleys to the east, where it had been present for 40 or more years according to photographs of its characteristic longhouses taken on early patrols in the Mendi valley. The *sa* cycle had all the appearances of a cult stripped of supernatural associations, leaving behind what was a key feature of earlier cults such as the *saybel* and *timp*, namely an exchange festival featuring dances and pig kills.

The *sa* cycle started like the earlier cults with the building of a special house, the *sa aenda*, comprising two longhouses built in the style of ordinary dwellings, facing each other across a *howma*. Men in the host *sem* sponsoring the *sa* agreed to build a section of the house comprising a room. Ongol joined with his *iyziy* and *haemay*, Hond, in seeing to the construction of their part of the house. They did not build it themselves but, following *sa* custom, contracted other relatives to do so. It took some weeks to amass the construction materials including *pel* stakes and sheets of pandan bark for walls, poles for ridge and rafters, and grass for thatch.

When the house was complete, the sponsors arranged a "hitting the *sa* ground" exchange to recompense the builders for their efforts. The payment included pearl shells, pork sides, and cash introduced by the pale-skinned newcomers. Ongol was not keen on the stuff they called money, which could purchase the manufactured things arriving from the outside world, and looked like unimpressive small pieces of colored paper, but others were including it in transactions and he had to move with the times. All of those

A *sa* longhouse.

sponsoring the house construction displayed their wealth together on the grass clearing before handing over payment to the house builders. Some of the younger men donned their second-best finery, faces painted and various bird feathers in their hair, and staged a celebratory dance around the clearing.

Two of Ongol's sons moved into the house with their wives and children for a month or so. He spent a couple of nights there, but the house was "green" and chilly and he was not comfortable. He left it to the younger members of his family, for whom it was an exciting diversion, particularly when anticipating the next stage of the cycle some months later. The next stage involved building the *pokaenda* house at the head of the clearing between the two longhouses. This resembled a carport in size and appearance, comprising four tree trunks sunk in the ground at each corner, supporting the eaves of a bark shingle roof. The ends were open and the sides roughly enclosed with a screen of cane grass stems.

The subsequent stage featured the "see the eaves thatch trimmed" dance, a metaphoric reference to the completion of the house, not a literal trimming of the eaves. Some of the guests attending stayed in the longhouses, and several young people engaged in *turmaen* there with the arrival of others from elsewhere. The sponsors again wore their second-best finery, while relatives associated with neighborhoods that had already hosted the "thatch trimming" dance donned full decoration including bird-of-paradise plume headdresses. They paraded through the *pokaenda* as they arrived and during the subsequent *tomp* dance around the clearing, chanting and stamping their feet, chopping at the tree trunk supports. This initiated the *sa* cycle for all to see. The next stage was some way off.

A *pokaenda* "house."

* * * * * * * * * * * * * * *

The pale-skinned newcomers evidently belonged to two *sem* that appeared to have little to do with one another, called in Pidgin (Papua New Guinea's lingua franca) either *kiap* [government officer] or *misin* [missionary]. The *kiap* represented the outside world's political incursion into the Highlanders' lives, the *misin* the supernatural one. It was the *kiap* "family" that imposed the colonial order on the tribal Wola valleys. After their reappearance at Kutubu, the government officers arranged for the clearance of land to accommodate a large airstrip at a place in the Mendi valley and established an administrative post there, which was subsequently to become the major town of the Southern Highlands Province. These developments had relatively little impact on the Was valley for a decade or so, other than the occasional government patrol passing through and issuing largely unenforceable directions, particularly that the people should stop armed hostilities.

It all changed when the administration decided to establish a patrol post at Nipa in the neighboring Nembi valley. The *kiap* soon established colonial government control over the region and not long afterward, the missionaries started to arrive. The patrol post was a place of fascination for people, who visited there in large numbers to look at what the pale-skinned strangers were doing. Although Ongol maintained that nothing would surprise him about these newcomers, after the "shock of seeing the metal bird land on Lake Kutubu," he was nonetheless impressed with what he saw. The Europeans brought in masses of exotic goods by airplane.

They constructed houses such as no one had seen before from all manner of foreign materials with roofs apparently made of the same hard shiny stuff as the new axes, only in enormous wavy sheets. The doors were large enough to walk, not crawl, through and were shut not by wooden slats but by slabs larger than shields that could swing and shut themselves. Moreover, at intervals around the walls they had smaller openings, somewhat like crawl-through doorways, only higher up, which looked as if open to the elements but when you tried to look inside you banged your nose on something hard and invisible. The Europeans filled their houses with all manner of strange paraphernalia that comprised things they sat on, cooked with, ate off, and slept on. It even included a small box that actually spoke and sang.

When the first vehicle arrived at the post, it predictably caused something of a sensation. It is hard to imagine the thoughts of people who, until then, had no reason to have invented the wheel. A cart would have been extraordinary, but a motor vehicle that went along under its own power was astonishing, and so large and powerful, carrying several persons or large amounts of cargo, more than 10 men could manage. It was about this time that people started to explain the arrival of the newcomers by referring to a myth about two brothers who used to live in their mountains, one black- and the other pale-skinned. The black-skinned brother was lazy and greedy, while the pale-skinned one was hard working and temperate. They lived together until one day the pale-skinned brother, tired of the other's selfish behavior, left him forever. The newcomers were clearly his descendants come back, as was evident from their industry and achievements with vehicles, airplanes, tinned food, manufactured goods, cotton clothing, and so on.

People visited the patrol post not only to marvel at the constructions and property of the pale-skinned newcomers but also to assist in the work. They

The government office at Nipa station.

heard that the Europeans made unimaginable payments of shell wealth, notably cowries and pearl shells, in return for help, and men flocked to give a hand. Initially the *kiap* needed considerable help to level the land for the airstrip, supplying interesting new tools to do the work, such as a highly effective digging stick with a wide blade, made of the same metallic material as the new axes. The large numbers of men that came from the Ak, Was, and Nembi valleys moved vast amounts of earth using only spades and picks. Some of the work was easy, it was "wealth for nothing," such as the marching up and down in military-like squads stamping their feet to firm up the surface of the airstrip, necessary to ensure that the wheels of landing planes did not sink in and tip them over. The arrival of the first plane was an unforgettable occasion, people scattering in fear at its approach, and for years afterward a small crowd would gather whenever an aircraft came in to land.

While men were pleased to receive what was to them such generous shell wealth remuneration, and the authorities were happy to disburse it, as it meant the cost of labor was consequently minimal, the increase in supply led to problems. The difficulties started before the colonial authorities arrived in their valleys. The impact of shell wealth inflation was a Highlands-wide phenomenon. The volume entering the region was enormous, particularly via the Central Highlands from the time of first contact onward, when Europeans realized how much the local population valued shells and what men would do to earn them. This wealth spread out across the Highlands through exchange and trade, reaching the Was valley before the colonial authorities imposed their control. It led to rampant inflation in the size of exchanges.

While previously a *injiykab* might feature two or three pearl shells, the bride's relatives now demanded a dozen or more. Everyone locally had equal opportunity to earn shell wealth, either for labor or food sold to patrols, and so nobody was any better off relative to anyone else. Ongol, like others, became increasingly perplexed at the increasing size of transactions, which inflated in size beyond their wildest previous dreams of avarice. He found himself increasingly in dispute, as people demanded evermore shells in exchange transactions. He was engaged in a series of *haypuw* transactions to relatives for their assistance in the previous armed hostilities and saw their demands increasing wildly and disconcertingly. Transactions were becoming unmanageable. It was inevitable that devaluation would occur, not of highly valued shells, but other things such as bird plumes, local salt, and black palm bows, no longer acceptable in exchanges, driven out by shell inflation. In a few years, pearl shells and pigs, together with cash, subsequently came to dominate in all transactions. It was a dramatic change from a local perspective.

The generous times were not to last for long. The arrival of the vehicle at the post signaled the start of a corvée system of labor to construct and maintain four-wheel-drive tracks. The authorities required all able-bodied men and unmarried women to work on tracks for one day a week; they called it "Monday work." Many initially thought that it was a good idea and would bring European-style development to the region, but they soon became disillu-

Some men sit chatting outside the *lotu* church as they wait for the service to start.

sioned when this did not arrive. The authorities also required each settlement to build and maintain a large thatched house for the use of visiting patrols. There was no remuneration, but those who decided to boycott the work were arrested if a *kiap* patrol officer made a spot check and were sentenced to a spell in the jail, where they were required to work scything grass on the patrol station all day.

The forced labor was an aspect of the new colonial regime, which extended inordinate and unheard of power over people's lives to a few young Australian officers. They forbade any fighting with weapons, which many thought a good thing, and they intervened in serious disputes, imposing their law and punishment on those they judged to be in the wrong, which often involved a jail term. The colonial authorities also started to demand annual taxes from all adults, which local people greatly resented; failure to pay also brought a jail sentence. Fortunately for Ongol, he was judged too old to conscript or tax. The authority wielded by the few *kiap* was unknown in their Was valley's stateless, egalitarian society, and it was perplexing, even capricious sometimes, although it accorded with the many other puzzling changes occurring with the outside world's arrival. While some of these changes were unwelcome, overall most people approved of the coming of patrol officers and missionaries.

* * * * * * * * * * * * * *

The boat episode confirmed, indeed epitomized these perplexing impressions in the Was valley. It started with one of Ongol's young nephews returning excitedly from Boiya to say that there were many men carrying a strange object shaped rather like a house roof down the valley toward them. At their head was Master Laus (Mr. Rouse[1]) the missionary from Lake Kutubu, a small, wiry figure, reminiscent of a mushroom under his wide brimmed Australian bush hat. They said that the thing was the Europeans' equivalent of a dugout canoe, such as the Foi people use to travel on the lake, only much larger. Why anyone should be carrying a "canoe" through their mountains was a mystery. They learned the answer the following afternoon when amid much excited hollering and strained grunting the boat arrived at Tombem, where the party carrying it deposited it upside-down on the *howma*. It was not an enormous hollowed out tree trunk, as Ongol and his kin had expected, but rather a clinker-built rowing boat. Up-ended on the grass it looked, someone said, like the gigantic elytra of a chafer beetle[2] and they called it the "water beetle."

After a smoke and eating some baked sweet potato tubers offered to them by the Tombem residents, the party of carriers departed back up the valley to spend the night with relatives. They had apparently done their bit in transporting the boat that far and it was up to those living at Tombem to carry it further on its journey, which they learned with incredulity was to Lake Kutubu. The dinghy, constructed by a boat builder in Queensland, was beyond the cargo capacity of light Cessna aircraft that could land at the small lakeside airstrip. Thus, the valiant missionary had decided to transport it there by flying it to Mendi, the nearest airstrip capable of handling the freight airplane. From there, he planned to transport it by four-wheel truck to the Nembi valley, and from there on the "backs of natives." When the men from Boiya told the Tombem residents that Master Laus was paying each a large pearl shell for his efforts, they were keen to enroll as carriers. If they had been aware of the labor involved, they may not have been so eager.

The next morning nearly all the able-bodied men from the Tombem area and several women, too, set off for the lake with Master Laus striding along in front, shouting out largely incomprehensible directions. The solidly built boat was much heavier than they had anticipated, and it took several men along the gunwales on either side to carry it. In addition, there were two enormous paddles with wide spatula-shaped ends that someone had to carry. As they started to climb the watershed of the Was valley, they realized what they had let themselves in for, and even Master Laus started to have his doubts about the doability of the remaining leg of the journey through the forest. At the steeply sloping ridge summit, they resorted to lashing lengths of rattan vine to the bow and hauling the boat up, some heaving pulley-like around the trunks of a pair of large trees while others pushed at the stern. They had to resort to this tactic on several of the mountain slopes they negotiated on the path to Kutubu. They reversed the procedure when descending steep inclines, tying the rattan vine ropes to the transom and lowering the boat bow first, which was easy work compared to hauling it up. On the first occasion adjacent to Mount Pega, they almost lost control and Master Laus fretted about the damage to the keel, but there was nothing for it. He told men to cut and put branches on rocky sections of the path to protect it. Otherwise, it glided easily on the slippery clay of the forest path.

The next challenge was crossing the raging Was River, just up from Ngoltimaenda where there was a vine suspension bridge. It was clear that they could not carry the boat across the river on the flimsy bridge. They would have to float it over. The prospect did not please Master Laus who could see his craft dashed to pieces on the rocks, but he had no other ideas. They decided to undertake the crossing a short distance downstream where the river widened for a stretch and was not so turbulent. They lashed rattan vines to the bow and stern. Some men took the bowlines across the river via the bridge. By pulling on the bow while others held the stern line taut to stop the boat from swinging downstream into the rapids, they hauled the "water beetle" across the river. They almost lost it in midstream where the strong current swept it sideways but the men on the far bank saved it by anchoring their line around a large tree and pulling like fury. They used the same tactic at the other rivers they had to cross, including the Ak, Muwsez, Haegaip and Mubi.

They stayed that night on the other side of the Was River in some relatives' houses. Other nights they camped under hurriedly erected lean-to shelters of leafy branches, lighting blazing fires to keep warm. Master Laus slept under the up-turned boat, supported on one side by a couple of forked sticks under the gunwales so that he could crawl in and out. Someone carried his bedding, change of clothes, and tinned food rations in a backpack. The boat arrangement was like a deadfall trap, Ongol's nephew commented, not realizing his prescience. One morning as they sat roasting sweet potato tubers, the morning's mist rising around them, the men became aware of muffled banging and shouting. They realized that it came from the direction of the boat, situated a little way off to give Master Laus his required privacy. Some of them went over and found the red-faced missionary trapped under the heavy boat, which had slowly pushed the forked sticks into the soft ground during the night. They tried not to laugh as they lifted it up to let him out because they knew that Europeans stood on their dignity and could be humorless. However, they could not contain themselves when the angry little man crawled out and scurried off into the nearby underbrush. "He was busting for a pee," they told everyone, "that was why he was so ratty," for he was "shamed at the episode."

It was evident by the time they reached the Muwsez River that the journey was going to take considerably longer than they had anticipated, with women and some men having to return to the Was valley to harvest and bring further food for everyone. In addition to carrying and hauling the boat across the mountainous terrain, they often had to cut down vegetation to widen the path, which further slowed down progress. They had bruised and sore shoulders and barked shins from stumbles with the heavy boat. While grumbling about the folly of the enterprise, they arrived at a consensus that Master Laus was not paying them enough for their troubles. With the timing typical of Highlanders, who instinctively know the best time to strike a deal, that is when the other party is most vulnerable, they put the boat down on a remote forested ridge between the Muwsez and Haegaip Rivers and announced that they were not going on without another pearl shell each for their efforts. The missionary realized that he was in a corner and conceded more easily than they expected to their demand. They pulled the same stunt a second time as they approached the Mubi River, and after some harder bargaining secured a handsome promise of three pearl shells each.

The terrain toward the lake was relatively level and they made better progress there, finally arriving—aching and tired—at a small navigable creek that flowed into the lake. They happily put the "water beetle" on the water, where they saw the purpose of the two cumbersome paddles. After rummaging in his backpack and producing a pair of oarlocks that he slotted into holes in both gunwales, Master Laus dropped a paddle into either and proceeded to row off down the creek toward the lake. The Tombem party followed, arriving at the mission station by the lakeshore to see Master Laus proudly showing his wife the boat and telling her how much easier it would be from now on to travel around the lakeside longhouse settlements.

Later, the weary men queued up excitedly, their eyes almost watering at the sight of the large crate of pearl shells from which the missionary paid them three shells each as agreed previously. It was well into the afternoon. He told them that they could sleep in the meeting hall at the mission station. Before going inside to sleep, they sat around a large fire eating, smoking, and talking until late, for truth to tell they were frightened to sleep in a location so close to the Foi cannibals, with their fearsome sorcery reputation. The anxiety was contagious, especially after someone became convinced that he heard strange sounds in the dark, which they attributed to a sorcery force seeking its victim. When they finally went into the mission hall, they could not settle, and finally one man decided to climb up into the roof space to avoid any sorcery force. "It will not be aimed up here," he reasoned. Soon the others joined him, and they spent an uncomfortable night cramped together in the clammy and stuffy space, dozing fitfully.

In the morning, two strange sounds startled them. The first was a loud clanging that brought them tumbling down out of the roof space. Although they had heard talk of it summoning people to *lotu*, it was the first time that they had heard a bell ring. They inspected the large brass object with interest, tapping it to make it ring. The other sound came later from the lake. An extraordinarily loud buzzing brought everyone running to the shore, the Foi too. There they saw Master Laus traveling at amazing speed in his new "canoe," leaving a trail of white-foam-flecked waves in its wake. He had attached a high-powered outboard motor to the stern, which had, fortunately for the Tombem carriers, fit into the Cessna's small cargo hold. The sound would disturb the peace and serenity of the lake for years to come as the missionary went about his evangelizing business—only to be trumped some years later by the industrial clatter that would accompany the sinking of an oil well adjacent to the lake.

The Tombem crowd, not wishing to spend another scary night among the Foi, left later that morning for their Highland valley home. A couple of them, Ongol's sharp nephew included, took the opportunity to trade for *wombok* before departing, although no one was keen to offer to help carry the long bamboo tubes back, shoulders aching after the arduous trip to the lake. The journey of the boat would go down in local legend; the embellished story might even become an incredible myth. The authors certainly had some trouble making sense of it when related to them only a year or so later.

* * * * * * * * * * * * * *

Our arrival upset the straightforward dual classification of Europeans into government or mission, prompting some confusion. People initially associated us with the government "family" as we arrived with a *kiap* and armed police patrol, which made them suspicious of our intentions and reluctant to have us live in their community. During a vociferous argument with the patrol interpreter, some young men showed their displeasure in an aggressive bow-and-arrows-waving display of defiance, to which the *kiap* put an abrupt stop by ordering two police officers to discharge their .303 rifles into a nearby earth bank. The government had established its clear military superiority in earlier skirmishes; one man had as a reminder of a previous incident a badly deformed left hand due to a bullet wound. We subsequently learned that they feared we were there to annex their land, as Europeans had elsewhere, for a patrol station (such as locally at Nipa) or a plantation (seen by migrant laborers, such as one of Ongol's sons, elsewhere in Papua New Guinea). We inadvertently exacerbated these worries by starting to survey gardens soon after our arrival, as part of our study of the Was valley economy.

We thought it best to withdraw and find somewhere else after this apparently disastrous approach, but the *kiap* insisted that we stay a night or two camping in the patrol house and see what might be arranged with further discussion. In his opinion, we could expect the same suspicious unwelcoming reception wherever we went in the district. A series of, to us unintelligible, negotiations took place over the next couple of days in Pidgin and Wola, involving the patrol officer, the interpreter, and some men. We saw no women, children, or older men at this time. When not bystanders, we went on short exploratory walks in the vicinity, accompanied by some young men, visiting nearby men's houses and communal grass clearings and a vine suspension bridge. Finally, the *kiap* told us that the men had agreed that we could take up residence in the patrol house, which was to be refurbished as it was in a rather dilapidated state. What had apparently swayed opinion in our favor was the agreement that we should pay for the renovation and extension of the house, and the prospect that we would pay for further services when living there.

When we returned as agreed a few days later, we were disappointed to see that scarcely any work had been done on the house, a coastal style thatched structure of woven split cane walls over a wooden frame. We

Weaving split cane walls for the anthropologists' house.

decided to camp in the adjacent small house used by police officers on patrols, to assist in the work to be done on the renovation of our house, and to start collecting some basic information on the community. Several weeks of cramped living followed, without which we doubt the refurbishment of the house would have been completed. Finally, we moved into what reminded us of a gigantic newly woven basket such as we had on the front of our bicycles in Cambridge, topped with a worryingly insubstantial looking grass roof (no imaginary concern as it turned out, as we spent many a night sleeping under a large plastic sheet during heavy rainstorms). The confusion that had marked our arrival continued to characterize our relations with the local population. When those working on the house realized that we both intended to sleep in the same room, they urged the building of another one, or better still a separate house, following their residential arrangements. Ignorant of men's concerns about female pollution, we brushed the suggestion aside—house building had taken up quite enough time already.

Relations between women and men remained a source of puzzlement between us for some time. We shudder to think how ill-mannered and insensitive we must have appeared. The lengths to which individuals went, for instance, not to step over one another's persons or possessions were incomprehensible and almost comical to us. They would screw themselves up into an uncomfortable ball to stop us from stepping over their legs and snatch away any belongings such as net bags that were in our path. On one occasion, one of us was tripped up and sent spread-eagled into the laps of others by someone attempting to stop us from stepping over him, to the amusement of

The anthropologists' house at Honael.

all present. We soon learned that it was the height of rudeness to step over someone or his or her possessions. To do so is insulting, although it was some time before we understood why. The implications regarding men's fears of pollution only dawned slowly on us, as did so much else. Looking back, people were surprisingly tolerant of our abysmal ignorance and poor behavior.

The issue of what pale-skinned "family" we belonged to exercised people's minds for some time. They gradually formulated a new category for us but they found it hard to understand what we were doing. It took a while to convince them that we were not government, with patrol officers generously helping us with logistics. The missionaries helped us too, even though we did not share their beliefs, and told them and local people so. It became evident that we got on equally with both of these European "families" but were not part of either. When we gave the standard anthropological reply to queries about our purpose—namely that we wished to learn about and document their culture to inform others elsewhere about it, to further the goal of mutual understanding—it hardly cleared the fog. This explanation met at first with complete incomprehension. Some could not believe that powerful Europeans should be interested in their way of life. Others could not see what there was to understand, as their ways were so obvious to them, there was nothing to tell. They were disinterested rather than reticent about discussing their lives. It seemed improbable that we could not comprehend what was going on around us.

The extraordinary ignorance that we showed, and the naiveté of our questions, served eventually to convince them that we really had no idea how they conducted their lives. Our persistence over many months eventually persuaded them, incredible as it seemed to many, that we genuinely wanted to learn about their ways. Nonetheless, individuals rarely volunteered explanations, only our constant child-like querying brought forth information; even today it is the same after decades working in the Was valley, although now they have reason to assume that we must understand their lives. The consensus that finally emerged was that we were from the "big school" family, the label we used to describe a university. The majority came to accept us, if not with enthusiasm then tolerance. We are grateful to them for allowing us to pry uninvited into their lives and for their forbearance as we sought to make sense of their sociocultural world, asking sometimes insensitive, stupid, and even impertinent questions.

While those living in the Was valley may have found it hard to believe that we could be interested in their lives, they were very interested to learn about ours. They were first-rate anthropologists. We were the first opportunity they had to see Europeans close-up, and our house and activities became the focus of considerable local interest. People would wander around the two-room dwelling inspecting everything closely, and it is testimony to their honesty that we lost nothing more than a couple of tins of fish. There was much "oohing" and "aahing" over things, and many questions. The Coleman pressure lamp was an object of particular interest and there were disputes over whose turn it was to light it, when they had mastered the procedure. On one occasion, Hond sat for a long time looking intently at our small transistor radio; when we asked what he was doing, his relatives told us that he was watching to catch a glimpse of the little people he assumed were inside making the noise that he heard.

The confusions continued, each side puzzled by the behavior of the other. We were slow learners. We should have welcomed our mutual misunderstandings, for anthropologists are taught to expect and use them to further understanding of new cultural worlds, such differences opening up unexpected avenues of inquiry. Nevertheless, it was not easy living in a state of ongoing perplexity. Something that we found difficult to adjust to was the constant demands from individuals that we give them things. Among the first words we recognized in the Wola language was *njiy* [give (me)], which one hears constantly. It seemed that, since they had agreed that we could live on their land, they expected us to share all that we had with them. They had their eyes particularly on our sacks of rice and cartons of tinned fish. We explained that we depended on this food as we had no gardens, but it made little difference. Individuals also regularly turned up with empty cans asking for kerosene. We failed for a long time to see their demands for what they were: a key to their social life. Instead, we allowed them to annoy us. These demands derived from their social experience, where giving and receiving feature prominently. They were treating us the same as they treat one another; why should we have expected anything else?

The Was inhabitants were unwittingly inviting us to enter their exchange world, and our reluctance presumably baffled them. They probably could not understand why we did not wish to participate with our wealth. By demanding things from us, they were offering us the opportunity to show generosity and so earn social esteem in their eyes, as open-handedness is the way to social renown. When we gave individuals things, their behavior confused us even further. We expected some show of gratitude but instead they just took what was on offer, sometimes with what seemed to us a scowl on their faces, and on occasion to our consternation, they would refuse to accept what we offered and demand more or something else. Again, they were treating us no differently than they did each other. We came to observe the same behavior whenever they received things from each other, notably when they engaged in formal wealth exchange transactions, when hard negotiations were usual and heated arguments possible. A related issue is the absence of any word equivalent to "thank you" in their language. When persons are given something, they invariably take it without a word. After some years, we grasped that to say "thank you" would be to acknowledge a superior position to the giver and one's indebtedness, contradicting the egalitarian nature of sociopolitical relations.

We were clearly far wealthier than those living in the Was valley, coming from the European *sem* that was exerting unheard-of power over their lives, so why should they show us any gratitude? Their culture's equality ethic led them to expect us to share our wealth with them. Why should we have so much more? The value that people living in the region put on equality was to turn into the focus of much of our work. The valley's stateless political-economic arrangements fascinated us when we became aware of them, contrasting so strongly with our class-structured society's condemnation of some to drudgery and poverty while others enjoy privilege and wealth. The contrast between the local egalitarian order and the invading hierarchical colonial one was stark. In the Was valley all enjoy the same standard of living and no one has the authority to direct and coerce others' behavior, whereas the invading order extended inordinate power over people's lives to a handful of colonial officers, able to demand resources and even deprive persons of their freedom.

Chapter 12

The Stateless Order

$\mathcal{H}$ow is the Was valley population able to ensure equal relations between all and prevent some from gaining power over others and grabbing more for themselves? It was while inquiring into this, or more particularly how they contrive to ensure social order in such a stateless political context when individuals wrong one another, that Ongol told us the Kot saga one day. Initially, for some months after our unannounced arrival in the Was valley, Ongol kept his distance, like other older men and women, unable to comprehend what we were up to. When word spread that we gave visitors twist tobacco and newspaper (to roll novel cigarettes), salt to season food, and on occasion tinned fish and rice, he decided to pay us a call and see for himself. He was a mellow, elderly man when we knew him. He was a reluctant informant at first, as he could not understand what we were doing in his locality and what we might do with any knowledge he imparted to us. We slowly came to interact increasingly, until he became a daily visitor to our house and a valuable friend and source of information about life in the Highlands as related in this book.

The Kot saga came up when we were discussing what happens when close relatives come into serious dispute. We had previously talked about what goes on when persons in different localities wrong one another and what occurs when the disputants are distantly related residents in the same locality. And we had established the centrality of the principle of revenge. We wandered, hypothetically I thought, onto the question of how relatives might deal with someone who was a psychopath and would not behave properly toward them and others no matter what pressures were brought to bear on him or her, it being inappropriate for close kin to take revenge on one another. The Wola however are not happy talking in the abstract. The response to a generally worded question asking what would happen if someone did such-and-such invariably meets with the query, "Who did that and where?"

It was perhaps inevitable, therefore, that we should get onto Kot's story. It was a sign that we had won Ongol's confidence that he broached the issue at all, a painful and difficult one for him. He recounted how he regretted burdening his descendants with a series of *haypuw* obligations that he was unable to meet during his lifetime. During the discussion, he related in detail the various reparation and reimbursement transactions resulting from the armed conflicts, and how he was currently preparing with his brothers and sons to make another reimbursement exchange. These were of great concern to him, one of many indications of the centrality of such sociopolitical exchanges in people's lives. The discussion furthered our understanding of the *ol komb, showmay enjay, haypuw,* and *ol bay* interrelated series of reparation and reimbursement exchanges, which until then we had only observed as separate events.

We were gradually beginning to see the interconnections between the various transactions of wealth that featured so prominently in Wola life. It was part of the understanding that was gradually formulating itself in our minds as to the workings of the stateless political-economic regime. We have touched on it a number of times in this book. It is, in summary, as follows.

The value put on individual political autonomy poses challenges for social order for the dense, sedentary, stateless population of the Was valley. It is easier to understand how those living within the same neighborhood manage, because they are related to one another (inevitably with kinship governing land tenure). Kin are less likely to quarrel seriously. They observe shared conventions that they are brought up to value, founded on an unspoken recognition that it is in all their interests, living close to one another, to regulate their behavior to make possible the cooperation that benefits all. Nevertheless, even kin have disputes sometimes. Sanctions to discourage them include the withdrawal of kin support from wrongdoers, such that they forfeit the benefits of sociability that their behavior challenges.

Individuals also avoid openly infringing the expectations of their kin with regard to observing the customs of self-regulation because if they behave otherwise, they will damage their reputations. The social arrangements exploit in a covert way their desire for status and respect, which shared cultural values guide, to reaffirm order without openly detracting from their personal political, albeit socially circumscribed, autonomy. When a dispute occurs, others present act as an informal jury by expressing their opinions. The subsequent actions of disputants, knowing the majority view, will influence their reputations. If the majority view suggests the accused is in the wrong, then that person should concede to the plaintiff or lose respect; this process occurs without anyone forcing compliance and infringing personal sovereignty. Settlement often features compensation that goes beyond indemnification of a wrong; as an act of exchange (which defines sociability for the reciprocally motivated Wola), it marks the continuation of amicable relations disrupted by the dispute.

People acknowledge an obligation to observe the expectations of self-regulation toward kin and friends living elsewhere with whom they have ongoing relations. They may behave with less consideration toward others, although the intertwined relations between the residents of neighborhoods reduce the likelihood of blatantly unsocial acts. If a dispute occurs between such distantly related or unrelated persons, they are more likely to resort to force than to discussion to settle their disagreement. While the threat of aggression is an aspect of all political relations, in both stateless and state-based societies, frequent acts of personal violence are usual in many acephalous polities, particularly those of large tribal populations such as those in the New Guinea Highlands, which are among some of the most belligerent. The downside of the value these people put on equality is that physical aggression is a common feature of life. When they disagree and become frustrated, they are likely to come to blows, as readiness to do so is necessary to defend yourself from others dictating to you against your will. In pushing these informal arrangements to their limits, Kot's behavior starkly revealed their contours.

If a fight breaks out and a fatality occurs, the result is open armed hostilities. The kin of anyone killed violently have a moral duty, as we have seen, to seek revenge on those responsible and on their relatives. To appreciate the logic of conflicts we have to understand why this injunction exists, that is why individuals acknowledge an unquestioning duty to wreak vengeance, not why they observe it, either out of grief, fear of losing face, or sanctions from others. Disputes occur when individuals intrude on one another's space more than is accepted as necessary to everyday life. They should try to settle their differences without encroaching on each other's freedom of action and equal rights more than is necessary to reach a fair resolution. If they cannot agree on the rights and wrongs of the issue, they may lose their tempers, and, frustrated, resort to violence in an attempt to force their view on the other party against its wishes. In essence, violence seeks to deprive persons of their freedom to hold different positions on an issue.

If there was no danger of revenge, those involved in disputes might try to force the other party to agree with their views routinely. Social life beyond a small circle of kin would be unimaginable if people could wrong and kill with impunity those toward whom they recognized no obligation to regulate their behavior. Furthermore, this initially anarchic state of affairs would give those who are physically stronger access to power, which would presage the end of the egalitarian order that rests on the axiom that no persons have the means to subject others to their will and rob them of their right to equal political freedom of action. The moral obligation to seek revenge prevents this by mobilizing a group against anyone who attempts to force a kinsman to act against his wishes, killing him as he struggles to defend his sovereignty. The threat of armed conflict further acts to discourage people from turning readily to violence in dealing with distant kin and strangers, because those responsible for hostilities assume large responsibilities. They are answerable for all relatives who die fighting; they are accountable for the extensive series of reparation exchange transactions that follow, which are usually so onerous, as Ongol's experiences show, that a person's descendants remain liable for two or three generations.

The pursuit of hostilities, or any collective action (rituals, dances, wealth exchanges, pig festivals, etc.), presupposes people coordinating their actions.

There are no rules stipulating that individuals should support certain corporate groups (constituted by descent, residence, or whatever), an issue over which considerable debate has occurred in the New Guinea Highlands. Action-sets may correspond closely with neighborhoods, but this does not imply that they are political corporations. It results from residential proximity. People are more likely to join in an activity with those they reside among than with those living elsewhere. The "collectivities" are temporary gatherings of persons who think that it is in their personal interest to coordinate their actions to achieve certain ends. They may never come together again with exactly the same membership. Various considerations prompt persons to join, such as concern for their "name," a wish to involve themselves in and share the glory of an event, or the desire to take advantage of the benefits that come from several persons joining forces to do something. They do not act wholly selfishly, but as Melanesian individuals; they act according to cultural values that prompt them to consider kin interests, such that the concerns that lead them to participate or not will reflect to some extent their relatives' expectations.

Coalitions are not random alliances. Some have a predictable composition, such as for exchanges where people know who will be transacting what with respect to others. Kin interaction informs their composition. Neighborhoods, where related residents interact daily, act as nodes around which groups collect through connections spreading out from those living there. Such geographical locales are close-knit networks, beyond which residents maintain separate, albeit overlapping, networks of relations. Action-sets form through connections radiating out from those who propose an event. They can count on some relatives in their neighborhood, with whom they interact frequently, making up the core for the event, and possibly some of their relatives from elsewhere joining in and recruiting a few people from their networks. Individuals may potentially join activities initiated at several places where they maintain social relations, notably through acknowledged exchange obligations to some residents there.

In many societies, the organization of people into groups presumes some kind of leadership—but not in the Was valley. Here any collective act emerges from the interaction of all participants; no leaders facilitate it. They reach decisions and coordinate their actions by discussing them until the majority opinion emerges; the exception is when hostilities suddenly erupt, when sides emerge spontaneously according to actors' interpretations of their revenge obligations. Participants commonly arrive at an agreement over a period through discussions of the proposed event, maybe never all coming together to do so but engaging in smaller groups, between which some actors move. All have an equal right to voice their views in these discussions, trying to persuade others to act in ways that best suit their interests. Success depends largely on the benefits that their proposals offer to those they are trying to persuade.

Some men may have more influence than others and a better chance of swaying plans to their advantage, although they cannot force others to follow their wishes by virtue of the respect they enjoy. Those who excel in activities that all are socialized to value, earn respect and some influence. They are the *ol howma*, such as Ongol. While "grass-clearing man" status threatens equal relations, escalation into political power is averted; renowned status is achieved and not inherited; action-sets dispense with leadership, and so on. Individuals are motivated to act for self and kin, not any group they may misguidedly seek to lead. They achieve recognition and limited sway by excelling in activities pivotal to the finessing of the opposed interests of individual autonomy and social control. These focus on sociopolitical exchange, all agreeing that persons aspiring to respected *ol howma* standing have constantly to show that they are skillful managers of wealth. Finally, this brings us to exchange.

* * * * * * * * * * * * * * *

The above brief discussion of the informal stateless Wola polity indicates the centrality of exchange to the egalitarian order. Organized into a wide-ranging institution with social rules obliging involvement, Wola transactional arrangements extend on the exchange aspect of all human interaction to further cooperation in an otherwise fractious, dense population where considerable autonomy is granted to individuals. Give-and-take in sociopolitical transactions demands far-reaching collaboration. Exchange obligations sustain sociality, requiring persons to interact and cooperate on specified social occasions. An *injiykab* unites new affines, not only by acknowledging the establishment of fresh relations but also as the first transaction in a series that marks a marriage and furthers steady relations. The ramifying sequence of mortuary transactions focuses interest on and bolsters relations undermined by a death. Similarly, the reparation series that follows a violent fatality is not just compensation, it is a declaration by the party responsible that it was involuntary and does not wish the death to end the relationship with the deceased's kin.

While disagreements occur and poor payments can lead to arguments prejudicial to social order, the overall effect of obliging people to pass wealth around is its reaffirmation. The implications of formal exchange arrangements are evident in individuals' stance on informal debt transactions. They enter into these with any kin or friends who can help them when they need something urgently, often a valuable to meet an exchange obligation. If they think they can get away with it, persons may renege on such debts. They can try it, because they enter into such deals privately—they may, figuratively speaking, "whisper" requests (not wanting their embarrassment widely known)—unlike transactions in the formal exchange sphere, which are public and put significant pressure on them to meet their responsibilities or lose face. The withdrawal of people from relationships, often after disputes over failures to meet exchange obligations, further accounts for individuals endeavoring to meet their transactional commitments. To do otherwise will disrupt social interaction with those who judge them unreliable, and they may not have their support when needed.

The concern persons have for their social standing buttresses these interests; reputations depend on living up to the customary arrangements that ensure the constant circulation of wealth. Failure to meet exchange obligations not only causes trouble but also tarnishes social reputations; whereas those who excel in this transactional world "have names." This draws on the competitive aspect of exchange to encourage individuals' wholehearted participation. By definition, they have continually to pass valuables around to promote sociality; success is not measured by what they own but by what passes through their hands.

We see here how exchange resolves the apparent conflict that exists in this stateless context between collective and individual interests. It has two aspects, on the one hand it engenders sociability and supports communal relations, and on the other, it allows competition and appeals to individual concerns. Self-interest is a feature of human behavior and drives people to compete; in the Was valley this means giving more than the other person, and so attain social rewards such as renown and influence. By competing in this manner, individuals promote sociality, which is in the wider interests of the community. The balance achieved between individual and collective interests through exchange allows for a degree of personal political autonomy that is difficult for those living in politically run states to comprehend. The competitive side of exchange persuades people to meet their obligations without any need for authority figures to force them, trespassing on their apparent liberty to decide their own actions. This is a key issue in any egalitarian stateless order that seeks to extend the maximum political freedom to persons compatible with the continuance of orderly social relations.

The political order of the Was valley continues to feature exchange. The Europeans left the Southern Highlands almost as abruptly as they arrived, within a few years of the independence of Papua New Guinea. Many residents in the Was valley expressed regret at their departure, having adjusted to colonial rule and judging it preferable on balance to their previous ordered anarchy. They were still in awe of the outsiders' technology and heard that it would be available to them through "development," including education. They took the view that the colonial government saved them from their fractious selves. Subsequent events proved them correct, although it would probably have only been a matter of time, if experiences elsewhere are any guide, before they tired of the imposed colonial order dominating their lives in disagreeable ways. Local discontent with colonial rule, notably its intervention in dispute settlement, was evident early on and fueled later events. The Australian administration and subsequently the Papua New Guinea government subjected the Was population to law courts and prison for less than two decades before the nation-state collapsed across the region. Without strong central government, notably an effective police force, people saw the system as ineffective, if not subversive, and returned to their old ways of dealing with differences. The previous stateless order reasserted itself vigorously with the resurgence of so-called tribal fighting.

The Was valley is effectively independent of central government jurisdiction currently, but things have not returned to as they were for most of

Ongol's life. People are in contact with the world beyond their valleys and some travel elsewhere, although there is considerable danger of criminal assault by strangers, particularly in townships such as Mendi and Mount Hagen. Previously, it was unheard of for people to hold others up and rob them, but such criminal behavior is common today across the Highlands. Some people have access to firearms, which not only feature in armed hold-ups and shootings but also make armed hostilities more lethal when they break out locally. Ongol knew hardly anything of this new world, living securely in his own neighborhood.

* * * * * * * * * * * * * *

The *sa* exchange cycle illustrates the intriguing accommodation of opposed communal and individual interests. The next stage in the cycle was the *hiyl kombayay*—transversely butcher—meat distribution and accompanying dance. A two-day affair, it featured the killing of cassowaries as well as pigs. The men hosting the event sought to obtain birds, either in exchange or through trade. As the date approached, they became increasingly eager to do so, especially ambitious individuals seeking to enhance their social standing. Ongol possessed one jointly with two of his sons, which was received in a daughter's *injiykab*. They kept the bird in a small stake cage on the side of their house yard. In the weeks before the event, the hosts also had to complete the preparations necessary for any pig-kill festival, both the physical preparation of the communal clearing and the meeting of outstanding exchange. It was a hectic and stressful time.

Pigs on display tethered to stakes across the clearing before a *sa* festival kill (in the background, cassowary cages are in a line).

A few days before the event, those with birds built cages in a line down the center of the grass clearing. They would display their birds there. They also arranged to bring pigs to the clearing on an agreed day and tether them to rows of stakes in a "pig stake display" to announce the forthcoming *sa* event. Ongol took the opportunity to speak about the fine display of animals and invite people to attend the festival, although few heard him above the excited chatter, even speaking at the top of his voice. Some younger men also went to other neighborhoods, doing the "carrying the man tree leaf" to announce the coming dance, shouting "*tuw-uw-uw*" as they came along paths and rushed onto clearings to perform an exuberant circular bobbing and chanting dance. They urged those they met to participate in the coming dance, particularly if the young men had previously taken part in a *sa* dance at the others' place, as this creates an obligation to reciprocate. The more dancers taking part, the more memorable the event.

At dawn on the first day, men with cassowaries met on the clearing and slaughtered the birds by wringing their necks through the bars of their cages, before dragging them out and finishing them off, if necessary, with a club. They carried the dead birds into the surrounding dense cane grass and hid there before anyone else arrived. They donned second-best decoration, sporting a pompom of cassowary feathers and face designs in white clay painted on charcoal black foundations. They also prepared the birds for the coming dance by grooming their ruffled feathers and tying a short length of vine to one leg and around the neck to stop the head from swinging back and forth. They waited patiently for the other dancers to assemble on the clearing, wearing full decoration topped with bird-of-paradise headdresses, torsos glistening black with charcoal and cosmetic oil.

The majestically decorated dancers paraded, stomping around the clearing in troops of five men or more wide and, chanting at the top of their voices, sometimes passing through the *pokaenda* renovated for the event, swinging their axes at the tree trunk supports. A fully decorated adolescent girl danced, twisting around at the front. When the dance was in full swing, those hiding in the surrounding cane grass with the cassowaries burst forth in single file and joined the dancers, forming an outside row to their phalanx so that the spectators could see the birds they carried on their backs. Ongol's chest swelled to see his son carrying their cassowary in the dance. He was too old now to participate in such events and watched with the others. But he would not remain a spectator for long. The dancers carrying the heavy cassowaries could only manage a few circuits of the clearing before tiring and dropping out.

After they withdrew, men took the birds to their homesteads to prepare for cooking, leaving the other dancers to continue until it threatened to rain, when plume owners with headdresses hired out to dancers took their valuable feathers before they became damaged. The dance degenerated into a large circle of young women and men in second-best finery, whooping it up until the rain compelled them to take shelter. Meanwhile, at their homesteads, the cassowary owners plucked and butchered their birds and heated

Men dancing with cassowaries.

stones for earth ovens, with columns of smoke curling up into the sky across the neighborhood. Some collected bundles of the filamentous feathers, pulled out by the handful, to make pompom headdresses later. Ongol took charge of proceedings in his men's house yard, although most of the time was spent chatting and smoking with relatives. Many relatives were present, expecting a cut from the bird, and he and his sons deliberated for some time before distributing the meat. It was a successful occasion, and they retired that evening in good spirits with high expectations of the next day.

Again at dawn on the second day, men and women converged on the clearing, leading pigs by tethers tied to a front trotter. The pig kill followed the pattern of other festivals. You may have tired of reading about these accounts of pig killings, but you will be aware that they are central to Wola life, marking the high point of many events, rather like grand celebratory parties for us. The clearing filled with the sound of squealing pigs terrified at the smell of blood, followed by thick clouds of smoke and the odor of singeing bristles. While men butchered the majority in the standard way to give two sides of pork displayed over the poles around the edge of the clearing, a few they butchered in the transverse fashion. As a man of standing, Ongol determined to butcher one of his largest pigs in this way, which involved eviscerating the animal and cooking it whole. When he and his sons removed the carcass from the oven later in the afternoon, he cut it transversely in three parts with an axe, rendering the head and front legs, the rump and rear legs, and the middle of the torso. He presented these to groups of relatives with whom he had enjoyed close exchange relations over the years—who had assisted him with earlier reparation payments following armed conflicts.

Sides of pork displayed on a *tok* pole.

Many months elapsed before the next stage of the cycle, the *sa aend liy* [hitting the *sa* house]. It involved another large *tomp* dance in full bird-of-paradise decoration, men parading and chanting around the clearing where the tumbledown *sa* houses had stood previously. Again, young men toured other neighborhoods beforehand announcing the event and recruiting dancers. The "house hitting" refers to the behavior of visitors who roam around the host's neighborhood with a licence to damage property. They uproot and help themselves to crops, such as tobacco cultivated under the eaves of houses; they pull up fence stakes and make fires with the wood; they fell casuarina and pandan trees; and they have even been known to set fire to houses. Ongol and his sons kept a watchful eye on their homestead overlooking the clearing. There were some tense moments, such as when Hond found a youth helping himself to food from the small mixed vegetable garden adjacent to their house and then chasing him off shouting, "Do you want to taste this sweet potato?" waving his clenched tuber-like fist at him.

The destruction of property is a response to the taunting chants of the dancers praising their transactional successes and the grandeur of their *sa* event compared to the "rubbish" efforts of those elsewhere. If they are so successful, they will be able to sustain such damage, and have to stand by to prove it. The event's hosts prudently remove all valuables from their houses, storing them with relatives who live elsewhere, as the marauders may help themselves to anything they find, except for pigs, which they must not molest. Ongol realized that he had reached the "fallow period of life" when he thought how unimpressed he was by the event, unlike the *kem* and *saybel* all those years before. He was looking forward far more to the final stage of the *sa* cycle, another large pig festival. Unfortunately, however, he would not see the end of the exchange cycle.

Distributing joints of pork.

* * * * * * * * * * * * * * *

When we were about to leave the Was valley and return to Australia one time, Ongol told us that he felt unwell and thought that he was suffering from *saem tokay* [peeled heart] at seeing us go. In part, he was probably expressing regret at the prospect of the supply of twist tobacco and tinned fish stopping in addition to losing our company. The *saem* is the pericardium tissue surrounding the heart, which the Wola believe can peel away when a person is deeply sad, frustrated, or jealous, and can result in death. It was decided that we should arrange for a *holhae* procedure to ensure the strength of Ongol's heart and forestall any peeling of the *saem* tissue.

One afternoon someone who knew what to do killed one of our pigs. He removed its tongue and esophagus, together with the windpipe, with lungs and heart attached by connective tissue. He wrapped the bloody bundle in a parcel of *taziy* and *hongok* fronds. He took a handful of the blood-dripping leaves in one hand and the pig's organs parceled with leaves in the other and wiped these across Ongol's chest from under his armpits to his sternum while muttering a spell. After this, he had Ongol lie on the ground, facing upward. After dipping the bundle of organs in the pig's blood, he held it over Ongol so that blood dribbled on his chest. When he had finished, he put the pad of bloody leaves on the bark sheet baffle above the fire in the foyer of the men's house where it was left to dry out. The officiant received the tongue, esophagus, heart, and lungs, plus a generous cut of pork, for his services. Ongol and his relatives shared the remainder of the meat with us, which they cooked in an

Roasting tidbits of meat at a pig kill.

earth oven in the corner of the men's house yard. Ongol did not die of a "peeled heart."

If we are fortunate, we pass away as we enter the world, not aware of the event, dying peacefully while asleep one night. This was not Ongol's fate. His death was in keeping with the violent and tragic deaths of Kot, his *mboliy* [cousin] Kombaem, and Pes. It was the fault of his daft brother Hond. It was late one afternoon and Ongol sat in the foyer of their men's house scraping sweet potato tubers to put in the hot ashes to bake. Hond had gone to a nearby garden to collect some spinach leaves to cook, too. There was a dull thud of an explosion and the fireplace erupted, spraying hot embers and scalding oil onto Ongol's chest and stomach. His *weray* Wat and one of his *waenay* [daughters] heard his pained shriek and ran up to the house to find him swearing "*arrghh sezinda*" as he brushed the debris off his body. The girl, who was a quick thinker, grabbed a nearby gourd, thankfully full of drinking water, and poured it over his chest to wash off the burning material and relieve the pain. Ongol said something about the missionaries thinking that they had driven away their *towmow*, but these spirits were clearly still around, as he knew all along. "Look, the ones residing under the fireplace as snakes have attacked me in an unheard of way." He died holding this belief.

What had happened was that Hond had acquired a prized tin of mackerel and put it to heat in the ashes of the fire. He had gone to fetch spinach to eat with the fish, fully intending to share the treat with his brother. What he did not know was that you cannot treat a tin of fish like a sweet potato tuber, that is, after tearing off the label, just bury it in the embers. He was unaware that before heating it up you must first pierce it. Ongol spent an uncomfortable night, indeed several troubled days and nights, we heard. Unfortunately for him the wounds became infected and festered horribly, oozing pus, his skin peeling off to reveal red raw flesh. One of his sons walked to the medical aid post at Nipa station, a journey that Ongol was too weak to make, and came back with a tube of calamine based cream that they applied to his burns, which probably made matters worse as it caked hard over them. Ongol passed away some two nights later in an agonized delirium.

Ongol's family buried him in a grave on the edge of the *howma* where he had strutted many of his transactional triumphs. The administration and mission had forbidden raised coffins or exposed graves. His resting place is under the graceful casuarina trees just below the knoll on which stands the men's house where he spent much of his life. When we returned, we gathered a large bunch of wild flowers that we placed on his grave, propping the flowers up at the head against the low fence that surrounded it. It was, his kin thought, a nice exotic touch. More to the point, in their eyes—if, in turn, exotic in ours—we also made a late contribution to his *ol gwat* mortuary exchange. They were preparing for the final stage of the *sa* cycle when he passed away. They decided to combine the funeral pig kill and pork distribution with the cycle's final kill, after delaying it for a period to mark their mourning. It was a fitting occasion for someone of such *ol howma* status.

The final stage in the *sa* cycle is the *sa liy* [*sa* kill], a grand pig-kill festival. It followed the same pattern as other kills with some additional flourishes. Again, sometime before the event, participants lined up all the pigs they planned to kill, tethered to stakes across the clearing, and Ongol's relatives recalled sadly the speech that he had made a few years previously, boasting about the display of animals for that *sa* event. Some men took the opportunity, while inspecting one another's pigs, to arrange to swap sides of pork at the kill or to exchange pearl shells and cash for sides of pork. This practice characterizes the final *sa* kill, and men make such arrangements up until the day itself. Another is the presentation of wealth by men to their wives' relatives in the "children kunai-grass" transaction, where they hang valuables around the necks of their children and tell them to take these to their mother's relatives who are present. Another transaction that marks

Erecting the fence around a grave, similar to Ongol's last resting place.

this stage is the "on the pig's back" exchange where men repay publicly with interest those who have loaned them wealth during the *sa* cycle. Ongol's sons had inherited responsibility for his transactional obligations and met them generously, which would have won their father's approval.

We all follow our own unique journeys from womb to grave during our brief stays on Earth. Ongol's was one of many thousands of such journeys that occurred in the Was and surrounding valleys during the twentieth century, and so far as one can talk of any single life as typical, his illustrates many of the features and events that characterized life in the region during that time. He did not think that it was remarkable, although he considered himself a significant person by his culture's standards, as a "grass-clearing man." He would probably be surprised to know that you, the reader, were interested enough in his life to have read this book. But he would be pleased to know that you were sufficiently curious about the ways of his world and would hope that you have learned something of value contrasting his life with your own.

Notes

Chapter 1
[1] *Elaeocarpus polydactylus*
[2] *Pandanus antaresensis.*

Chapter 2
[1] *Cordyline fruticosa*, the *kal* cultivar.
[2] All of the *sor kem* ritual spells are in the neighboring Huli language and unintelligible to most Wola speakers if they heard them.
[3] *Probosciger aterrimus.*
[4] The point is either *doba* (*Caryota rumphiana*) or *waeb* (*Caryota* sp.) black palm that comes from lower altitudes in the Lake Kutubu region.
[5] *Smilax leucophylla.*
[6] This chunky cut comes from the back of the animal's neck.
[7] *Paradisaea minor.*
[8] *Acorus calamus.*
[9] *Dicrancloma* cf. *blumei.*
[10] *Cryptocarya laevigata.*
[11] *Trema orientalis.*
[12] *Rubus rosifolius.*
[13] *Desmodium repandum.*
[14] *Ficus iodotricha*, that has bulbous maroon fruits.

Chapter 3
[1] *Cetonia* sp.
[2] *Litoria iris*
[3] *Trema orientalis.*
[4] *Psophocarpus tetragonolobus.*
[5] Again, the spell is in the Huli language.
[6] *Pandanus julianettii.*
[7] *Miscanthus floridulus.*

[8] *Poa saruwagetica.*
[9] *Impatiens* sp.
[10] The *ondal* variety of *Miscanthus.*
[11] *Garcinia* sp.
[12] *Hoya* sp.
[13] *Elaeocarpus dolidrostylus* spp. *collinus.*
[14] *Cryptocarya* sp.
[15] *Oenanthe javanica.*

Chapter 4
[1] Southern beech *Nothofagus* spp.
[2] *Nastus obtusus.*
[3] *Smilax leucophylla.*
[4] It is in the Huli language.
[5] *Commelina diffusa.*
[6] In some places people use a stone called a *kuba* wrapped in leaves, which they say also dulls the senses of enemies so that they are unaware of their presence.
[7] Again in the Huli language.

Chapter 5
[1] *Boletus* sp.
[2] *Evodiella cauliflora.*
[3] No one could confirm if this name related to the early morning dew that had wetted the couple's legs.

Chapter 6
[1] A large variety of plants, if fallowed only briefly, whereas the coarse grass *Ischaemum polystachum* will dominate if left fallow for longer.
[2] *Agrostis avenacea.*
[3] *Phalanger vestitus.*

Chapter 7

1 *Laportea decumana.*
2 *Piper* sp.
3 *Cyathea magna.*
4 *Opodiphthera joiceyi.*
5 *Rapanea* sp.
6 *Lycoperdon maximum*
7 *Chisocheton ceramicum*
8 Rhinoceros beetle (*Papuana* sp.).
9 Longicorn beetle larvae (*Olethrinus tyrannus*).
10 *Dicliptera papuana.*
11 *Pandanus adinobotrys*
12 *Marattia* sp.
13 *Campnosperma brevipetiolata.*
14 *Syzygium* sp.
15 *Charmosyna papou.*

Chapter 8

1 *Pteroptyx* sp.
2 *Dicksonia grandis.*
3 *Pometia pinnata.*
4 *Dobsonia moluccensis.*
5 A strip of skin and fat from either side of the chest and around the base of the neck.
6 *Scincella elegantoides lobula.*
7 *Sycorycteris australis.*

8 *Graptophyllum pictum.*
9 The "a" sound is added at the end of each refrain for rhythm.
10 *Bubbia* sp.
11 *Cyathea* spp.
12 *Zingiber officinale.*

Chapter 9

1 The spell is in Huli language.
2 Again in the Huli language.
3 Again in the Huli language.
4 *Ptiloprora guisei.*
5 *Medinilla* sp.
6 *Ganophyllum?* sp.

Chapter 10

1 *Casuarina oligodon* and *Cinnamomum* sp.
2 *Gulubia* sp.

Chapter 11

1 The Wola often pronounce the "r" as "l" at the beginning of a word, such that the New Britain town of Rabaul, known to some labor migrants for example, is called Labaul.
2 *Digenethle* sp.

Glossary

ab   father/father's brother (uncle)/father's father's brother's son (2nd uncle)
ab saend bay   fighting with insults
am   mother
aumuw shor   lungs, literally "heart leaves"
aysha   mother-in-law
boliy   sister-in-law
boliy tumay   incest, literally "sister climbing"
bomboraenda   a leafy bower behind a men's house where *towmow* sometimes reside
buragaib kalay   a type of offering
dayngeltay   hungry-time-origin grass
em   garden
enza   men's house
gwat or *ol gwat*   the first payment in mortuary exchange sequence
gwat kaend   payment of pigs and sides of pork in mortuary exchange
habuwk   a payment made to someone for performing a ritual
haemay   brother/male parallel cousins (male speaking)
hay   cross cousins
haypuw   reimbursement payment to intermediaries in a reparation exchange
hobaen   a type of tree; a pronged implement used during the *shobez ak* rite
hogol   groomwealth
holhae   a curing procedure using a pig's heart and lungs
hombera   funeral
hongok   tree fern
hort bay   attenuated bridewealth
howma   communal grass-clearing
hul tort   sorcery, believed to be most powerful
hungnaip aenda   ancestor stones house
hungnaip or *hungnaip haen*   ancestor stones (largely prehistoric objects)
injiykab   bridewealth
iyziy   son
jiya luw waen bay   a courting procedure, literally "kill and dry a frog"
kem or *sor kem*   palm cockatoo; name of a ritual

195

kem nais   adolescents who play part in *sor kem* ritual
kiap   Pidgin for government officer
kinja   green tree frog
kiya   s/he says
komay   retributive divination believed to find out a wrongdoer in sorcery
konay   mind
kongol   piper bush
kot bay   yodel
kwimb   moss
leb   sweet flag plant
lotu   Pidgin for church
maeruw tinjil   an infant with a baby sibling
mai   maternal uncle/nephew (sister's son)
mashoraenda   house for *saybel* festival where pig offerings made, literally "taro-leaf house"
mat nuw   afterbirth, literally "carry bag"
mboliy   sister/ female cousin (man speaking)
misin   Pidgin for mission
miyt kaerat   tobacco tar
mogtomb   poisoning/poison
moma   grandson/grandfather
moraret   those who initially pay reparation on behalf of others responsible for armed hostilities
moray nais   participants in the *iysh ponda ma henday* famine ritual
muwnaenda   lean-to structure housing *hungnaip* stones (same as *hungnaip aenda*)
njiy   give (me)
ol bay   mortuary transaction, literally "man maker" repayment exchange
ol gwat   see *gwat*
ol howma   renowned man, literally "grass-clearing man"
ol iysh   small stakes used in sorcery-curing rites, literally "man stakes"
ol komb   exchange that is part of reparation sequence
ol sond beray   divination performed to ascertain cause of premature death
ol sond   a death compensation payment
ol tobway   mortuary transaction, literally "man maker," investment part of *ol bay* exchange
omok   variety of edible greens
ongol   a type of tree
ongor goiz   late contributions to *injiykab* "bridewealth" transaction
pel   beech tree/wood
pes   bed of soft leaves (nappy)
sa   an exchange festival cycle featuring dances and pig kills
saem tokay   a sickness involving "peeled heart" syndrome
saend   armed hostilities
saend howma   area across which fighting occurs
saend iysh shor   leaf funnel used to detect lookouts and ambushes, literally "fight tree leaf"
saend mariy pay   to take the fight to the enemy, to outflank them, literally "carry the fight"
saend pa biy   the end of armed hostilities
saend pol   period when armed hostilities go dormant, literally "fight sleeps"
saend tay   the originators of armed hostilities, literally "fight source"
saybel   a ritual to promote well-being

sem   family (may also serve surname-like)

semgᵉnk   small family/ies

semonda   large family/ies

sezinda   a swear word derived from the name of the place where a massacre occurred

shiyp   a type of tree

showmay   pig

showmay enjay   exchange that is part of reparation sequence, literally "live pigs"

showmay hentiya   a pig rope

showmay tok   horizontal pole on which pork displayed at pig kill

shumb   elder-in-law

shumba tenj   netted hood worn by mother-in-law, literally "elder hat"

shwimb   a type of tree

sor kem   see *kem*

taz iysh   payment made to *tort* sorcerer, literally "pig wood" payment

taziy   parsley

ten howma   renowned woman, literally "grass-clearing woman"

ten sab liy   payment by groom's to bride's kin after *injiykab*, literally "woman marsupial hit"

tenda   women's house

timp   a cult cycle

tomtay   arrow with a plain point made of black palm wood

tort   an unseen malicious force featuring in sorcery

towmow habuwk bay   payment made to person officiating at ritual, literally "spirit
stand make"

towmow   spirit/ancestor spirits/ghost

turmaen   courting songs/sessions; engaged persons

waen   woolly cedar tree

waenay   daughter

weray   wife

wezow   life force/soul/ reflection/shadow

wok   a type of tree

woktoiz   a kind of sorcery

wombok   cosmetic oil tapped from tree at Lake Kutubu.

Further Reading

Readers interested in knowing more about various aspects of life in the Wola-speaking region will find the following helpful:

Crittenden, Robert. 1982. Sustenance, Seasonality and Social Cycles on the Nembi Plateau, Papua New Guinea. Unpub. Ph.D. thesis, Australian National University, Canberra.

Hides, Jack. 1936. *Papuan Wonderland*. London: Blackie and Son.

Lederman, Rena. 1986. *What Gifts Engender: Social Relations and Politics in Mendi, Highland Papua New Guinea*. Cambridge: Cambridge University Press.

Nihill, M. W. 1986. Roads of Presence: Exchanges and Social Relatedness in Anganen Social Structure. Ph.D. dissertation, University of Adelaide.

Reeson, Margaret. 1972. *Torn Between Two Worlds*. Madang: Kristen Press.

Reithofer, Hans. 2006. *The Python Spirit and the Cross: Becoming Christian in a Highland Community of Papua New Guinea*. Göttingen: Göttinger Studien zur Ethnologie Bd. 16.

Ryan, D'Arcy. 1961. Gift Exchange in the Mendi Valley. Ph.D. thesis, Sydney University.

Schieffelin, Edward and Robert Crittenden (eds.). 1990. *Like People You See in a Dream: First Contact in Six Papuan Societies*. Stanford: Stanford University Press.

Sillitoe, Paul. 1979. *Give and Take: Exchange in Wola Society*. Canberra: Australian National University Press, and New York: St. Martin's Press.

Sillitoe, Paul. 1983. *Roots of the Earth: The Cultivation and Classification of Crops in the Papua New Guinea Highlands*. Manchester: University Press, and the University of New South Wales Press.

Sillitoe, Paul. 1988. *Made in Niugini: Technology in the Highlands of Papua New Guinea*. London: British Museum Publications and [1989] Bathurst: Crawford House Press.

Sillitoe, Paul. 1996. *A Place Against Time: Land and Environment in the Papua New Guinea Highlands*. Amsterdam: Harwood Academic [Gordon & Breach].

Sillitoe, Paul. 2003. *Managing Animals in New Guinea: Preying the Game in the Highlands*. London: Routledge (Environmental Anthropology Series Vol. 7).

Sillitoe, Paul, Pamela Stewart, and Andrew Strathern. 2002. *Horticulture in Papua New Guinea: Case Studies from the Southern and Western Highlands*. Pittsburgh: Ethnology Monograph No. 18.

Smith, Graham. 1974. *Mendi Memories*. Melbourne: Thomas Nelson.

The following films also depict aspects of Wola life and visually comple-
ment the above studies:

Bird of the Thunderwoman. Australian Broadcasting Commission, 1979.
The Nature of Things: The Mendi. Canadian Broadcasting Commission, 1974.